CONTRACTING IN JAPAN

Economic arrangements, Ramseyer writes, are structured and implemented with the intent and hope that they will be carried out with "care, intelligence, discretion, and effort." Yet entrepreneurs work with partial information about the products, and people, they are dealing with. *Contracting in Japan* illustrates this by examining five sets of negotiations and unusual contractual arrangements among businessmen and women, in Japan. In it, Ramseyer explores how sake brewers were able to obtain and market the necessary, but difficult-to-grow, sake rice that captured the local terroir; how Buddhist temples tried to compensate for rapidly falling donations by negotiating unusual funerary contracts; and how pre-war local elites used leasing instead of loans to fund local agriculture. Ramseyer examines these entrepreneurs, discovering how they structured contracts, made credible commitments, obtained valuable information, and protected themselves from adverse consequences to create, maintain, strengthen, and leverage the social networks in which they operated.

J. Mark Ramseyer spent most of his childhood in provincial towns and cities in southern Japan, attending Japanese schools for K-6. He returned to the US for college. Before attending law school, he studied Japanese history in graduate school. Ramseyer graduated from Harvard Law School in 1982. He clerked for the Hon. Stephen Breyer (then on the First Circuit), worked for two years at Sidley & Austin (in corporate tax), and studied as a Fulbright student at the University of Tokyo. After teaching at UCLA and the University of Chicago, he came to Harvard in 1998. He has also taught or co-taught courses at several Japanese universities (in Japanese). For his contribution to mutual understanding between Japan and the US, Ramseyer was awarded the Order of the Rising Sun, Gold Rays and Neck Ribbon, by the Japanese government in 2018.

CAMBRIDGE STUDIES IN ECONOMICS, CHOICE, AND SOCIETY

Founding Editors

Timur Kuran, *Duke University*
Peter J. Boettke, *George Mason University*

This interdisciplinary series promotes original theoretical and empirical research as well as integrative syntheses involving links between individual choice, institutions, and social outcomes. Contributions are welcome from across the social sciences, particularly in the areas where economic analysis is joined with other disciplines such as comparative political economy, new institutional economics, and behavioral economics.

Books in the Series

PAUL DRAGOS ALIGICA, *Public Entrepreneurship, Citizenship, and Self-Governance*

TERRY L. ANDERSON and GARY D. LIBECAP, *Environmental Markets: A Property Rights Approach*

SHELBY GROSSMAN, *The Politics of Order in Informal Markets: How the State Shapes Private Governance*

MORRIS B. HOFFMAN, *The Punisher's Brain: The Evolution of Judge and Jury*

RANDALL G. HOLCOMBE, *Political Capitalism: How Political Influence is Made and Maintained*

ROGER KOPPL, *Expert Failure*

PETER T. LEESON, *Anarchy Unbound: Why Self- Governance Works Better Than You Think*

MICHAEL C. MUNGER, *Tomorrow 3.0: Transaction Costs and the Sharing Economy*

JENNIFER BRICK MURTAZASHVILI and ILIA MURTAZASHVILI, *Land, the State, and War Property Institutions and Political Order in Afghanistan*

ALEX NOWRASTEH and BENJAMIN POWELL, *Wretched Refuse?: The Political Economy of Immigration and Institutions*

BENJAMIN POWELL, *Out of Poverty: Sweatshops in the Global Economy*

JEAN-PHILIPPE PLATTEAU, *Islam Instrumentalized: Religion and Politics in Historical Perspective*

JARED RUBIN, *Rulers, Religion, and Riches: Why the West Got Rich and the Middle East Did Not*

VERNON L. SMITH AND BART J. WILSON, *Humanomics: Moral Sentiments and the Wealth of Nations for the Twenty-First Century*

CASS R. SUNSTEIN, *The Ethics of Influence: Government in the Age of Behavioral Science*

Contracting in Japan

*The Bargains People Make When Information is Costly,
Commitment is Hard, Friendships Are Unstable,
and Suing is Not Worth It*

J. MARK RAMSEYER

Harvard Law School

CAMBRIDGE
UNIVERSITY PRESS

Shaftesbury Road, Cambridge CB2 8EA, United Kingdom

One Liberty Plaza, 20th Floor, New York, NY 10006, USA

477 Williamstown Road, Port Melbourne, VIC 3207, Australia

314–321, 3rd Floor, Plot 3, Splendor Forum, Jasola District Centre, New Delhi – 110025, India

103 Penang Road, #05–06/07, Visioncrest Commercial, Singapore 238467

Cambridge University Press is part of Cambridge University Press & Assessment, a department of the University of Cambridge.

We share the University's mission to contribute to society through the pursuit of education, learning and research at the highest international levels of excellence.

www.cambridge.org
Information on this title: www.cambridge.org/9781009215725

DOI: 10.1017/9781009215763

First published 2023

A catalogue record for this publication is available from the British Library.

Library of Congress Cataloging-in-Publication Data
Names: Ramseyer, J. Mark, 1954– author.
Title: Contracting in Japan : the bargains people make when information is costly, commitment is hard, friendships are unstable, and suing is not worth it / J. Mark Ramseyer, Harvard Law School, Massachusetts.
Description: Cambridge, United Kingdom ; New York, NY, USA : Cambridge University Press, 2023. | Series: Cambridge studies in economics, choice, and society | Includes bibliographical references and index.
Identifiers: LCCN 2022055204 (print) | LCCN 2022055205 (ebook) | ISBN 9781009215725 (hardback) | ISBN 9781009215763 (ebook)
Subjects: LCSH: Contracting out – Japan.
Classification: LCC HD3860.J3 R367 2023 (print) | LCC HD3860.J3 (ebook) | DDC 658.4/0580952–dc23/eng/20230224
LC record available at https://lccn.loc.gov/2022055204
LC ebook record available at https://lccn.loc.gov/2022055205

ISBN 978-1-009-21572-5 Hardback
ISBN 978-1-009-21571-8 Paperback

For H and K:
May all your adventures be as rich as the
voyages of the Calamity Cookie

Contents

Acknowledgments

Earlier versions of several of the chapters have been published separately: J. Mark Ramseyer, Contracting for Terroir in Sake, 46 *Law & Social Inquiry* 666 (2021); J. Mark Ramseyer, The Fable of Land Reform: Leases and Credit Markets in Occupied Japan, 24 *Journal of Economics & Management Strategy* 934 (2015); J. Mark Ramseyer, Social Capital and the Formal Legal System: Evidence from Prefecture-Level Data in Japan, 7 *Journal of Legal Analysis* 421 (2015); Review of K. Suenaga, The Story of Japan's Ohmi Merchants, in the *Japan Forward*, Nov. 12, 2020; J. Mark Ramseyer, Water Law in Imperial Japan: Public Goods, Private Claims, and Legal Convergence, 18 *The Journal of Legal Studies* 51 (1989). I am grateful to the journals for allowing me to use them in this book.

I gratefully acknowledge the generous financial support of the Harvard Law School.

I received helpful comments and suggestions from Yasuhiro Arai, Arivek Avedian, Stephen Bainbridge, Lisa Bernstein, Sadie Blanchard, Jack Donahue, Alexander Evans, Penelope Francks, Yoshitaka Fukui, Tom Ginsburg, Mary Ann Glendon, John Haley, Todd Henderson, William Hubbard, Masaki Iwasaki, Temple Jorden, Heiko Karle, Mitsuhiko Kimura, Paul Lagunes, Salil Mehra, Curtis Milhaupt, Yoshiro Miwa, Jason Morgan, Carl Mosk, Minoru Nakazato, H. Ramseyer, K. Ramseyer, Eric Rasmusen, Frances Rosenbluth, Zen'ichi Shishido, David Skeel, Richard Smethurst, Henry Smith, Frank Upham, David Weinstein, and participants in workshops at the Bank of Japan, Columbia University, ETH Zurich, Harvard University, Hitotsubashi University, the Japanese Law & Economics Association, Kobe University, Kochi University, the Korean Law & Economics Association, Nishimura & Asahi, Northwestern University,

Notre Dame University, Seoul National University, Tel Aviv University, the University of Chicago, the University of Pennsylvania, the University of Tokyo, and Yale University.

Lake Nojiri, Nagano (if only, if only)
Summer 2022

1

Introduction

Twenty to thirty kilometers east of Kyoto, Omi lies on the coast of Lake Biwa.[1] There, during the Tokugawa (1600–1868) period, the Tokaido and Nakasendo highways crossed. Those routes and others tied the Kyoto-Osaka area to nearby Ise; to Edo (Tokyo); to the mountainous but prosperous Shinano (Nagano) area; to the Japan Sea coast; and to the more distant Tohoku region to the northeast. "Highway" may be a euphemism, of course. These were footpaths, sometimes along the coasts, sometimes through the mountains.

Over time, the merchants from Omi came to specialize in interregional trade. The economy was growing, and producers were increasingly specializing by region. The division of labor is limited by the size of the market, wrote Adam Smith. If only they could sell their goods more broadly, the producers could focus on innovation and scale economies and capitalize on their comparative advantage. The Omi merchants gave them that chance. Pottery, medicines, sake, soy sauce, and textiles – the merchants bought from each community and sold as they went.

Along the various highways, Omi merchants built a vast network of branch offices – by the late 1920s, more than 1,100. Through the networks, they collected information about supply: which regions produced what style of goods, which craftsmen produced the highest quality, and which techniques involved the lowest costs. Through the same networks, they also collected information about demand: which consumers wanted what style of fabric, which villages wanted what flavor of soy sauce, and what price people were willing to pay for each product in each area. Knowing who made what and who wanted what, they matched producers with buyers across the country.

---

[1] This discussion is based on J. Mark Ramseyer, Review of K. Suenaga, *The Story of Japan's Ohmi Merchants*, in the *Japan Forward*, November 12, 2020.

During the Tokugawa period, the Omi merchants did this without a post office, a bank, or a national court system, much less Google and the Internet. In the twenty-first century, we email and telephone our sales agents and branch offices. A few decades ago, we used express mail and UPS (in Japan, sokutatsu and takkyubin) and eventually turned to fax machines. Out of our central offices, we monitor the accounts for all of our branches.

Should a customer fail to pay, we take him to court. Should a salesman steal, we call the police. We deposit our cash in government-insured banks. We monitor our inventories, scan barcodes to record deliveries and sales, and reconcile accounts at the end of each day. If we lack the capital to survive a warehouse fire, we buy insurance.

The Omi merchants had access to none of this. To communicate, they met in person. To travel, they walked. They could not entrust cash to national networks of banking outlets. They could not sue for damages in reliable and predictable legal systems. Merchants in Brooklyn and Chicago used to worry about items they shipped that "fell off the back of the truck." During Prohibition, they hired Meyer Lansky and Bugsy Siegel to ensure that fewer cases fell off the back. Omi merchants had no way reliably to know what anyone had even loaded onto a truck (and actually, they had no trucks).

To maintain honesty within their networks of agents and branch offices, the Omi merchants created, cultivated, and grew their own networks of personal, social, and "ethnic" ties. They hired mostly people born within Omi. They intermarried. They devoted themselves to a common Jodo-shin (True Pure Land) Buddhist faith. They sent a young man to a branch office only after they had trained him in the home office for multiple years and observed his abilities, weaknesses, and – crucially – character. To maintain his loyalty, they required him to return to the home office every few years. To motivate him to look out for the good of the house, they keyed his wages to its profitability.

Obviously, there is nothing peculiarly Japanese about any of these problems. Neither is there anything peculiarly Japanese about the way that the Omi merchants approached them. Across a wide range of societies, merchants have intermarried. They have supported common religious institutions. They have lived and worked within guilds laced with gossip networks that conveyed information about each other's trustworthiness. To increase both the depth and breadth of information and the weight of their normative sanctions, people everywhere have cultivated and maintained networks of dense and interlocking ethnic ties and focused their transactions within them. They did the same in Omi.

* * *

At stake in the Omi world were information and reliability: The Omi traders needed both access to information and the ability to increase transactional reliability. Like merchants everywhere, they needed information about the producers from whom they bought and the consumers to whom they sold. They needed information about their market rivals. They needed information about their own agents. And like merchants everywhere, they needed counter-parties to their transactions whom they could trust. They needed ways to insure that even their own agents did not cheat them.

Omi merchants did not follow commercial statutes. During the Tokugawa period, there were no commercial statutes to follow. They rarely relied on formal courts. Tokugawa judges were more honest and sophisticated than the judges in many pre-modern court systems, but they lacked much expertise in commercial behavior. Instead, the Omi merchants followed their own customary norms of commerce and negotiated and enforced their contracts within networks of interlaced personal ties that both conveyed information and provided sanctions against opportunistic behavior.

Information and reliability mattered in 1950s Wisconsin too. At the end of the decade, Wisconsin law professor Stewart Macaulay famously "discovered" that Wisconsin businessmen negotiated and enforced their contracts within defined social networks. They hired lawyers who paid attention to formal legal rules and procedures, but they themselves seemed often simply to ignore those rules and procedures. Rather than draft a contract carefully, sometimes they preferred "to rely on 'a man's word' in a brief letter, a handshake, or 'common honesty and decency' – even when the transaction involves exposure to serious risks" (Macaulay 1963, 58). Complained one lawyer to Macaulay: I am "sick of being told, 'We can trust old Max'" (Macaulay 1963, 58). When they sued a defaulting counter-party, the businessmen used lawyers, and the lawyers fought over the contractual terms. When they settled the disputes out of court, however, the businessmen "frequently settled without reference to the contract or potential for actual legal sanctions" (Macaulay 1963, 61).

In both mid-twentieth century Wisconsin and early nineteenth century Omi, successful merchants needed access to information, and they needed reliable contractual counter-parties. In Wisconsin, the businessmen mixed both formal and informal strategies. They could check courthouse records for real estate title and security interests. Were a counter-party to cheat them, they could sue. If the counter-party had assets, they might even collect.

By contrast, Omi traders had no real access to formal strategies. The Tokugawa courts were honest enough. If cheated by a party with substantial enough assets, they might even be able to collect. But government records were unlikely to provide much by way of current and reliable information. And against most defaulting counter-parties, the courts could not give much real relief.

Such are the themes I explore in this book, and they concern one obvious question: How do businessmen and businesswomen obtain the information and transactional reliability they need to conduct their business? Modern business executives have access both to formal legal mechanisms and to informal social networks. The formal mechanisms constitute the heart of traditional law school education. The informal mechanisms have remained less fully explored.

In this introductory chapter, I begin by summarizing (very briefly) the (well-known) formal mechanisms by which contracting parties have tried to insure access to information and transactional reliability: court-enforced contract enforcement (Section I.A) and vertical integration (Section I.B). I then turn to the way in which business executives structure their arrangements within their social context. I first review the classic economics-related studies on the relation between contracting behavior and social ties (Section II.A). I then turn to the parallel literature in sociology and political science on "social capital" (Section II.B) I explore how that social capital can facilitate information acquisition and augment transactional reliability (Section III.B). I conclude by discussing how participants "endogenize" that social capital: how they can and do deliberately structure a dense network of personal relations around their transactions (Section III.C).

I Formal Legal Enforcement

A Contract

1. Introduction. – Access to information and transactional reliability work in tandem. With better information, business executives are more likely to trade with a counter-party who is well matched. They are better prepared to meet any stress that the relationship might encounter. Knowing that the other party has access to information about his own behavior, the counter-party is himself less likely to try to defraud.

What is more, when a transaction is more reliable, the contracting parties are more willing to invest in relationship-specific assets and skills; earning a return from those assets and skills, they will be less likely to find termination profitable. Providing information to one's counter-party constitutes exactly such a relationship-specific investment: The contracting parties are incurring a cost to exchange information that they each will find valuable only in the context of their relationship.

Hence the conclusion: Legal institutions that enforce the terms of an agreement increase both transactional reliability and the amount of information that the contracting parties will find it profitable to exchange.

2. Transactional reliability. – Modern formal legal institutions serve at least two key functions relevant here. First, they potentially extend the range of parties with whom a business executive can profitably trade. The point follows from jurisdictional reach. Formal institutions can enforce compliance from those counter-parties who are subject to the jurisdiction of the court. For most modern societies, this jurisdiction will extend at least to the boundaries of the nation state (and sometimes even beyond). By contrast, informal institutions exert power only within a party's social network. They induce compliance only from those parties subject to the social sanctions of the group.

As a result, rational wealth-maximizing parties to a contract can use the courts as a way to expand their set of potential contract partners beyond those amenable to informal social sanctions. For any business executive, some potential business partners will lie beyond the range of their informal networks. In such situations, court-enforceable legal sanctions potentially extend the bounds of profitable contracting. As Richard Epstein (2008, 279–80) put it:

In strong, well-functioning legal systems, parties continue to rely on a full range of affective and interpersonal ties to facilitate both exchange and cooperative arrangements. But at the margin, they know that they can be a bit less selective in choosing their trading partners or business associates and in negotiating the terms of their agreement because they have the legal machinery of the state to backstop their mistakes.

Second, the formal legal system will potentially set the contours of the terms by which the parties settle disputes out of court. In cases involving contracts, modern legal systems generally provide a non-breaching party with expectation damages: The profit he could reasonably expect to earn had the counter-party not breached. Given that both parties can generally settle a dispute out of court more cheaply than through trial, rational parties will settle most disputes informally.

When parties to a contract do settle out of court, the legal system potentially sets the contours of their informal settlement. When rational wealth-maximizing parties decide to terminate a relationship, they negotiate – in the famous words of Robert Mnookin and Lewis

Kornhauser (1979) – "in the shadow of the law." As scholars in law and economics have shown in detail, they settle their endgame disputes within a "settlement window" determined by their respective estimates of the probable litigated outcome, their costs of litigation, and their costs of settlement. In Lisa Bernstein's words (2015, 569):

> A buyer is … unlikely to sue for breach of contract (or have a credible threat to sue) unless the amount he can recover (net of litigation costs, switching costs, secrecy costs, and reputation costs) exceeds the present value of the marginal benefit of continuing to deal with this supplier, rather than the next best supplier, in the future.

Crucially, the expected legal outcome sets the contours of the out-of-court settlement only when the parties have decided to terminate their relationship. Firms (or Midwestern business executives, observes Bernstein) draft contract terms in order to structure the dissolution of a relationship if and when they decide it no longer works. They do not intend the terms to bind them while the relationship remains viable. So long as they find the relationship profitable, they routinely adjust and change their course of dealing to keep it mutually advantageous.

Faced with a contract breach, explains Bernstein (1996, 1999), firms distinguish between those relations they want to keep and those they want to terminate. The former, they work to preserve, and in doing so may ignore completely the terms that a court would impose in court. The latter, they terminate and do so in Mnookin and Kornhauser's shadow of the law. The terms they apply to the relations they want to preserve can – and often do – differ dramatically "from the terms of transactors' written contracts, which contain the norms that transactors would want a third-party neutral to apply in a situation where they were unable to cooperatively resolve a dispute and viewed their relationship as being at an end-game" (Bernstein 1996, 1796).

3. The effect of price. – When transacting across the market, a firm can increase the incentive of its contracting partner to keep its word by increasing the price it pays. Obviously, firms do not generally increase profitability by raising the prices they pay. They raise profitability through higher prices only if those prices induce a contracting partner to so increase its reliability that the firm can produce in a way otherwise not possible.

At stake are the rents that a contracting party can expect to earn from the relationship. If the rents are sufficiently high, the party will find it profitable to pay more to insure that the relationship continues. If information disclosure will increase the viability of the contractual relationship, rational parties will each disclose additional information. They will continue to invest in the relationship-specific attributes (like information) until they have reduced the return on the contract to market levels.

More generally, consider this the contractual analogue to the concept of "efficiency wages." Sometimes, an employer can raise profitability by raising wages. It can do so when those higher wages raise productivity by an amount that more than offsets the higher wage costs. The classic example is Henry Ford. He had conceived a new manufacturing technique: the assembly line. To make the technique work, he needed workers who would stay on the job. He needed workers who would accumulate experience and then draw on that experience to engineer the hundreds of changes necessary to make the assembly line work. As long as he paid the going rate in Detroit – $2.50 per day – workers quit as they pleased. Ford doubled the pay to $5.00, and workers now stayed on the job. They studied the assembly line and made it work.[2]

B Vertical Integration

If one plausible way that formal legal procedures can increase access to information and contractual reliability is through contract law, another is through merger. On the one hand, two contracting parties can use the formal contract apparatus to buy and sell their goods and services to each other. On the other, they can use the merger apparatus to work together within a single firm.

In the classic language of economics workshops, the parties can either "make or buy." If "to buy" is to contract through formal legal mechanisms, "to make" is to use those same legal institutions to merge. As early as 1937, Ronald Coase explained the choice – like so much else – through transactions costs. Rational parties will place the two counter-parties within a single firm when the transactions costs of contracting across the market exceed the transactions costs of administering a transaction within the firm. They will contract across the market when the transactions costs of internal organization exceed the costs of market contracting.

In the 1980s and 1990s, scholars tried to explain mergers through the extent that the firms relied on assets whose value was specific to the transaction. Such a transaction-specific investment would generate "quasi rents," they explained. Should the two parties try to contract for the assets across the market, those rents would create incentives for

---

[2] Raff and Summers (1987); see also Shapiro and Stiglitz (1984).

them to try to "hold up" each other (e.g., Klein, Crawford & Alchian 1978; Williamson 1985). The point is obviously true. Unfortunately, as an explanation for actual mergers, the concept lacked much empirical currency. Scholars had initially focused primarily on one historical example (the GM-Fisher Body merger). That example, however, turned on factors later shown to be entirely orthogonal to the "transaction-specific asset" hypothesis (Casadesus-Masanell & Spulber 2000; Coase 2000). When scholars did find other applications, many of them involved clearly nonstandard venues like government procurement (e.g., Masten, Meehan & Snyder 1991).

In his own theory of the firm, Oliver Hart (Grossman & Hart 1986; Hart & Moore 1990) instead suggests that the question of whether to merge or contract turns on whose involvement is most important to the value of the key assets. Assets, he reasons, should be owned by the firm whose involvement raises the value of those assets to its highest use. As Halonen-Akatwijuka (2019) summarized the argument:

If … assets are so complementary that they are productive only when used together, they should have a single owner. … Furthermore, if there are such strong complementarities between an asset and a party that the asset is productive only with that party, then this indispensable party should own the asset.

If the land is most valuable when used for the production of sake, for example, it should be owned by the entity whose role is most important in producing that sake (see Chapter 2).

Crucial to our discussion here, formal merger (or vertical integration) does not solve the problem of either information acquisition or transactional reliability. Coase's point – as important now as in 1937 – is that a merger will change the nature of the transactions costs involved. Sometimes a merger will reduce the level of transactions costs – and when it does, rational parties will tend to merge. Sometimes it will increase the level of the transactions costs – and when it does, rational parties will contract across the market. But in either case, some transactions costs will remain.

Posit two contracting parties, A and B. When they contract as independent parties across the market, they bring interests that sometimes diverge. Because they are each residual claimants to their separate businesses, they each have an interest in diverting as much of the residual revenue stream as possible to themselves. Toward that end, they may find it advantageous to renege on their bargains (hence the problem of transactional reliability). Given that risk of opportunism, they may hesitate to disclose much information to each other (hence the problem of information acquisition).

Now suppose that A buys B's business. B (or someone else named by A as B's replacement) will continue to operate the assets and people that constituted B's business, but now under A's ownership. In effect, B (or his replacement) now works as a paid agent of A. Given that A has a claim to the entire residual revenue stream from the combined A-B business, he no longer needs to worry about how B splits the stream. After all, no one splits the stream at all.

Instead, however, A does now need to worry about B diverting the firm's revenue stream to himself as hidden compensation. He can take money from customers under the table. He can steal assets from the firm. He can steal the most profitable business opportunities for himself. If not pecuniarily inclined, he can simply stop working hard. A no longer worries about splitting the residual income stream with B; instead, A now worries that B will divert revenue before it ever reaches that residual level.

Hence the importance of Coase: When (a) the potential loss from divergent interests in the residual revenue stream exceeds (b) the potential loss from the efforts of an in-house agent to increase his pecuniary or non-pecuniary compensation, the parties will tend to join together in a single firm. When the latter exceeds the former, they will tend to contract across the market. Call it "transactions costs" if you will – but vertical integration does not eliminate informational and reliability problems. It may reduce those problems, but never to zero. It may eliminate the problem that arises from having two independent claimants to a business's residual revenue stream. But in eliminating that problem, it simultaneously compounds the problem that arises from employing an agent with his own selfish interests.

II Informal Enforcement

A Introduction

No one relies exclusively on formal legal institutions, of course. No one ever did. Legal scholars traditionally focused on those institutions, and many scholars in economics have done the same. Yet in both fields, over the course of the last century, scholars have increasingly also studied the way that people integrate their formal legal tools into the social world within which they live and work (Section B). Simultaneously, sociologists and political scientists have used a different set of terms to explore a largely overlapping phenomenon (Section C).

B The Classic Examples

Scholars examining the relationships among formal legal institutions and social context focus on several closely observed studies. In all of these classic studies, the authors examined a relatively small and insular community. Throughout – whether explicitly or implicitly – they focused on the way that the parties involved increased the reliability of their transactions and the information to which they had access.

1. Macaulay. – The modern literature begins with Stewart Macaulay (1963). As described above, Macaulay's Wisconsin businessmen transacted with people they knew. They transacted with them because they knew them (had better information) and could trust them (could more reliably predict transactional performance). "At all levels of the two business units personal relationships ... exert pressures for conformity to expectations," wrote Macaulay (1963, 63). "The top executives of the two firms may know each other. They may sit together on government or trade committees. They may know each other socially and even belong to the same country club."

Macaulay's businessmen knew each other from a variety of fora. They could use those fora to obtain information. And they could rely on those fora to induce the other to perform.

2. Landa. – If Macaulay saw himself as a sociologist, Janet Landa (1981) tied her studies to modern economics. Landa examined Chinese middlemen in the Southeast Asian rubber market. There, she (1981, 350) found trade dominated by several clans bound together through "a tightly knit kinship structure" and "linked together in complex networks of particularistic exchange relations." An "ethnically homogenous middlemen group," she called them. The clan functioned as "a low-cost club-like institutional arrangement," she (1981, 350) explained, "an alternative to contract law and the vertically integrated firm."

These Chinese middlemen traded, Landa and Robert Cooter (1984, 15–16) continued, within "a repository of trust that reduces the probability of breach on a contract between insiders." Through their personal ties, they were able "to rely upon informal means of enforcement of contracts." As Richard Epstein (2008, 280) explained Landa's work, "the group members tend to cooperate with each other because they have common ties of kinship that antedate their business relationship." They understand that "to treat someone badly on the job is to risk social censure and ostracism, which in turn makes breach more costly than would otherwise be the case."

3. Ellickson. – Robert Ellickson (1986, 1991) identified much the same apparent irrelevance to the formal legal system among the farmers and

cattle ranchers of Shasta County, California. As the cattle roamed, they damaged fences and ate crops. For the most part, found Ellickson, the residents settled their resulting disputes without going to court, and without even following the rules a court would enforce.

Ellickson's rangers interacted with each other regularly, and across a wide range of issues – and could expect to continue to interact indefinitely into the future. Because they thought their norms better suited to their micro-economy than California property or tort law, they "discourage[d] members from taking intermember disputes into the legal system" (Ellickson 1991, 250). Despite the logic of law and economics scholarship, claimed Ellickson (1986, 672), Shasta county rangers did not resolve their conflicts "in the shadow of the law." Instead, they settled them "*beyond* that shadow" (Ellickson 1986, 672; ital. orig.).

4. Bernstein. – Lisa Bernstein (1992) studied the New York diamond market. There, she (1992, 140) observed that "the diamond industry has long been dominated by Orthodox Jews." She found that the merchants deliberately shifted their highest stake transactions outside the ambit of the US legal system (Bernstein 1992, 133). Within "the diamond industry, extralegal contracts are the dominant contractual paradigm," wrote Bernstein. Rather than turn to the courts, merchants construct a market where "enforcement depends on social ostracism or reputational damage" (133).

Their religious ties, Bernstein posited, gave the Jewish merchants both access to relatively high levels of information about their contracting partners and an ability to punish those who reneged on their promises. The Orthodox community provided, she (1992, 140) explained, "geographical concentration, ethnic homogeneity, and repeat dealing." Within this world, traders organized their industry "to minimize the cost of obtaining information about dealers' reputations" (133).

5. Greif. – Finally, Avner Greif (1993) examined long-distance commerce among eleventh-century Maghribi Jewish traders in the Muslim Mediterranean world. Greif did formally what Bernstein and Ellickson did informally: He modeled the ties among traders and agents as an indefinitely repeated game. He then examined the historical record and found that the members of the community did indeed share information with each other and enforce honesty by punishing violators mutually and multilaterally.

These traders "deterred opportunism in bilateral agency relations [through] a credible threat of losing future profitable relations in the traders' broader community," wrote Greif (2012, 445). The traders could rely on this informal punishment strategy because they traded through "coalitions," Greif contended; Bernstein (2019) more plausibly argues that they could punish opportunism because they traded within "small-world networks."

6. "Law and social norms." – Parallel to these studies, several legal scholars in the 1990s developed a corpus of largely non-empirical scholarship on "social norms" (see the synthesis by E. Posner 1998, 2002). They focused – at the obvious risk of over-simplification – on several points: on the importance of information, on the gains from repeated trades, and on the cost of ostracism.

First, the scholars focused on the informational advance that norms and rules could provide. "Norms and rules, whether publicly or privately created, embody and convey information," explained Avery Katz (1996, 1749):

> They cannot be followed unless information is transmitted regarding their substantive content; they cannot be enforced unless information is transmitted regarding who has obeyed them, who has violated them, and who is to impose any associated punishment or reward.

The more people gossip, the more information they collect. The better their information, the more they know about their neighbors. And the more closely they follow what their neighbors do, the more secure their collective norms.

Second, the scholars concluded that people follow communal norms in order to retain the chance to trade. They earn returns from their trades that they do not want to jeopardize. Those future gains from trades, in essence, become a hostage that they sacrifice should they renege from the communal standards of behavior.

Last, should anyone try to deviate from communal norms, others enforce the norms by boycotting him. That boycott – ostracism – was in most cases the ultimate sanction. The parties enforced expected behavior, wrote Richard Posner (1991, 366), by tying behavioral norms to an "implicit threat of ostracism, that is, of refusal of advantageous transactions."[3]

C Social Capital

1. The concept. – As economists and law professors studied social norms and private legal systems over the course of the last several decades, several political scientists and sociologists pursued a parallel project.

---

[3] See also R. Posner and Rasmusen (1999) and E. Posner (1998, 554); on ostracism, see Ramseyer and Rasmusen (2020).

During the same period, they studied the way people invest in their relational networks. Through these networks, people gather information about each other and develop the mechanisms by which to induce each other to comply with broadly shared communal norms.

The scholars called it "social capital." More than anyone else, it was political scientist Robert Putnam (1995, 2000) who popularized the concept in academic circles. Putnam hit a chord (and sold books) when he suggested two decades ago that the modern American malaise might stem from a decline in "social capital." Sociologists replied by noting antecedents in their own discipline. They pointed to the concept in Durkheim and Marx (Portes 1998, 2). They cited more recent discussions by James Coleman (1988, 1990).

But it was Putnam who brought the theme home. It was he who introduced it to political science, to economics, and to the chattering classes more generally. As Putnam articulated the idea, people invest in social capital within their communities by building, maintaining, and strengthening their ties with each other. They help the PTA. They join the Rotary Club. They coach soccer leagues. They attend churches and synagogues.

In the course of doing all this, Putnam's citizens created social capital: the byzantine network of reciprocal favors and obligations that let them overcome the collective action problems that would otherwise plague their communities. With social capital intact, they volunteer. They deter petty crime. And together, in the words of Blanche Dubois, they come to depend on the kindness of strangers.

Build ties, and people behave. Integrate them into dense and crosscutting networks of social connections, as Saegert and Winkel (2004, 220) put it, and they come to "share a sense of mutual obligation, shared norms, and trustworthiness." Make friends, and "[i]nformation flows freely and from multiple channels." Convey that information, and people know what they need to know to punish those who misbehave: "norms of behavior are reinforced in many settings and sanctions for violating these norms can be effectively brought to bear."

Coleman (1988, 1990; see Burt 2000, 351) gave the classic statement of social capital. As he articulated the concept, residents enforce their communal norms best if they keep a network of overlapping ties dense enough to create "closure" (Coleman 1988, S105):

Norms arise as attempts to limit negative external effects [by some members] or encourage positive ones. But, in many social structures where these conditions exist, norms do not come into existence. The reason is what can be described as lack of closure of the social structure.

Posit two societies, explained Coleman (1998, S105–S107). In one, members maintain ties with other members that do not intertwine. A knows B and C, but B and C do not know each other and neither do they know anyone else in common. Without such mutual connections, they find it harder to punish people who violate important norms:

> In an open structure ..., actor A, having relations with actors B and C, can carry out actions that impose negative externalities on B or C or both. Since they have no relations with one another, but with others instead (D and E), they cannot combine forces to sanction A in order to constrain the actions. Unless either B or C alone is sufficiently harmed and sufficiently powerful vis-a-vis A to sanction alone, A's actions can continue unabated.

If members do maintain intertwined ties, the society is "closed." Should anyone deviate from the norms, many in the network will know, and many can punish (Coleman 1998, S105–S107). "In a structure with closure," Coleman continued, "B and C can combine to provide a collective sanction, or either can reward the other for sanctioning A." As Ronald S. Burt (2000, 351) put it, "network closure facilitates sanctions that make it less risky for people in the network to trust one another." It "enables local monitoring," write Hillmann and Aven (2011, 486). It helps "ensure that members know how their exchange partners behaved in the past, whether the behavior complied with community norms or not, and if these partners should be trusted in future transactions."

2. Variation. – Social capital is, as Saegert and Winkel (2004, 220) put it, "a property of groups." To be sure, it "can derive from a variety of individual actions, motivations, and expectations and can be used for individual as well as collective benefit" (Saegert & Winkel 2004, 220). But at root it is a group attribute. Stolle and Rochon (1998, 50) probably overstate their case in describing a reference "to an individual's social capital" as "a category mistake." But as Burt (1997, 339; see 2000, 346) explains, if human capital describes the abilities that an individual develops, "social capital is the contextual complement to [that] human capital."

Putnam compared the social capital in the US across time. He saw in the modern US a fall in social capital and lamented the decline. Social capital mattered to Putnam, because he thought the capital key to democratic governance. In Northern Italy, he noted, residents maintained a more vibrant democratic order than in the south. They maintained it through (Putnam's first canonical example) the vast number of choral societies they joined. In the 1950s, US residents maintained their democratic order through (his second canonical example) the bowling leagues they joined. Unfortunately, claimed Putnam, in the twenty-first century, they bowl alone.

Charles Murray (2012) compared the social capital in the US across regions. He contests any notion that American social capital has declined across the board. It remains intact in professional communities, he argued, even as it has vanished from among the working class. He calls the former "Belmont," after the affluent Boston suburb, and the latter "Fishtown," after the blue-collar Philadelphia neighborhood of that name. In America's Belmonts, social capital remains high – and people read the newspaper, vote, attend churches or synagogues, volunteer at schools, marry, bear children within marriage, and stay married. In its Fishtowns, social capital has disappeared. With social capital high, in Belmont people keep their promises; with that capital gone, in Fishtown they rely on neighbors at their peril. In Belmont, people trust; in Fishtown, they cheat.

3. Positive and negative groups. – This is all a bit ingenuous, of course. Communities enforce a wide variety of norms, and not all of them promote democracy. Much less do communities necessarily confront poverty, shield the vulnerable, or exploit new opportunities. In the 1930s, choral-society-rich Northern Italy turned fascist (Riley 2005). When the Soviet empire collapsed, Serbs embedded in dense networks of social ties massacred their Bosnian Croat and Muslim neighbors (Chambers & Kopstein 2001, 842).

By far the most telling example, however, involves the Nazis. Through historical narrative, Berman (1997, 402) shows "how a robust civil society actually helped scuttle the twentieth century's most critical democratic experiment, Weimar Germany." The "high levels of association," explains she (402), "served to fragment rather than unite German society."

Satyanath, Voiglaender, and Voth (2017) make the same point econometrically. From city directories, they calculate the density of civil associations (not just political associations, but "sports clubs, choirs, animal breeding associations, or gymnastics clubs"; 2017, 491) in Weimar Germany. With that density, they then predict the speed at which the Nazi Party grew. The denser the associational networks, the faster the spread of Nazism. Conclude Satyanath, Voiglaender, and Voth (2017, 520), "where there were more grass-roots social and civil organizations, the Nazi Party grew markedly faster."

III Structuring the Social Context

A Introduction

The Omi merchants hired their agents and branch managers from within the Omi world. They did so deliberately because of the contractual advantage that the policy presented. More generally, they did not just contract within a social context; they deliberately manipulated that social context to contract to their private advantage. They chose people about whom they had relatively full information and obtained that information through their social connections. They chose to deal with people whom they could monitor, who would be subject to informal social sanctions, and who would jeopardize future profits should they renege – all factors correlated with their places within that social context.

Further, Omi merchants required their agents and branch managers to invest in their ties within the Omi world. Successful merchants and industrialists did not take their social context as exogenous. Instead, they self-consciously created and shaped the social context within which they did business. They invested in their friendships, ties, and connections. They encouraged the people with whom they dealt to learn to know each other. If social context could facilitate the acquisition of information about potential partners, they invested in that social structure. If it could increase their ability to monitor their contractual partners, if it could increase their ability to learn what their rivals might be doing, and if it raised the odds that their contractual partners would perform as promised – if social context could do any of this (and often it can do all of this), they deliberately invested in that structure.

What one can say about the Omi merchants, one can say – and Macaulay, Landa, Ellickson, Bernstein, and Greif did say – about merchants elsewhere. They deliberately structure their transactions within social networks that enable them to elicit information and to increase transactional reliability (Section B). And they deliberately structure those networks to strengthen their transactions in turn (Section C).

B Exploiting Social Capital

The relevance of this social capital to business contracts stems from two characteristics: First, within a world with high levels of social capital, information travels. Potential contracting parties have better information about each other; once they enter into a contract, they can more readily monitor each other's behavior; they can more accurately gauge the state of the market and the actions of their competitors.

Second, within a world of "closed" (Coleman's term) social capital, contracting parties can more effectively draw on informal social sanctions to induce their partner to perform his part of the bargain. Because the community at large can observe contractual performance, contracting parties effectively post a larger share of their future profits as a bond.

The bond both helps assure a partner's contractual performance ex post and increases the credibility of his promises ex ante.

Put in those terms, these observations confirm the logic behind the classic studies by Landa, Bernstein, and Greif. These writers studied communities bound together through high levels of social capital. Landa described the expatriate Chinese merchant community in Southeast Asia. Bernstein described the Orthodox Jewish community in New York. And Greif described the Maghribi traders in North Africa. These were small and distinctive ethnic groups. They were groups shunned by the surrounding society. And they were groups that had cultivated within their insular community dense and interlocking networks of personal and social ties.

Restated, although Landa, Bernstein, and Grief did not use the term "social capital," the groups they studied were indeed groups with high levels of closed social capital. Through the dense networks of interlocking ties, group members obtained information about potential trading partners. They monitored their trading partners. And they manipulated the mechanism of social exclusion to induce their trading partners to keep their word. Within these densely intertwined communities, information about contractual trustworthiness traveled. And precisely because it traveled, contractual partners could trade on their partners' reputation for probity and post their own profits from future transactions as a bond for their own performance.

C Building Social Capital

Shrewd contracting parties do not just exploit social capital; often, they also create it. In fact, often they actively structure their contracts to promote the network of relationships that together constitute social capital. Lisa Bernstein (2015), for example, recently turned to heavy industry manufacturers in the Midwest and explicitly draws on the social capital literature. "The governance frameworks created by the [contracts used by these manufacturers] promote the growth of trust-based relationship-specific social capital," she explains (2015, 589). They "create conditions that support the emergence of repeat dealing relationships which in turn grow relational capital that is valuable to firms." And they create the "frameworks [that] facilitate the types of investments, norms, and interactions that are commonly associated with the emergence of trust. ..."

Through their contracts, the manufacturers deliberately build, maintain, and extend the social networks that together constitute social capital. Bernstein (2015, 599) uses the term "structural social capital" to refer to "the positions of a firm and its contracting partner in a relevant net-work of firms." In turn, she (2015, 599) continues, a "network is simply a set of connections between individuals or between organizations (here, firms)." Crucially, firms do not take these connections as given. Instead, the "connections can arise from prior deals between firms or prior social and business connections between their employees." They can and do actively promote the connections.

"These links enable firms in the network to convey 'privileged informa-tion about one another to other network members'," continues Bernstein (2015, 599). Recall Coleman's discussion of informational consequences to network "closure." The links, Bernstein (2015, 599) writes, affect:

"a counter-party's reputation among future business partners".... As a conse-quence, when a transaction is embedded in a network, the hostage value of reputa-tion is much greater than when a transaction is between two firms with few, if any, connections to other firms in the relevant market....

Social context, in other words, is not exogenous. Contracting parties need not – and do not – take that context as a given. Rather, they can create among the people with whom they contract a network. They can maintain that network, nourish the network, and grow the network. In the process, they increase their ability to obtain the information they need to choose contracting partners, to monitor their existing partners, and to scrutinize their potential rivals. In the process, they also increase their ability to har-ness informal pressures against partners who would consider reneging on their deals.

* * *

Businessmen and businesswomen – whether producers, merchants, or anyone else – need information: They need to know what their suppliers can provide, what their customers want, what their rivals offer, and what, more generally, will happen tomorrow. Businessmen and businesswomen also plan ahead by entering into agreements with other men and women. In doing so, they hope their counter-parties will keep their word. Toward that end, they do what they can to increase the reliability of their agreements.

In most modern, wealthy societies, businessmen and businesswomen exploit the advantages that the formal legal process can afford. When transacting across the market, they draft contracts that detail contingencies and specify terms that courts will enforce. When cross-market transactions grow too expensive, they integrate vertically. Using the formal legal pro-cess, they combine the contracting parties into one unit.

Yet even in modern, wealthy societies, businessmen and businesswomen do not rely solely on the formal process. They do not even rely mostly on the formal process. Instead, they contract within networks of social contacts that enable them both to gather information and to encourage contractual compliance. They do this deliberately. They search for counter-parties who live and operate within their own social networks, and they deliberately construct such networks around their transactions.

In the book that follows, I illustrate these observations through five sets of real-world business arrangements in twentieth- and twenty-first-century Japan.

Chapter 2: Contracting for Terroir in Sake. Over the course of the last century, Japanese consumers have gradually lost their taste for sake. A few producers in Kobe have dominated the mass market through economies of scale. Smaller regional brewers have steadily gone out of business. In this environment, a small cohort of ambitious (and perhaps desperate) brewers have tried radically to shift direction. Rather than continue as is, they have moved to create a market for unambiguously delicate and subtle high-end sake that showcases the environmental variation French chateau call "terroir."

To create their new *terroir* sake, these brewers must convince local farmers to grow the high-risk and high-cost varieties of rice optimized for premium sake. The necessary arrangements involve extraordinarily complex incentive and informational requirements. Yet the parties almost never draft elaborate contracts with verifiable terms and rarely vertically integrate. Instead, they try to encircle their transactions with dense networks of social capital and then use terminable short-term contracts and high prices to give them the flexibility they need.

Rather than pursue either elaborate contracts or vertical integration, in other words, brewers (i) deliberately cultivate a dense network of social capital around themselves and their contracting farmers. They then combine (ii) short-term renewable (and conversely, terminable) contracts, (iii) "efficiency wage" level payments, (iv) close monitoring, and (v) free intervention. Ultimately, this combination generally gives the brewers all the control over the farming process that they need.

Chapter 3: Contracting for Quality in Fish. Japanese fishermen traditionally fished individually. Through their hamlet, they held a collective property right in the coastal waters. But though they policed the waters together, they fished the waters by themselves.

Given the returns to modern equipment, fishermen now face economies of scale that reward capital investments. Because of those scale economies, the traditional small family firms find it hard to compete against their larger rivals. To survive in this environment, some entrepreneurial fishermen are moving deliberately upscale. Rather than try to sell on the mass market, they create and service a niche market for premium, high-quality fish. They have talent and are willing to invest time and effort, they reason. They will target the niche that rewards that deliberate care.

To compete in this market, the entrepreneurial fishermen have purposely raised the stakes: They try to post their broader reputations as bonds in ways that make them as vulnerable as possible. Many of these fishermen then sell directly to customers over the Internet. The resulting human contact and potential for repeated transactions enhance promissory credibility and encourage trust. Sometimes, they work together through their local fishing union. The union fosters trust by monitoring and certifying the quality of the members. The union places the community's collective reputation at stake. The union monitors its members to prevent free-riding.

By posting their reputations widely, the fishermen increase their vulnerability to a dissatisfied customer. That such a customer can communicate with other customers on the web dramatically raises the stake to the fisherman. And that is why the strategy works. In effect, the fisherman uses his contracts to create among his customers the (Internet-based) overlapping ties that constitute social capital. When selling publicly on the Internet, the fishermen enable their buyers to contact each other; in the process, they build a network that lets them more credibly promise high quality, precisely because their buyers can contact each other, learn how they have behaved in the past, and punish them if they renege.

Chapter 4: Contracting for Geothermal in Hot Springs. Although Japan holds the third largest geothermal energy potential in the world, it has kept it largely undeveloped. The problem: The largest geothermal deposits lie in vacation centers with a thriving industry of hot springs hotels and inns. The hotel owners worry that new geothermal wells will run their wells dry. The geothermal developers argue that this cannot happen and can point to some solid science behind their claims. By Japanese property law, however, in many communities the hot springs owners hold the potential right to veto a geothermal plant.

Suppose geothermal energy generates larger returns than the risk it poses to hot springs. Logically, the two groups ought to be able to negotiate prices and terms that let the developers proceed. Yet except in a few areas, they have not done so.

Two reciprocal contracting problems have stymied the industry. First, geothermal developers cannot credibly promise incumbent hot springs owners that they (the incumbent owners) can collect expectation damages in case the geothermal wells do damage the hot springs. The hot springs industry is over-developed in Japan, and existing wells randomly go dry on a regular basis. Owners know that if a geothermal developer were to harm a well, they may not be able to prove causation in court – there are simply too many other possible explanations. In effect, the developers find it hard credibly to commit to compensating them in full ex post.

Second, the developers must negotiate with the hot springs hotel owners seriatim, and no one hotel owner can credibly promise that all subsequent owners will also negotiate in good faith. In many communities, Japanese hot springs owners potentially hold a customary right to protect their steam and hot water through injunctions ex ante. Because each owner may have (not "certainly have," but may have) a right to hold up the entire geothermal project, the geothermal developer faces sequential negotiations, each of them a bilateral monopoly, and each of them a possible holdup.

The few geothermal plants in operation disproportionately involve cases where the developer and the hotel owners were able to solve these twin contractual problems and make the necessary credible commitments. Sometimes, in the case of the smallest geothermal plants, the parties solved the problem through vertical integration: The hotel owners build the geothermal plants themselves. Sometimes, the geothermal developer made the promise of ex post compensation credible through technology: He pipes hot water to the springs directly from the geothermal plant. Unfortunately, many (if not most) geothermal projects lack enough hot water to cut this deal.

And sometimes, the hotels solved their offsetting collective action problem by negotiating through their trade association or town government. They harness the networks of local social capital, in other words, to control would-be deviants through threats of social ostracism. Necessarily, however, this requires levels of cohesion and social capital that many villages (especially those in the steadily deteriorating rural countryside) no longer have.

Chapter 5: Contracting for Credit in Agriculture. In describing the land reform program in 1947–50 Japan, scholars routinely claim that it raised productivity. In fact, it did nothing of the sort. Land reform in Japan slowed rather than hastened the growth in productivity.

Scholars miss the effect of the land reform because they miss the constraints on agricultural credit contracts in developing societies. Farmers in pre-war Japan faced two potential sources of funds: local elites and banks. Of these, the local elites had both the informational and the informal enforcement advantage. They lived and worked within the local social capital network: They knew the potential borrowers, the land, the various local micro-climates, and the agricultural technology. Members of the community itself, they could readily harness the social sanctions necessary to compel performance informally.

Should local elites try to advance money directly as a loan, however, they needed to create a security interest in the land that the farmer bought with it. Literate and numerate as these investors assuredly were, most lacked the university education necessary to manipulate the legal procedures involved in creating security interests. Banks had the university-trained officers who could create the security interests, but they were not local. As outsiders, they lacked the informational edge in the local credit market that the village elites enjoyed.

Leases gave local investors a simple but effective way to protect their funds. Rather than lend farmers the money directly, they bought land with the funds and leased it. If a farmer began to act strategically, the local investors could begin to activate the social sanctions by which to discourage the farmer from defaulting on the rent. If a farmer did default, they simply evicted him and moved on. The process was easy to understand and simple to enforce. Through it, the funds moved to the farmers who presented the best projects, and farmers and investors jointly economized on the transaction costs inherent in credit market arrangements anywhere.

The post-war land reform program reduced agricultural growth rates by interfering with the allocation of credit. A tenancy contract is a lease, and a lease is a capital market transaction. By precluding the use of leases, land reform effectively increased the cost of capital, reduced the amount of credit, and reduced the accuracy with which investors could target that credit.

Post-reform, farmers owned almost all the land, but many of them lost their access to the most efficient source of capital: The local elites tied into the networks of community social capital. Post-reform, farmers were richer, but no longer had the most efficient access to the extra funds they needed to repair dikes, to fix sluices, and to experiment with alternative equipment, fertilizers, and pesticides. Cited regularly by development economists and World Bank and UN officials as an example of the way redistribution can increase the rate of productivity growth, the Japanese land reform program did nothing of the sort. Instead, it slashed it.

Chapter 6: Contracting for Mercy in Buddhism. In the 1960s, Japanese women began asking temples to perform commemorative ceremonies for the fetuses or children (the term is obviously loaded) they had aborted.

They still do. Physicians have been able to perform abortions legally since 1952, and many women have had them. The ceremonies do not fit within the classic rituals offered by the temples, but many Japanese women find them helpful. They ask for the services. The temples respond.

Increasingly, in other words, temples offer memorial services for children (as the temples discreetly put it) who "were not able to be born." Many women ignore all this: They have their abortions and move on. Some, however, have found the experience more troubling and turn to the temples for comfort. In both Japan and the West, scholars feigned outrage at this "commercialization" within the religious community.

Yet the temples do not have much choice. As a church rather than sect (as Weber and Troelsch called it) – or a low-tension rather than high-tension religious group (as Rodney Stark put it) – Japanese Buddhism has not demanded much of its parishioners. Instead, priests have stood ready to offer counseling and ritual as needed during the existentially troubling passages in life. In exchange, local communities effectively kept the temple on retainer. The temples cannot rely on their parishioners to give voluntarily; low-tension groups never can. Instead, they counted on their local parishioners to enforce a donative obligation on each other through the elaborate networks of community social capital – through the tightly intertwined social ties in the traditional neighborhoods, towns, and villages.

Traditional temples broadly supplied two types of services: those they could price and sell on the market (if they had to do so) and those they could not. On the one hand, they supplied rituals associated with funerals. If necessary, they could have priced these services. On the other hand, traditional temples also offered more generalized support during difficult phases of life: compassion, comfort, and guidance from (in the best of all worlds) a priest who has known a parishioner and his or her family for years. These latter services complement the formal rituals, but cannot readily be priced. Obviously, they are not impossible to price. Hypothetically, village priests could charge by the hour like a Freudian analyst. But they rarely do, and even in the West Christian priests and ministers and Jewish rabbis hesitate to sell their support by the hour.

In the traditional closed village, none of this mattered, because the members of the community (through their tight networks of social capital) enforced on each other an obligation to support the temple as necessary. In the modern urban environment, people no longer provide that generalized support. As a result, the temples exist in an inherently non-viable situation: They provide two sets of complementary services, but face market competition for the priceable services and no way readily to charge for the non-priceable services.

The memorial service for the aborted children developed in part as a priceable ritual that could substitute for what in another era might have been informal compassion, comfort, and guidance. With sufficient generalized revenue support enforceable through a tight network of community social capital, a priest might have offered a troubled woman that compassion directly. With no source of support except in the highly competitive and anonymous market for fee-for-service transactions, modern priests find that support hard to fund.

* * *

It should go without saying, but I say it anyway: for the sources of information about the contracting practices involved, see the various materials cited, either in footnotes or in parenthetical form. Many of the contracts involved are oral, and I rely on secondary materials about the contracts.

* * *

Such is the gist of what follows. I take five sets of negotiations. I examine the way people have tried to obtain information they needed and to protect themselves from adverse consequences. I discuss the ways they tried to structure their contracts to avoid having to involve the courts in resolving any disputes that might arise. I explore the ways that they tried to make credible their commitments to cooperate. And I study the way they have tried to create, maintain, strengthen, and leverage the social networks within which they negotiated, policed, and performed the agreements they made.

2

Contracting for Terroir in Sake

Three aging train cars creaked along the weed-covered single track and wended their way up the Nagano valley toward the station. If a train were to come from the opposite direction, it would have stopped in the station while the other passed. But that rarely happened. Trains in either direction barely came once an hour. Mostly, they served high school students commuting from the scattered hamlets to the central school a few train stops away.

After cresting the mountain range, the train stopped at Kurohime Station. The station served several of the hamlets in the Shinano village. In 1960, 13,700 people lived in Shinano, and 60 percent of them farmed. By 2015, barely 8,500 lived in Shimano anymore, nearly 40 percent of them were 65 or older, and barely 760 of them farmed (Shinano 2019).

Were a traveler to leave Kurohime Station, he would walk past one shuttered building after another – windows broken, siding unhinged, and front rooms littered with trash. Never mind the distance to the sea, but a sushi restaurant operated here during the booming 1980s. Tokyo vacationers came in their BMWs back then. No longer. An electrical appliance shop once did business. So did a bakery, a supermarket, a pottery shop. The stores are all closed now. With no demand for the land, owners have no incentive to clear the buildings. Instead, they have boarded them up and left them to rot. Tattered Communist Party posters hang from the walls.

A mile down the highway, past more abandoned storefronts, the traveler would pass a booming pachinko gambling establishment. He would pass a similarly booming funeral home. On the other side of the street from the gambling parlor, he would locate the one remaining supermarket. And behind the supermarket, he would find a small complex of buildings. Some are small, with faded creosoted wooden paneling. The rest are sheathed in slowly rusting metal siding. This is the town brewery, the creator of Matsuo sake.

If the traveler came with an appointment, the firm president Takahashi, son of the chairman of the board Takahashi, would proudly meet him in the entryway. Everything about the young president contrasts with the environment. Heir to the 150-year-old family brewery, he is young. He is energetic. And he is extraordinarily articulate. He will happily offer a visitor tastes of several of the firm products. Ask him questions, and he will begin to describe his firm's philosophy of "terroir."[1]

Takahashi uses the French word. The ever-so-glossy *Wine Spectator* (Steiman 2014) defines it as "all the physical elements of a place that can affect the character of wine made from it, … the sum total of a site's constants, including soil composition, latitude, elevation, contour, sun exposure and climate…." Of course, *Wine Spectator* also reminds the reader that "[m]ost of us certainly can cite the different characteristics we expect from a comparison of say, Chambolle-Musigny with Nuits-St.-Georges…." Certainly? Never mind – Takahashi will happily explain that he buys the rice from several farmers in the tiny hamlet of Arasebara on the foothills of nearby Mt. Madarao. They grow premium sake rice varieties optimized for Nagano. And with that Arasebara rice, he has fashioned a sake that he hopes captures the character of the mountainside hamlet. Six times, he has won the national sake championship (*junmai daiginjo* and *daiginjo* divisions).

Sixty kilometers away in Nechi valley sits the Watanabe brewery. But 60 km only as a crow or drone might fly. The 2,500-meter Mt. Myoko lies between. Were a traveler to attempt the trip by train, he would spend 2-1/2 hours and find the rails single-tracked at the Nechi end as well. On an average day in 2018, only four people used the Nechi train station. Were the traveler to try to drive, in winter and spring he would find the roads closed by snow. Headed by Yoshiki Watanabe, the sixth-generation head of the family firm, the Watanabe brewery uses local rice to showcase the terroir of the tiny Nechi valley hamlet. It too focuses on sake-optimized rice varieties, but also distinguishes its bottles by vintage. In 2010, it won the champion sake award (*junmai ginjo* division) at the London International Wine Challenge.

Over the course of the last century, Japanese consumers have gradually lost their taste for sake. A few producers in Kobe dominated the mass market through economies of scale. The smaller regional brewers steadily went out of business. In this environment, ambitious (and perhaps desperate) brewers like Takahashi and Watanabe have tried to create a market for

---

[1] Interview with the author, August 2019.

unambiguously delicate and subtle high-end sake that showcases environmental variation. To create their terroir sake, they must convince local farmers to grow the high-risk and high-cost varieties of rice optimized for premium sake. The necessary arrangements involve extraordinarily complex incentive and informational requirements.

Apparently, brewers and farmers do not address these requirements either through elaborate contracts with verifiable terms or through vertical integration. Rather than pursue either strategy, they seem (i) deliberately to cultivate a dense network of social capital and to combine (ii) simple and short-term renewable (and conversely, terminable) contracts, (iii) what economists call "efficiency wage" level payments, (iv) close monitoring, and (v) free intervention, to give the brewer close control over the farming process. Probably, they do not draft elaborate contracts or vertically integrate for a simple reason: Within dense networks of social capital, their terminable contracts paying high prices give them all the control they need.

I state the problem at issue (Section I). I discuss the process and history of sake brewing (Sections II and III). I explore the development of premium local breweries (Section IV) and turn to the contractual problems facing brewers who would create sake that reflects and showcases their distinctive terroir (Sections V and VI).

I The Problem

For their premium terroir sake, brewers need the right kind of rice. More specifically, they need (a) sake rice (far more difficult to grow than table rice) (b) of a variety optimized for their peculiar location (and, being an unusual variety, one without well-established best practices), (c) grown to the exacting standards required for premium sake, (d) but which standards are ones that the brewer can observe but often cannot specify at levels sufficiently verifiable for explicit contracting. The brewers need farmers whom they can trust – farmers on whom they can rely to produce rice at quality levels higher than that for which they could draft verifiable contract terms. Conversely, farmers need brewers they can trust – brewers who will compensate them as promised at the end of the harvest.

The brewers can choose their farming partners carefully; the farmers can gauge whether to trust the brewers to pay the prices promised. Toward building that trust, the brewers and farmers may deliberately structure the contract to build a network of social and personal ties around each other; alternatively, the brewers might integrate vertically into farming. Neither the brewer nor the farmer knows how best to grow the difficult and temperamental rice. The brewers would like to be able to intervene in the farming process; the farmers do not know whether to trust them.

II Sake

A The Drink

At least some version of sake dates to prehistory. Migrants from Korea or Sakhalin (no one knows which) brought wet rice agriculture to Japan sometime around the third century BCE. Probably Japanese began to drink a fermented rice drink soon thereafter.

In the two millennia since, sake has played a prominent role in Japanese culture. Seventh- and eighth-century poets sang praises to it. The fifteenth-century bakufu elites paired the "Way of tea" with a Zen'ish "Way of sake." No one knows how it tasted back then, but everyone drank it. Farmers drank it, merchants drank it, and swordsmen drank it.

Over time and across the country, the brewers doubled as bankers. Fans of classic cinema will remember Mifune playing off the village brewer against the village brothel owner in Kurosawa's 1961 *Yojimbo*. In premodern villages, the sake brewers were often among the richest. They financed paddies, irrigation networks, and entrepreneurship more generally (see Chapter 5).

Sake brewing is easy to describe, but uncommonly hard to execute well. Through the fermentation process, yeast turns sugars into alcohol. Yet rice contains no sugar. To create the sugar, brewers need first to add mold (*koji*) to a small amount of steamed rice (*koji mai*). The mold then transforms the starch in the kernel into a sugar. To this starter, the brewers add additional rice (*shubo mai* or *moto mai*) and yeast (*kobo*). This creates a culture (*shubo*), to which the brewers will add more mold, steamed rice (*kake mai*), and water. They take this last step multiple times. They precipitate out the solid particles. And they typically close the process by heating the mixture to kill the active ingredients.

B The Industry

Before the 1868 Meiji coup, most sake production was local. Most major towns (and many small ones) had their local brewer. Out of the local rice, the brewers brewed the sake for their local customers.

For a few years after the coup, production remained local. In 1876, brewers operated 26,000 breweries (Ninomiya 2012, 58; Suzuki 2015, 71).

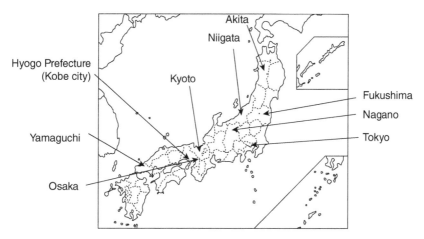

Figure 2.1 Japan

Soon, however, this changed – as the incipient transportation network allowed the most efficient producers to exploit economies of scale. By 1899, nearly half the breweries had disappeared, and only 15,000 remained. By 1942, the number had fallen to 7,000, and by 1958 to 4,000. In 2017, barely 1,378 still survived (Osake N.D.).

Today's 1,378 breweries vary enormously. The 11 largest each brew more than 10,000 kl of sake. Together, they employ over 4,300 employees and produce 47.5 percent of all sake (2017 data). Another 838 firms brew less than 100 kl each. Together, they employ 7,600 people and produce only 5.1 percent of all sake. Indeed, 830 of the breweries are seasonal firms that run only during the winter.[2]

Most of the biggest brewers operate from the Nada area of Kobe or the Fushimi area of Kyoto (see Figure 2.1). Now a center of 1.5 million and the capital of Hyogo prefecture, Kobe also serves as a port to the massive city of Osaka to its east. Nada lies along the eastern coast of Kobe, where the brewers enjoy access to an unusually clear stream of underground water. They traditionally bought their rice inland, brewed it with that local water, and – even during the Tokugawa period – shipped the sake to ports as far away as the Edo (now Tokyo) capital (Ninomiya 2012, 51–53).

Nada and Fushimi remain the base for the very largest producers. In Table 2.1, I give the market shares of the ten largest modern firms. Of these ten, only Koyama Honke does not operate from either Nada or Fushimi.

[2] Kokuzei cho (2018b) (fiscal 2018 survey). The cool temperatures lower the risk of sake spoiling during the course of production. See Suzuki (2015, 10–11, 29).

Table 2.1 *Largest breweries, 2018*

A. By total production

	Location	Production (kl)
Hakutsuru	Nada	52,363
Takara	Fushimi/Nada	51,801
Gekkeikan	Fushimi/Nada	42,744
Koyama Honke	Saitama	25,874
Ozeki	Nada	20,025
Kizakura	Fushimi	15,391
Kikumasamune	Nada	14,559
Nihon sakari	Nada	14,306
Oenon	Nada/other	12,896
Hakushika	Nada	8,563

B. By Premium Production

	Location	
Dassai	Yamaguchi	6,270
Kubota	Niigata	1,483
Hakuryu	Niigata	1,048
Bon	Fukui	874
Koyama Honke	Saitama	839
Hakushika	Nada	601
Masumi	Nagano	583
Gekkeikan	Fushimi/Nada	501
Shiratsuru	Nada	480
Oenon	Nada/other	466

Note: Premium – Junmai ginjo
Source: Yoshio Ono, Shuzogyo keieisha no henkaku kodo [Transformation of Brewery Managers], Shiga daigaku keizaigakubu kenkyu nenpo, 26: 13–38 (2019); Shuin naki fushin ni ochiitta seishu shijo [The Sake Market that is Thrown into Instability without Reason], Shurui shokuhin tokei geppo, February 2019.

C The Rice

Japanese farmers grow about 8.6 million tons of rice a year (Norin N.D.a). Most of this they grow as table rice, and for 35.9 percent of the table rice, they use the variety known as *koshihikari*. It is an enormously popular rice. Even the second and third most popular varieties are *koshihikari* derivatives. Farmers grow the largest amount of table rice in Niigata prefecture along the Japan Sea coast (Okome 2016; K.K. Kaneko 2016).

For their high-quality sake, brewers use more expensive rice varieties optimized for the drink. This sake rice is not a different species.

Like the table rice, it still falls within the *Japonica* rice used in Japan, Korea, and China. But within *Japonica*, the varieties that farmers grow specifically for sake will not double for food. Sake rice simply is not a vegetable that consumers would choose to eat (Suzuki & Takada 2017, 140).

For their very best sake, brewers use only this sake-optimized rice. Difficult to raise and producing a smaller yield, sake rice costs substantially more than table rice. Because of this cost, brewers sometimes skip the sake rice entirely for their cheapest sake. Given that the taste of the sake depends most critically on the first steps in the process, even brewers who use some sake rice may use it only for the initial starter (as *koji mai*) and culture (as *shubo mai*). They then add cheaper table rice for the rest of the process (as *kake mai*; this is 70 percent of the total).[3]

In 2018, Japanese farmers grew only 93,000 tons of sake rice. Sake rice has a relatively large kernel (which brewers need in order to remove the outer layers that muddy the taste). Sake rice will absorb the mold (*koji*) into the heart of the kernel more readily than table rice and will often contain a large starchy (*shimpaku*) core. It will have low levels of fat and protein.[4]

Yamada nishiki is the *koshihikari* of sake rice – indeed, 36.8 percent (34,059 tons) of all sake rice (Norin 2018a). It is particularly hard to grow. Developed in the 1930s, it is unusually susceptible to disease and with a long stem is especially vulnerable to late season typhoons.

Yet where *koshihikari* grows well across most of the country, *yamada nishiki* thrives only in a few areas. By latitude, the main islands of the Japanese archipelago stretch roughly from San Diego to Portland. The northern island of Hokkaido contains enormous ski resorts; the southern island of Kyushu was once a semi-tropical tourist destination. The island chain is relentlessly mountainous, and the area near Nagano hosted the 1998 Winter Olympics. Rain falls massively on the western side as the winds sweeping off Siberia pick up moisture over the Japan Sea and then drop it when they hit the mountains. The eastern side is dryer. Given that the mountains are essentially volcanic, soil content varies widely.

Yamada nishiki grows best in Hyogo prefecture (not coincidentally, near the Nada brewers). It needs moderate temperatures – ruling out both the northeast and the south. It does best in valleys (ideally, positioned east to west), with good sun exposure, with a large temperature variation from day to night, with good drainage, and with a clay base (Takeyasu 2018, 69). More than any other prefecture, Hyogo offers these

[3] Koike (1995, 161–62); Maikoku (2014, 12).
[4] Daiginjo (2014, 2); Kadono et al. (2011); Koike (1995, 161); Saito (2015, 2).

conditions, and in 2018, Hyogo farmers grew 58.5 percent of the *yamada nishiki* crop (Norin 2018a).

Outside of Hyogo, farmers grow other varieties of sake rice. At 21,000 tons (22.7 percent of the total), *gohyakuman goku* is the next most common sake rice. Farmers in Niigata prefecture produced 46.1 percent of the variety. *Miyama nishiki* (6,000 tons, 6.9 percent), of which Nagano farmers produced 61.0 percent, is third (Norin 2018a).

III The Sake Market

A Relative Decline

As the twenty-first century opened, Japanese were drinking less alcoholic beverages. In 1990, they had drunk 100.1 liters per adult capita per year.[5] By 2000, they drank only 95.5 liters, and by 2010 only 82.3. Middle-aged men and women drink more than younger men and women, but they also drink more than the elderly. As Japanese aged, the fraction in middle age declined, and with it fell per capita alcohol consumption (Kokuzei cho 2018a).

Of what they were drinking, Japanese drank less sake. For over a century, they had been steadily switching from sake to beer (Table 2.2). In 1902, they had drunk 92 percent of their alcohol as sake and only 2 percent as beer. By 1952, they drank 31 percent as sake and 34 percent as beer. By 2000, they drank only 10 percent of their alcoholic beverages as sake and 71 percent as beer.[6] Some urban professionals were beginning to drink wine, and some were returning to the traditional drink of shochu (once a distilled rotgut for impoverished peasants and factory hands) as a mark of retro-cool. Having peaked in 1973 at 1.4 million kl, sake consumption fell by 2012 to 439,000 kl.[7]

The decline hit brewers everywhere. As noted earlier, across the country as a whole the number of brewers fell from 4,000 in 1958 to 1,378 in 2017. In Nada itself, the number fell from sixty-seven breweries in 1973 to twenty-nine firms in 2011. In 1973, those 67 had made 582,000 kl. In 2011, the remaining 29 made only 163,000 kl (Nihon 2013).

---

[5] And there seems to have been a modest increase in per capita consumption during the 1990s recession.

[6] Beer falls from 71 percent to 44 percent over the next decade. This change reflects a shift toward a new supermarket drink category loosely called "liqueur." It is not what Westerners think of as liqueur. Rather, these are sweet and fruit-flavored, easy-to-drink, and cheap canned cocktails.

[7] Ono (2019, 13); Maikoku (2014, 2).

Table 2.2 *Consumption of alcoholic beverages*

Total volume (1000 kl)		Sake %	Beer %	Shochu %	Wine %
1882	573	96.5		1.6	
1892	695	96.6	0.2	1.4	
1902	660	92.2	2.5	3.2	
1912	860	88.4	4.1	5.4	
1922	1,344	80.1	10.3	6.7	
1932	1,002	73.7	14.0	9.4	
1942	669	44.0	31.4	8.1	
1952	1,073	30.9	34.1	22.8	
1962	2,791	23.7	54.4	8.7	
1970	4,901	31.2[*]	59.4	4.1	0.1
1980	6,660	22.6	65.8	3.4	0.7
1990	9,035	15.2	71.5	5.8	1.3
2000	9,520	10.3	71.0	7.7	2.8
2010	8,515	6.9	43.6	10.8	3.1

[*] The total volume of sake consumed peaked in 1973.

Sources: Fujio Oana, Shuzogyo no suii [Trends in the Brewing Industry], Jokyo, 65: 307–311 (1970); Kokuzeicho no "sake no shiori" ... [The "Guide to Sake" from the National Tax Office], November 9, 2014, Hatena blog, available at http://longlow.hatenablog.com/entry/20141109/p1.

B Historical Context

1. Introduction. – Tastes change. Over the course of the last 150 years, Japanese consumers have adopted Western dress. They listen to Western music. They watch Western movies. And they have learned to drink Western beverages.

But the story is not just one of drinking fashion. It is also a story about science and politics. It is a story that involves technological progress on the one hand, but military aggression and regulatory pressure on the other.

2. The science. – During the early Meiji decades, the most entrepreneurial brewers studied and incorporated modern science. Tokugawa brewers had not understood the chemistry of fermentation. They did not understand yeast and did not add it. Instead, their rice fermented because of the yeast in the environment – because of the fungi that happened to live in the air and grew on brewery surfaces themselves.

Once brewers learned the biology of fermentation, they began to approach yeasts deliberately. Rather than rely on haphazard environmental cultures, they searched for yeasts that had produced successful drinks in the past. They cultured those yeasts and began to add them with care. In the process, they lowered the fraction of batches that failed and raised the quality of the sake they produced (Suzuki 2015, 114).

Brewers also learned to accelerate the creation of the initial fermentation culture (the *shubo*). In the traditional process (called *kimoto*), brewers let the environmental yeast grow in the rice–mold mixture and turn the sugars into alcohol (Ozeki 1996, 560). The yeast initially competed with other bacteria in the mixture. As the (naturally occurring) lactic acid bacteria steadily multiplied, however, they eventually killed the other bacteria and let the fermentation proceed. This process took about a month. By deliberately adding lactic acid at the outset, the brewers found that they could halve the time necessary to finish the culture.[8]

In 1941, brewers also discovered that they could increase the amount of sake from a given quantity of rice by adding brewer's alcohol (Suzuki 2015, 167–68). Many (perhaps most) brewers still do. They note that the alcohol stabilizes the sake and helps to prevent spoilage. When critics complain, some producers protest that they are not adding a chemical from an antiseptic modern factory, but instead the traditional shochu distilled drink. They argue that the alcohol enhances the taste of the sake and that pre-Meiji brewers had done something like this as well. All this may be true, but critics point out that the mid-twentieth-century brewers (working in interwar Manchuria, no less) did not add the alcohol for any of these reasons. They added it because rice was expensive, and adding alcohol cut the cost of production (Yamakata 1997, 344–45).

3. Regulatory constraints. – Social tensions rose steadily during the interwar years, and the government responded by increasing control.[9] As they had since the late nineteenth century, peasants continued to abandon the farms and move to the cities. There, they crowded into newly created slums. Some rioted, and in 1918, they rioted over the price of rice. Within this environment, political entrepreneurs organized communist and anarchist cells.

As the Tokyo government worried about the leftist cells, the army expanded its territory over the continent. It evaded efforts by Tokyo politicians to control it. It created a massive colony in Manchuria. And by the late 1930s, it had dragged the country into a war it could not win.

The government responded to the fiscal strains by adopting increasingly stringent controls over an ever-wider swath of the economy. Central to this

---

[8] Ozeki (1996, 560); Suzuki (2015, 111–16).

[9] Note that during the late nineteenth and early twentieth century, the tax on alcohol was the single largest source of government revenue. Suzuki (2015, 102–03).

program, it began to control the market for rice. As it moved the country increasingly to a war footing, it relentlessly intensified this control.[10]

The Allied (effectively American) occupation government continued much of the pre-war control structure. Although Shigeru Yoshida dismantled the bulk of the program when he replaced socialist Tetsu Katayama as prime minister in 1948, he retained many of the controls over rice. During the next two decades, the government allocated rice among the brewers by quota. It had begun the quotas in 1938, but continued them after the war. A brewer could use the rice allocated to him or her, but (unless he or she bought another brewer's quota) could acquire no more.[11]

C The Nada-Fushimi Response

Deregulation would eventually come, but only after sake brewers (in response to the regulation) had so badly depreciated sake quality as to alienate most of their sophisticated potential customers. It was not until 1969 and 1974 that the government finally dismantled the regulatory strictures on the sake and rice markets.[12] Over the four preceding decades, brewers had learned to weather regulatorily created rice shortages. Now they needed to survive in a competitive market. To that goal, they would find their learned strategies badly mismatched.

The brewers had focused almost entirely on making sake as cheaply as possible. In 1922, a chemist had developed a synthetic sake that used very little (if any) rice.[13] With this technology, brewers had developed what would become the infamous "treble sake." Although they started with rice, mold, and water, they added a variety of other ingredients that let them treble the amount of drink they could produce from a given quantity of rice.[14]

Synthetic sake remains on the market and is often used for cooking. The treble-sake drink it spawned constituted a large part of the market in the 1950s and only disappeared in 2006. It had been the very worst sake. By 2006, too few people wanted to drink it to warrant production anymore.[15]

---

[10] Ozeki (1996, 426); Ito (1981); Furuichi (1996).
[11] Ono (2019, 22); Shibuya (2020, 89); Ninomiya (2015); Nishinomiya (1989, 226–27, 263); Suzuki (2015, 147–55, 164–82).
[12] Ono (2019, 22, 25); Ninomiya (2015, 492); Ito (1981); Ozeki (1996, 425–26); Suzuki (2015, 199); Sando (2018, 2019).
[13] Ishiguro (2015a); Ono (2019, 23); Ninomiya (2015, 472–73).
[14] Ishiguro (2015a); Ninomiya (2015, 472–73, 482–85); Ono (2019, 23); Yamakata (1977, 344).
[15] Ishiguro (2015b, 2015c); Nishinomiya (1989, 264–5).

In this desultory market, the Nada and Fushimi brewers did have name recognition. When during the 1950s and 60s they lacked high-enough rice quotas to meet the market demand, they simply filled the resulting shortage by buying additional sake. They bought it from less well-known regional brewers in bulk and resold it under their own names (Ono 2019, 24). They did not buy this bulk sake from brewers with whom they maintained long-term relations. Instead, they merely bought the available sake on the spot market: One brewery needed more sake; another had more than it could sell. In 1975, the Nada giant Hakutsuru brewed 109,000 koku (1 koku = 180 l) of sake; it sold 404,000.[16]

Note the obvious implication of these bulk sales: By mid-century, cheap sake was everywhere the same. By deliberately controlling the chemical transformations involved – standardizing yeast quality, introducing lactic acid, adding alcohol, and scientifically controlling quantities and timing – brewers had eliminated nearly all random variation. In the course of shifting to mechanized and sanitized processes, they had cut most of the variation not only in their own output but also from brewer to brewer as well (Ninomiya 2015, 473).

Although the government deregulated much of the rice and sake markets in the early 1970s, the Nada-Fushimi brewers continued to position their sake as a low-cost mass-market beverage. They focused first on price. Japan had not been rich in 1960, and they had positioned their drink as a low-cost beverage for ordinary Japanese. By the 1970s, Japanese were no longer poor, but the mass-market brewers continued to make the same drink.

In fact, the Nada-Fushimi brewers kept this strategy through the end of the century. The number two Gekkeikan firmly controlled a solid presence as the Budweiser of Japanese sake: ubiquitous, cheap, and defiantly working class (see generally Kawaguchi & Fujimoto 2007). The number four Ozeki found its own niche for cheap sake in a one-drink-quantity bottle that it distributed the country over: "One Cup Ozeki," they called it. In 1965, One Cup was 0.9 percent of Ozeki output. In 1967, Ozeki loaded the One Cup into vending machines, and by 1991, it constituted 34.0 percent of Ozeki output (Ozeki 1996, 334–35).

Consistent with this mass-market strategy, in the 1970s, the Nada makers began to sell sake in milk-like paper cartons. The cartons save money, fit in refrigerators, and look aggressively anti-gourmet. Ozeki introduced its first paper-carton sake in 1976. By 1983, carton sake constituted

---

[16] Yamakata (1977, 390); Ninomiya (2015, 488).

18.7 percent of its output (Ozeki 1996, 368). Gekkeikan introduced paper cartons in 1980 (Gekkeikan 1987, 178). By 2000, paper-carton sake was about 40 percent of all sake volume; by 2016, it constituted more than half (Osake N.D.).

IV Craft Breweries

A Introduction

As Japanese grew wealthier, many consumers developed a taste for premium alcoholic drinks. Tariffs came down (Ishiguro 2015c), and good scotch and cognac offered a complexity lost in most other distilled drinks. French and Napa wines presented subtleties that the Nada-Fushimi brewers had long since erased from sake.

In the competition for mass-market alcohol, the regional sake brewers could not win. The contest rewarded investments in the large-scale equipment that generated economies of scale. The Nada-Fushimi brewers brewed a drink that differed little from maker to maker and competed mostly by price. Unable to beat that price, the local brewers steadily disappeared.

It was within this rapidly deteriorating market that a few local brewers gambled on premium sake. They gambled big.

B The Premium Niche

1. The formula. – To shift their product upmarket, brewers focused first on three elements. They stopped adding brewers' alcohol. They removed more of the kernel's coarse-tasting outer layers. And they used costly sake rice varieties for a larger fraction of their rice.

a. Junmai. Pivotal to the rediscovery (or perhaps invention) of premium sake was the concept of *junmai* (meaning "pure rice"). By mid-century, Japanese brewers had learned to cut costs by adding brewers' alcohol to their sake. In doing so, they could use less rice and routinize, stabilize, and mechanize large-scale production.

Local brewers offered a return to a conceptually simpler but practically more difficult drink: sake made only with rice, mold, water, and yeast. This was a costlier process. It required nearly twice as much rice and (if the brewers are to be believed) more patience, subtlety, and expertise. They were rediscovering the classical sake-brewing tradition. In truth, they brewed a sake that was almost certainly much better than anything in the nineteenth century. But never mind. They were returning sake to the pre-mechanized, pre-adulterated pristine past.[17]

A mid-sized Fushimi brewer named Tamanohikari had made the first of the post-war *junmai* in 1964 (Ishiguro 2015b). It continues to proclaim that fact boldly on its company website. Steadily after the 1980s, local brewers began to focus on *junmai* sake. Many jettisoned their mass-market lines and started producing only *junmai*.[18]

b. Ginjo. Local breweries also began to focus production on their *ginjo* and *daiginjo* offerings. To make sake, brewers do not directly steam the rice kernels. Instead, they first mill (grind) the rice to remove the germ and some of the outer layers. Those layers contain material that introduces unwanted flavors into sake. Mill the rice first, and the drink will present a cleaner taste. It will also cost more to produce.

To make ordinary sake, a brewer might grind off as little as 10 to 20 percent of the kernel. To make *ginjo* sake, he (or she – most are men) will remove 40 percent, and to make *daiginjo* (meaning "great *ginjo*"), he will remove 50 percent. He will also need to ferment the rice at a lower temperature, and at a slower pace. The process is obviously more expensive. A sake that is both *junmai* (no alcohol added) and *daiginjo* (50 percent removed) will require six times as much rice as an ordinary sake.[19]

The *ginjo* (and *daiginjo*) sakes offer a cleaner taste than ordinary sake. Fans describe them as crisp, delicate, aristocratic, and clear. Note that the *ginjo* technique is relatively new. Several Hiroshima breweries produced the earliest versions of *ginjo* near the beginning of the twentieth century. A mid-sized Fushimi brewer, Tsuki no katsura, produced the first *daiginjo* in 1966.[20]

c. Rice variety. The regional brewers also began to focus heavily on premium rice varieties. Recall that brewers add rice at three stages. They mix a small amount with the mold (*koji mai*), add a larger amount when they introduce yeast and start fermentation (*shubo mai*), and then add the majority in later stages (*kake mai*). For mass-market sake, brewers might use table rice for all three processes. Those selling into the middle-tier might use table rice for the third stage, but sake rice for the first two (Saito 2015, 1).

Brewers selling into the premium market sometimes use only sake rice for the entire process. Recall that the sake rice varieties tend to grow only in limited areas and that the *yamada nishiki* grows primarily in Hyogo.

[17] Ishiguro (2015b); Tamanohikari (N.D.); Shibuya (2020, 83).
[18] Sando (2018); Akita (2019a); Tamanohikari (N.D.).
[19] Shibuya (2020, 83); Kokuzeicho (N.D.); Suzuki (2015, 52–53).
[20] Ono (2019, 26); Ishiguro (2015b, 1966); Suzuki (2015, 89, 160–61).

Some regional growers simply import Hyogo *yamada nishiki* for their sake. Others mix local sake rice varieties with imported *yamada nishiki*. And still others – the terroir breweries described below – will focus primarily or exclusively on distinctive local varieties.

2. The Dassai success. – Asahi Shuzo's Dassai brand embodies the premium local-sake boom. As a success story, it has also inspired beleaguered small breweries the country over. The Asahi sake brewery (unrelated to the company that makes Asahi beer) had been founded in 1948 in Yamaguchi prefecture in southwestern Japan. As sake consumption fell, it found itself in dire straits. Total sales had plummeted to 97 million yen (at the approximate conversation rate of 100 yen per dollar, $970,000).

In 1984, Hiroshi Sakurai took over as third-generation head of the family firm. He was thirty-four, the firm was failing, and he gambled big. The firm had been making ordinary sake. He jettisoned the line and over the next several years would develop a clear firm policy: He would make only *junmai*; he would make only *daiginjo*; and he would use only *yamada nishiki*. Not only would he only make *daiginjo*, he made history in 1992 when he introduced a *daiginjo* milled down to the last 23 percent.

As of 2005, Dassai still sold only 216 kl. By 2010, sales had trebled to 776 kl, by 2013 to 2,052 kl, and by 2018 to 6,270 kl. Some of its bottles now sell for close to 40,000 yen (about $400). By 2018, it was far and away the largest maker of premium sake (Table 2.1).[21]

At about the time that the third-generation Sakurai arrived at Dassai, the brewers' trade association for Niigata prefecture made roughly the same collective gamble. Faced with the secular decline in sake consumption and the scale economies in Nada and Fushimi, the Niigata brewers together decided to move upmarket (Ono 2019, 25). With a source for water with very low mineral content and the local *gohyakuman goku* sake rice, they have cultivated a distinctive Niigata taste, which they describe as *tanrei karakuchi* – light and dry. Largely, they have succeeded. After Dassai, the two breweries producing the most premium sake are both Niigata firms (Table 2.1), and by total volume, Niigata ranks third after Hyogo and Kyoto.

Akita prefecture hosts an unusually large number of very high-end breweries as well. Like Niigata, Akita provides low-mineral water and distinctive local sake rice varieties: *Akita sake komachi* and *miyama nishiki*. When the *Sake Time* gourmet news ranked the top twenty bottles in 2020, five were from Akita (Zenkoku 2020a). Three each were from Nagano and Fukushima, and none were from either Hyogo or Kyoto.

---

[21] "Dassai" (2013); Yamaguchi (2018); Nihon (2018).

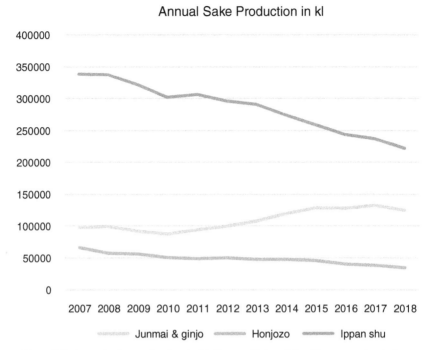

Figure 2.2 Annual sake production in kl. Source: Kokuzeicho, *Shuzo nendo ni okeru seishu no seizo jokyo to ni tsuite* [Regarding the Production Circumstances, Etc., of the Brewing of Sake], various years

3. The industry transformation. – Steadily, one-time local breweries like Dassai have begun to transform the sake industry. Overall, Japanese continue to drink less alcohol (Table 2.2). They also continue to drink less mass-market sake (Figure 2.2). From 2007 to 2018, sales of ordinary sake fell from 339,000 kl to 222,000 kl. Those of the intermediate category *honjozo* (described in Subsection C, below) fell from 67,000 kl to 35,000 kl.

Over the same period, however, premium *junmai* and *ginjo* sales rose from 98,000 kl to 125,000 kl. This is the growth that the regional breweries have driven. By total 2018 production, nine of the top ten breweries were in either Nada or Fushimi (Table 2.1). Yet of the top producers of junmai ginjo sake, only four of the top ten were from Nada or Fushimi, and none of the top five.[22]

---

[22] Exports have been increasing. In 2018, the value of the exports had reached 22.2 billion yen (Nihon 2019a). Of the exports, 58 percent are of the premium sake described in Section IV.C. The largest export market is the US. To the US., 87 percent are of the premium sake (Kokuzeicho 2018c).

During the war-impoverished and heavily regulated mid-century, Nada-Fushimi breweries had cultivated a competitive advantage in low-cost production. Exploiting their economies of scale, they had focused on the mass-market sector. Hyogo producers still brew 85 percent of their sake as general (*futsu* or *ippan*) sake (2014 numbers). The Kyoto producers brew 90 percent as general. By contrast, in Dassai's Yamaguchi prefecture, producers brew barely 21 percent of their sake as general.[23]

The regional brewers have deliberately crafted a new image. For decades, sake was a drink that middle-aged men (especially working class men) drank in dirty bars on their way home from work. They drank it heated in small ceramic cups. By contrast, the regional brewers have nurtured an image of sake drunk by urbane thirty- and forty-something gourmets. They drink it cold, in long-stemmed wine glasses (Ono 2019, 13).

The regional brewers present sake as a distinctively Japanese drink, but one to be savored by these successful young professionals. On its website, Niigata brewer Kikusui describes sake as a drink for all seasons. There is a sake to drink when relaxing with friends at a restaurant. There is a sake for men to drink while flirting with a waitress. And there is a sake for women to drink while recalling their first crush, continues Kikusui, while commiserating with each other over the sadnesses that only women can know, or while (alluding to a well-known passage in the *Tale of Genji*) trashing the actual men in their lives (Kunifuda N.D.).

4. Extensions. – Encouraged by the success of Dassai and its hundreds of competitors, entrepreneurial sake brewers experiment with a wide range of new approaches. Recall that since the Meiji period, brewers have added lactic acid to eliminate competing bacteria and accelerate fermentation. Some regional brewers have returned to the earlier fermentation process (*kimoto*) and use no lactic acid at all.[24]

Some brewers experiment with other long-discarded techniques. One Akita brewer abandoned stainless steel containers for the earlier wooden vats. The vats require more work cleaning and repairing them, but they "bring a deeper taste to the sake," claims the brewer. Another brewer turned to the panoply of other wooden hand tools that brewers had discarded. Another abandoned added yeast and relies on the wild yeasts living in the brewery. Yet others – like the Watanabe brewery in the Nechi valley – are introducing the concept of vintages.[25]

---

[23] Yamagata (2015); see generally Shibuya (2020, 86).
[24] Sando (2018); Akita (2019a).
[25] Akita (2019a); Saito and Yamada (2017, 18); Bumu (2015).

Some brewers have revived discontinued local rice varieties. Despite the dominance of *yamada nishiki, gohyakuman goku,* and *miyama nishiki,* in 2019, farmers grew 119 different varieties of sake rice. Many are new, experimental varieties. Others are varieties farmers discarded long ago as sake production centralized in Nada-Fushimi and brewers converged on homogeneous tastes.[26]

And still other brewers cater to the distinctly modern demand for "organic" and "sustainable" products. A wide variety of regional brewers include sake made from low- or no-pesticide and low- or no-chemical fertilizer rice. Kikusui advertises itself as "an environmentally friendly business" that donates a share of its revenue to the World Wildlife Fund (Kobayashi 2004). The Izumibashi brewery in Kanagawa promotes its "sustainable" production techniques.[27]

C Certification

In 1990, the government introduced a standard certification regime for the terms *junmai, ginjo,* and *daiginjo.* It had graded sake by a different metric for much of the mid-century, though nominally by quality. It had also taxed the brewers according to those quality grades, however, so brewers began to manipulate the grades to lower their tax bill. By the end of the twentieth century, the earlier grades had ceased to reflect quality, and the government repealed the system.[28]

Under the new 1990 certification regime, the tax office defined several of the new premium categories.[29] The rules have changed modestly over the years, but as of 2020:

JUNMAI: sake with only rice, yeast, and rice-based mold (*koji*).
GINJO: sake in which each kernel is milled to 60 percent or less of its initial size and in which any brewers' alcohol constitutes less than 10 percent of the weight of the rice.

---

[26] Zenkoku (2019); Norin (2018a).
[27] Kobayashi (2004); Sando (2019); Miyajima (N.D.).
[28] Ishiguro (2015c); Ono (2019, 22); Iga (2008, 152). For much of the period, the quality designation turned on the level of alcohol (before and during the war, watered sake – known as "goldfish sake" on the theory that it had so little alcohol that fish could live in it – had been a problem) and the level of additives. Breweries could avoid the higher taxes by not submitting their sake for measurement and taking the lowest grade. For more detail, see Suzuki (2015, 5; 147–58).
[29] The new certification standards were introduced in the National Tax Office order, *Seishu no seiho hinshitsu hyoji kijun wo sadameru ken* [Establishing the Display Standards for the Means of Production and the Product Quality of Sake], Kokuzeicho

DAIGINJO: sake in which each kernel is milled to 50 percent or less of its initial size and in which any brewers' alcohol constitutes less than
10 percent of the weight of the rice.

HONJOZO: sake in which each kernel has been milled to 70 percent or less of its
initial size and any brewers' alcohol constitutes less than 10 percent
of the weight of the rice.

Junmai offers classic nineteenth-century-style sake. Brewers use it to
showcase their distinctive flavors. *Ginjo* and *daiginjo* offer smooth, clear
tastes. Because differences attributable to soil, weather, fertilizers, and rice
variety tend to concentrate in the outer layers, however, *ginjo* and *daiginjo*
offer less variation across breweries. A *ginjo* with no added alcohol would
be called a *junmai ginjo*. *Honjozo* represents a sake intermediate both in
quality and in price between the other certified sakes and ordinary uncerti-
fied sake (*futsu* or *ippan shu*).

V The Invention of Terroir

A The Competitive Logic

The local breweries had sparked a renaissance in sake. By cultivating a taste
for quality, they had created a market where none had existed before. The
Nada-Fushimi brewers had responded to the war-time regulatory regime
by using technology to lower cost and generate consistent products, but
ignored the potential market for premium sake. The smaller local breweries
now exploited the resulting opportunity and succeeded.

Unfortunately for the local breweries, the Nada-Fushimi breweries can
compete in the market for *ginjo* and *daiginjo* if they choose. They will need
better rice. They will need to shift production technique. They will need
expertise. But they already have sophisticated equipment. They have capital. And if they lack the requisite experience and technique, they can hire it.

They can, and they have. All of the top mass-market producers (see
Table 2.1) have premium products. Ozeki still stocks its One Cup Ozeki in
vending machines, but it also offers an award-winning *junmai daiginjo* at
5,118 yen. Hakutsuru sells a 200 ml can of ordinary sake for 218 yen, but also
offers an award-winning *junmai daiginjo* for over 10,000 yen. Gekkeikan
sells its perennial working-class drink, but produces an award-winning
junmai daiginjo besides. Takara offers enough varieties in cardboard cartons to fill a refrigerator, but sells a *junmai daiginjo* to boot.

kokushi no. 8, November 22, 1989. The order is issued under the Shuzei no hozen oyobi
shuruigyo kumiai to ni kansuru horitsu [Law Regarding the Preservation of Liquor Tax
and Liquor Industry Organizations, Etc.], Law No. 7 of 1953.

What is more, a local brewery looking to move upscale will worry about more than Nada-Fushimi. It will face direct competition from Dassai and the Niigata-Nagano-Akita-Fukushima breweries that already dominate the "best sake" rankings. These breweries are local in name only. For the young Matsuo president in Shinano village, his competitors include the many premium breweries striving to replicate the Dassai success.

Crucially, the more successful two *daiginjo* rivals might be, the closer they will taste. Rice does indeed acquire flavors that reflect the mineral content of the water, the character of the soil, and the weather. But these differences are located almost entirely in a kernel's outer layers. Grind off 40 to 50 percent of the kernel, and rice loses most of that distinctiveness.[30] All too often, as one brewer cruelly put it, *ginjo* will be to sake what the "valedictorian" was to the high school class – never wrong, but never interesting either (Miyajima N.D.).

Hence the appeal of "terroir." If the Matsuo president in Shinano village and his peers around the country can convince consumers to distinguish and enjoy regional variation, they create a niche that the other breweries cannot readily fill. Perhaps small Niigata breweries like Watanabe can fashion a taste that reflects the windswept Nechi valley, the brutally cold winters, and the massive snowstorms. Perhaps Matsuo can fashion a taste distinctive to the Arasebara hamlet (population 219) on the foothills of Mt. Madarao. To be sure, even connoisseurs of the best French and Napa wines roll their eyes at some terroir claims; many sake fans retain a similar suspicion too. As one reader of an earlier draft put it, mostly this shows that people have too much money.

But what the Matsuo and Watanabe presidents and their allies hope to create is an appreciation for a wide variety of very different but each appealing sakes. In New York, a connoisseur might choose a white wine one night, a red another. Among the reds, he might choose a pinot noir one night, a cabernet sauvignon another. Among the pinot noir, he might choose a Cote de Nuits one night, a Givry another. If the Matsuo and Watanabe presidents and their allies have their way, the sake industry will offer connoisseurs' choices just as rich.

B Certification Problems

Give him half a chance, however, and President Takahashi will complain about his certification problems. He (and others championing terroir sake)[31]

---

[30] Ninomiya (2014, 469–70); Sugihara (2012); Miyajima (N.D.); Bumu (2015).
[31] See, e.g., Nihonshu (2019); Miyajima (N.D.); Shibuya (2020, 94).

would like to adopt something close to the French *appellation d'origine controlee* (AOC). Under AOC, a winery can advertise its offerings as coming from a given district – a system in which, as Orley Ashenfelter (2007) put it, the "best wines of Bordeaux are made from grapes (typically cabernet sauvignon and merlot) grown on specific plots of land and the wine is named after the property, or chateau, where the grapes are grown." Under AOC, the size of the certified district can vary, depending on how selective the winery chooses to be. A winery can market its product as a Bordeaux wine, as a Haut-Medoc (within Bordeaux), or as a Pauliac (within Haut-Medoc). Some Nagano breweries sell distinctively Nagano sake. Matsuo offers a sake distinctive to Arasebara.

In fact, Takahashi would like to go farther and certify rice variety as well. The French chateaux blend wines, but the AOC rules specify the grapes they can blend (e.g., Ashenfelter & Storchman 2016, 39–40). Premium California wineries usually specify the grape. For his non-terroir sake at the Matsuo brewery, Takahashi sometimes uses *yamada nishiki* from areas outside Nagano. But for his local sakes, he uses several different varieties. For some, he uses *miyama nishiki*, the standard Nagano premium sake rice. For others, he celebrates the more recent local alternative, *sankei nishiki*.

In 2015, the Ministry of Agriculture, Forestry and Fisheries (MAFF) bureau for northeastern Japan launched the "Tohoku Sake Terroir Project" (it too uses the French word). The surviving local breweries in the region were trying to move into premium sake, much like the Niigata breweries had done four decades ago. The bureau hoped to facilitate their shift by encouraging a distinctively northeastern taste. The MAFF bureau sponsored a study group. It met several times. It assembled a roster of eighty breweries that hoped to market sake with the new designation. Largely, however, it seems to have gone inactive.[32]

In any case, for breweries like Matsuo, the project did not go far enough. To qualify under the project, a brewery had to use local water, use at least 50 percent local (prefectural, or at least northeastern) rice, and communicate directly with its supplying farmers (Tohoku N.D.). For advocates of a narrower terroir approach, this was far too broad. The project proposed certifying the sake's prefecture. Yet Nagano has a population of 380,000, more than the entire Bordeaux area (population 250,000). In effect, the project would preclude all of the finer AOC partitions.

When Japan joined the World Trade Organization, it adopted a completely separate, national program for geographical certification (Kokuzeicho 2020).

---

[32] Tohoku (N.D.); Matsuo (2017, 42).

As of mid-2020, it had haphazardly approved four sake designations under the program. In 2005, it had certified the sake from the town of Hakusan on the Japan Sea coast: Local breweries could use the designation if they used local water and only Japanese rice (i.e., rice from anywhere in Japan) of grade 1. In 2016, they certified sake from the prefecture of Yamagata: Prefectural breweries could use the designation if they used local water and – again – Japanese rice. In 2020, they certified a much more finely partitioned designation for the Harima area of Hyogo: Harima breweries could use the designation if they used local water and *yamada nishiki* rice from Hyogo prefecture.

Alas, for terroir brewers like Matsuo, the government saved its ultimate insult for 2018. That year, under its WTO geographical certification, it designated "Nada Gogo." To advertise the certification, the Nada firms had to use local water. They had to use Japanese rice (again, from anywhere in Japan). And that rice had to be of at least grade 3 (rarely does anyone designate sake rice below grade 3).

Takahashi and his fellow terroir brewers have not constructed (either publicly through the government or privately among each other) a certification program – yet. But one should not try to explain too much. They want a program. They do not have one yet. And they have only begun to try.

VI Contracting for Terroir

A Introduction

For terroir offerings, breweries cannot obtain rice through the usual routes. For high-quality sake, more generally, some breweries specify desired rice variety and quality grade and buy it anonymously through intermediaries. For terroir sake, breweries cannot do this. They will need to contact local farmers and negotiate the transaction directly. In the process, they will encounter contracting problems common to buyers more generally – whether Midwestern heavy industry manufacturers, Japanese car companies, or Silicon Valley tech firms.

The brewers and farmers rarely draft elaborate contracts with verifiable terms; they seldom vertically integrate. Instead, they deliberately maintain extensive social networks. Within these networks, they combine short-term renewable (and hence terminable) contracts, efficiency-wage-level prices, close monitoring, and free intervention. In the process, they give the brewer close control over the farming process.

B The JA Cooperative Network

Most firms buy their sake rice through their local agricultural cooperative. More precisely, in recent decades, sake brewers have been buying about 70 percent of their sake rice through their prefectural sake brewers' association and the JA, the national network of Japanese agricultural cooperatives.[33]

Under this arrangement, each year, the brewers' association solicits rice orders from its members for the season two years hence. It places the orders with the agricultural cooperative. The cooperatives then distribute the orders among their membership.[34]

The brewers will use this sake rice mostly for their initial steps. Recall that they add rice in three broad steps: They mix a small amount of rice with the mold (the *koji mai*); they add more rice with the yeast (the *shubo mai*); and after the fermentation has progressed, they add the rest of the rice (the *kake mai*). Many (if not most) brewers use table rice for the third, high-volume step. They use this costlier sake rice primarily for the first two steps.

C Muramai

1. Classic. – In their official histories, the Nada-Fushimi firms recount the way they had insured a supply of high-quality rice before war. They had contracted directly with Hyogo farming villages, they write. Their problems had begun in 1874. That year, according to these standard industry accounts, the government started collecting taxes in cash. The Tokugawa domains had collected their taxes in rice and in Hyogo had carefully inspected the rice submitted. They had rejected low-quality rice and imposed penalties on those who had submitted it. Once the government adopted a cash tax, however, farmers switched to low-quality rice that they could easily market. Why the farmers would not be able to sell high-quality rice at high prices the standard histories do not say. They report only that the brewers found themselves without the high-quality rice that they needed for their sake.[35]

Somewhere around the turn of the century, Nada firms began contracting for high-quality rice from selected Hyogo hamlets. *Muramai*, they called the arrangements: "village rice." Some writers place the first *muramai* contract in the early 1890s with the Kamikume hamlet in Yoneda village. Others name the nearby hamlet of Ichinose in Yokawa village.[36]

---

[33] Suzuki and Takada (2017); Nihon (2018); Saito (2015, 3); Hirogaru (2018); Keiyaku (2018).
[34] Hayashi (2017, 55); Koike (1995, 163); Maikoku (2014, 13).
[35] See Hyogo (1961, 99–102); Daiginjo (2014, 4).
[36] See Ozeki (1996, 432); Hyogo (1961, 100); Saito (2015, 8–9); Sakamai (N.D.).

By the early twentieth century, the major Nada-Fushimi breweries were buying large portions of their sake rice from a portfolio of hamlets. The details of the arrangements varied, but usually the brewery agreed to buy a hamlet's entire crop. In return, the villagers promised to work to improve rice quality. The firms obtained a steady supply of quality rice. The villages obtained a reliable outlet at a good price.[37]

The parties waited to decide the price of the rice until November or December, after its delivery. At that point, a hamlet representative, the brewer, and the rice broker (if one were involved) met to negotiate the price. Usually, they adopted a standard discount (or more rarely a premium) from the *muramai* contract price for the original Kamikume hamlet. Despite the obvious possibility of corruption, the other brewers and hamlets apparently took this price as an honest reference point.[38]

The Kamikume price similarly followed negotiations among a hamlet representative, the brewer, and a rice broker. Given its larger significance, however, the negotiations could take time. Generally, the parties looked to such factors as the previous year's price, general economic circumstances, fluctuations in the spot market price for rice, and the annual yield. Reflecting their higher quality, *muramai* rice tended to sell for a premium over other sake rice.[39]

Crucially, brewers and hamlets did not always renew the *muramai* contracts. Instead, villages maintained their contracts only if they worked collectively and steadily to improve the quality of the rice they supplied. Those that did not, sometimes found their contracts terminated.[40]

2. Modern. – Some Nada-Fushimi brewers again maintain contracts with Hyogo hamlets, but these are not continuations of the earlier contracts. After the rice riots of 1918, the Japanese government had begun evermore intrusively to regulate the market for rice. As the country drifted into war during the 1930s, the army increased its control over the economy. During the earliest years of these rice-market controls, the Nada breweries had negotiated exceptions for their *muramai* contracts.

Yet the regulatory exceptions for the Hyogo *muramai* contracts did not survive the war. Given that the government retained many of its earlier

---

[37] See Toku A (N.D.); Mori (1983, 124–26); Ninomiya (2013, 311); Hyogo (1961, 98–104); Daiginjo (2014, 3).

[38] For lists of the muramai villages, see generally Ozeki (1996, 433) and Hyogo (1961, 89). For the pricing hierarchy in 1938 of the villages relative to Kamikume, see Mori (1983, 125).

[39] See Nishinomiya (1989, 197); Hyogo (1961, 99–109); and Mori (1983, 126).

[40] See Toku A (N.D.); Nishinomiya (1989, 197); Ozeki (1996, 432); and Hyogo (1961, 98–105).

rice-market controls after the war, neither did they reappear during the early post-war years. Only in the 1970s did firms reacquire their ability to negotiate their own supply contracts. By then, however, the Nada firms no longer produced much high-quality sake.

Nevertheless, some of the Nada producers did begin to negotiate *mura-mai* contracts again. By the 1970s, some of the firms wanted *yamada nishiki* for their best offerings, and the hamlets that had provided sake rice before the war now grew some of the best of the *yamada nishiki*. As of 1981, the 10 largest Nada brewers obtained their *yamada nishiki* through *muramai* contracts with 326 hamlets (Mori 1983, 126).

These new *muramai* contracts were not simple continuations of the old. Hyogo in 1980 was not the Hyogo of 1930. Within Yokawa village, 38 groups of farmers now sell to brewers. They include classic hamlets that produced the best sake rice before the war (Saito 2015, 9). But other villages that had maintained *muramai* contracts pre-war no longer do, while hamlets without pre-war *muramai* antecedents now do negotiate them (Koike 1995, 166; Nihonshu no korekara). The late nineteenth- century brewers and farmers negotiated the contracts that enabled the brewers to obtain the rice they needed for premium sake. By mid-century, regulatory restrictions killed the market for that premium sake. As the regulatory restrictions disappeared, the brewers began slowly to recreate premium offerings. To obtain the rice they needed for this sake, they began to contract directly with farmers. As they did, they turned to contracts much like the contracts they had used decades before.

D Direct Contracts

1. Introduction. – Should brewers want to make sake that reflects the weather and soil of their area, they will need to approach farmers themselves. If President Takahashi of the Matsuo brewery wants to make a sake that reflects the Arasebara paddies on the foothill of Mt. Madarao, he will need to approach the Arasebara farmers himself.

Increasingly, premium regional sake brewers are doing exactly that. Over the course of the past decades, brewers had been procuring about 70 percent of their sake rice through the agricultural cooperatives. In 2010, they bought 73.8 percent of their sake rice through the coop. By 2015, they bought only 58.3 percent. In 2011, Akita prefecture brewers directly contracted for 167 ha of sake rice. By 2014, they had 292 ha under contract.[41]

---

[41] 1 hectare (ha) = 100 ares (a) = 10,000 sq. meters = 2.47 US acres. Saito (2015, 3); Hirogaru (2018); Keiyaku (2018); Suzuki and Takada (2017); Hayashi (2017, 56).

Consider first the nature and structure of the contracts they use, and then how and when they intervene in the farming itself.

2. The nature of the contracts. – (a) Brewers pay a generous price. Regional breweries pay their farmers more than what they would pay the coop – sometimes substantially more. In his recent study of Akita brewers, Futoshi Hayashi (2017, 62) examines the way they set the price. Often, he finds, they simply add a premium to the coop's price. They do not use formulas that turn on the results of quality inspections, or on the methods that the farmers use to cultivate.

Instead, Akita brewers take what the farmer could obtain from the coop, and pay him substantially more. "We want a price where the farmers will want to raise sake rice even if table rice is selling for 20,000 yen [per 60 kg]," said one brewer. To do this, he needed to pay two or three times the usual price for table rice (Hayashi 2017, 62).

Prior to the war, the Hyogo brewers paid high prices under their *mura-mai* contracts as well. In 1933, Hyogo sake rice sold for an average 23.30 yen per koku (180 l); the Kamikume *muramai* rice sold for 27.30. In 1935, the Hyogo sake rice sold for 32.63, while Kamikume *muramai* went for 35.60. In 1937, the Hyogo average was 36.64 while Kamikume sold for 40.00. And in 1938, the Hyogo sake rice sold for 37.73, while Kamikume *muramai* sold for 43.10 – a 14.2 percent premium.[42]

(b) Brewers use renewable (and therefore terminable) contracts. A simple high price presents a risk of moral hazard, of course. A farmer can renege on the deal in myriad observable but not legally verifiable ways (a distinction at the core of Hart and Moore [1990]). The breweries mitigate this risk straightforwardly: They offer only one-year contracts. They renew the contracts if a farmer cooperates, and look elsewhere if he or she does not. Should a farmer adopt opportunistic strategies, he or she will find himself or herself next year without a high-priced contract.

The history of the *muramai* contracts in Hyogo indicates brewers do terminate contracts. Should farmers fail to live up to brewers' hopes, pre-war brewers did indeed refuse to renew the contracts, and turn to other growers.[43] Given the quick termination, however, one would not necessarily expect the parties to litigate disputes. At least on the Westlaw database, no record of any litigation over premium sake-rice quality remains.

---

[42] See generally Mori (1983). In the analysis that follows, I integrate the sake example with the modern literature on relational contracts. Note that there are strong similarities (and clear differences) with the contracts between new firms and venture capital investors.

[43] See Toku A (N.D.); Nishinomiya (1989, 197); Ozeki (1996, 432); Hyogo (1961, 98–105).

(c) Brewers select for the person. Over and over, the brewers insist that they "need to be able to see the farmer's face."[44] To obtain consistently high quality, they need to contract with men and women of character and ability. Were they obtaining their rice from the cooperative, brewers could specify the graded quality they want. From a farmer under contract, matters are more complex. They will take the rice the farmer delivers, and the quality of their sake for the year will turn in part on that rice.

Whether through opportunism or simple incompetence, a farmer can easily sabotage a brewer's product, and a law suit will not help. To be sure, brewers can specify some verifiable quality metrics. If a farmer failed to meet a metric, the brewer could sue for breach. But if any brewer ever did – again – no record of it remains on the Westlaw database. For the most part, Japanese farmers are low-income retirees with a tiny paddy of little economic value and a dilapidated two- or three-cylinder truck. Seventy-two percent of the farmers own less than a hectare of paddy (2.47 acres; Hatsuki 2015, 128), and the trucks are 50 horsepower machines that sell for as little as $7,000 new. If a farmer has few assets to attach, the brewer gains little from any claim for breach.

The brewers and farmers draft a contract to build a relationship. As Thomas Dietz (2012, 39) put it in his study of international transactions (where state enforcement is obviously problematic), a contract serves as "a communication document." It facilitates "mutual communication, but not the enforcement, of legal claims." Lisa Bernstein (2015, 562) made the same point about Midwestern heavy machinery manufacturers: Their contracts simply "are not designed to create incentives for performance." The brewers negotiate the contract to build a collaborative relationship. Toward that end, they pick their suppliers carefully. They pick by talent. They pick by character. And in the brutal candor of small towns the world over, they pick by family: Know a farmer's last name, explained the *muramai* chair for Yokawa village, and you know the quality of his rice (Nihonshu 2017).

(d) Brewers select for the land. And almost as often, the brewers insist that "to buy the rice, you need to see the land."[45] Brewers do not offer contracts on just any paddy; they select for the quality of the land. To raise sake rice properly, "you need to see the rice paddy," explained the Yokawa *muramai* chair (Nihon shu 2017). "You need to talk to the *yamada nishiki*." By soil, by location, by drainage, some farms produce better rice than others. The same is true in Burgundy and Bordeaux, of course. Even within

---

[44] E.g., Keiyaku (2018); Hirogaru (2018).
[45] E.g., Ozeki (1996, 432); Mori (1983, 124).

Yokawa village – the very origin of the *muramai* contract – some paddies yield better rice than others (Nihonshu 2017). The Miyajima brewery
(Miyajima shuzo website) in Nagano stresses the importance of water: The
fields upstream must not use heavy pesticide; the homes upstream cannot
discharge their sewage. It stresses the importance of sunlight, and it stresses
the importance of the wind patterns.

(e) Brewers monitor observable inputs. – Verifiable inputs can correlate with rice quality, and many brewers mandate the levels of the inputs
that do. Brewers often specify cultivation methods. Masaya Iga examined closely the contracts that one regional premium brewer maintained.
Should a farmer insist on using pesticides and chemical fertilizers at ordinary levels, the brewer offered no contract at all.[46] Should he or she agree
to use them at only low levels, the brewer might offer one price. Should he
or she agree to use none, the brewer paid a 50 percent premium (Table 2.3,
Panel A; Iga 2008).

Other brewers focus on yield – as in, they want low yields. Wine quality
tends to correlate inversely with vineyard productivity, and so it is with
sake.[47] As a result, both wineries and sake breweries contract to buy the
entire yield of a field. They then discourage farmers from ramping the productivity by adopting pricing formulae that track yields only up to a given
volume and pay nothing for any excess.[48]

(f) Sometimes (but only sometimes), brewers contract over observable
outputs. Brewers can observe rice quality and can verify that quality – in
part. They can measure the percentage of broken kernels. They can measure the level of protein in a kernel. And they can adjust the price they pay
by these verifiable measures (Hayashi 2017, 56).

And some do – but not all. The problem with setting price by verifiable
quality is precisely that it works and may work too well: It may skew an
agent's effort toward the verifiable measures, but away from other possibly
more important aspects of quality. Quality is a subtle thing, and only some
measures are verifiable. As Holmstrom and Milgrom (1991) point out, a
principal who pays his agent only by verifiable indices of quality may cause
the agent to bias his efforts away from aspects of quality not incorporated
into the pricing formula. If the cost of that bias is sufficiently high, the

---

[46] Verifying that the farmer used no pesticide (or only limited amount) would obviously
present a challenge.

[47] And for that reason, both wineries and sake breweries that focus on high-quality offerings try to avoid buying grapes or rice by the ton. Ashenfelter and Storchmann (2016, 30);
Hayashi (2017, 60); Firstenfeld (2008); Washington (2015, 3).

[48] Iga (2008); Washington (2015, 10) (grapes); Hayashi (2017, 62) (rice).

Table 2.3 *Two regional brewers and supplying farmers*

A. Brewer A:

	Exp	Age	kg	Ha	Price (A)	Pestic.	Fert.	Cont.	Notes
A1	40	60	2,640	60	20,000	Low	None	4	Contact through coop where A1 had sold quality eggs
A2	10	50	2,031	60	25,000	Low	Low	2	A2 took initiative, wanted to support local sake production
A3	8	40	2,310	60	25,000	Low	None	9	Knew A already; wanted to work together
A4	4		2,250	60	20,000	Low	Low	2	A4 took initiative; wanted to build community
A5	20	50	2,400	60	30,000	None	None	2	Introduced through natural foods seller; wanted to produce organic sake
A6	4	60	1,290	35	19,930	Low	None	2	A took initiative; wanted to support local community and economy
A7	4	40	362	30	25,000	None	none	0	Introduced through local politician
A8	2	50	2,160	60	25,000	Low	Low	0	A8 took initiative; wanted to support local community and build human relations with brewer
A9		60	1,800	50	17,650	Low	Low	2	
A10	5	30	810	30	30,000	None	None		Wanted to farm organically; brewer sympathized with farming philosophy

B. Brewer B:

	Exp	Age	kg	Ha	Price (B)	Pestic.	Fert.	Cont.	Notes
B1	10	70	1,225	30	20,000	Low	Low	2–4	B took initiative; wanted to support local community and economy
B2	10	70	1,505	39	20,000	Low	Low	2–4	B took initiative; wanted to support local community and economy
B3			4,458	87	20,000	Low	Low	2–4	
B4	5	50	1,020	40	60,000	No	No	2–4	Natural food connection; human relations important
B5	4	40	3,240	68	20,000	Low	Low	2–4	B took initiative; human relations important
B6	10	70	1,395	58	60,000	No	No	2–4	Introduced by B4; human relations important

(continued)

Table 2.3 *(continued)*

Brewer A is Yamana Shuzo, a brewer in Tamba city, Hyogo, specializing in premium sake. In 2006, Yamana consumed 42.4 tons of rice per year. Of these, it purchased 18.8 by direct contract. It promises to buy all rice produced on designated fields.
Brewer B is Taketsuru, a brewer in Takehara city, Hiroshima. Taketsuru advertises only versions of junmai sake. In 2006, it consumed 59.9 tons of rice, of which it acquired 12.8 tons by direct contract. Like Yamana, it promises to buy all rice produced on designated fields.
Notes:
Exp: Years of experience in sake rice production
Age: Age of male household head, deciles
kg: kg of sake rice supplied
Ha: hectare of land devoted to sake rice
Price (A): Yen per 60 kg
Price (B): Market price plus adjustments plus number in table, per .1 hectare
Pest.: Pesticide use – none or low
Fert.: Chemical fertilizer use – none or low
Contact: Number of regular contacts with brewery per year
Source: Masaya Iga, Seishu kyokyu taikei ni okeru shuzogyosha to sakamai seisansha no teikei kankei [The Relationship between the Sake Breyers and the Sake-Optimized Rice Producers under the Sake Supply Structure], Chiri gaku hyoron, 81: 150–78 (2008).

principal may rationally choose to offer instead a contract with only muted incentives. Wineries face the same problem. Grape quality turns in part on observable characteristics, but "more subtle characteristics are harder to measure" (Goodhue, et al. 2002, 98).

And so it is that many premium sake brewers omit quality measures from their pricing formula. Instead, they meet regularly with the farmers and discuss how better to raise that quality. If a farmer produces defective rice, they bring samples with them and talk to him about what to do (Hayashi 2017, 60). But when so many of the distinguishing measures of rice quality are observable but not verifiable, many of them rationally decide not to key their contracts to the verifiable measures of quality. Instead, they monitor and talk: They follow the progress of the rice, they talk with the farmer, they watch for potential problems, and they try to forestall a disaster before it arrives.

E Endogenous Social Capital

1. Introduction. – Let me restate the point: Rather than structure contracts on verifiable measures of output quality, the premium regional breweries intervene regularly in the farming itself. These brewers want farmers to use as little fertilizer and pesticides as possible (Hayashi 2017, 60). But they want much more. They want the farmers to watch the crop and to change as needed the steps they take and when they take them. Toward these ends

and more, the brewers monitor the progress of the crop. They may meet with the farmers, consult about schedules, and suggest new techniques. To encourage the farmers to welcome their intervention, they pay the high prices that they do. And to facilitate this collaboration, they do what they can to build trust. More specifically, they deliberately build the network of dense and overlapping personal and social ties that together constitute social capital.

The brewers and farmers negotiate contracts, in other words, to structure what they envision as a working, collaborative relationship. Lisa Bernstein (2015, 563) made a similar point about Midwestern manufacturers: They negotiate contracts "to create a framework for growing relational social capital and leveraging network governance." "Contracts serve mutual communication," wrote Dietz (2012, 39) in the context of software contracts. As Bozovic & Hadfield (2016, 988) put it in the context of technology firms: The parties negotiate their contracts to "coordinate beliefs" about what they intend to do, to create the "essential scaffolding to support the beliefs and strategies that make informal means of enforcement such as reputation and the threat of termination effective."

Turn to the component aspects of this strategy.

2. The brewers monitor intensively. – To gauge when and how to intervene, the brewers need information about a crop's progress. Toward that end, they monitor the paddy. For truly local operations, they can do this informally. The brewer lives in the area. He knows the weather. He can watch the rice grow in the paddy. Brewers more remote can engineer more elaborate arrangements. Dassai installs sensors in its farmers' fields to record rainfall and temperature (Nihon 2018). Other brewers follow the progress of the crops with drones (Sekai 2019).

3. The brewers intervene directly. – As necessary, these brewers then intervene. The necessity varies: Some farmers need it more; some brewers have more to offer. But in order to intervene, the brewers meet with their contracting farmers. Some hold conferences among all of their farmers. Some meet each farmer at the beginning of the season and then again at harvest. They may help the farmers plant the rice and then harvest it (Iga 2008, 158). Others meet with them on an ad hoc basis throughout the growing cycle. Masaya Iga (158) describes a brewer who meets with his farmers as often as nine times a year.

Should a crop fall short on some dimension, the brewers work with the farmer to devise a way to skirt the problem the next year (Hayashi 2017, 60). They review their farmers' plans (60). At root, they meet with their farmers to discuss and collaborate. Again, as Bernstein (2015, 576) wrote of

Midwestern manufacturers, the brewers "interact with their suppliers throughout the production, delivery, and quality assessment process to try and catch problems sooner rather than later …." They intervene in order to work with their suppliers to improve the quality of the rice they will obtain.

4. The brewers build social capital. – To enable this monitoring and intervention, the brewers work to build the "relational social capital" that fosters trust. "If you can see a farmer's face," explained several brewers, "it's easier to specify the quality you want."[49] "If you can see his face, both of you will feel as though you're making sake together," said another (Saitama 2017). Learn to know each other personally, and a brewer can communicate more effectively the type, quality, and quantity of rice that he or she needs (Matsuo 2017, 44).

The Miyajima (N.D.) brewery in Nagano wants its rice grown in an "environmentally sustainable" fashion. To work with its farmers to do this, it assures the public, it needs to be able to trust them. "This is not about finding farmers who will follow the terms of the contract," it explains. "We need to be able to talk with each other. We need to be able to trust each other. This is true everywhere in the world."

For this consultative approach to work, the brewers need farmers who can in turn trust them. President Takahashi of the Matsuo brewery has lived in Shinano village all his life. His father ran the brewery before him, and his grandfather before that. He lives within a dense network of "structural social capital" in which information about how he treats one farmer will travel quickly to all of his other suppliers.

But this structural social capital is not just an attribute of birth. It is also a characteristic that firms can – and do – deliberately build. More specifically, they deliberately build Coleman's "closure" among their farmers. They deliberately build ties among their farmers that would let them (the farmers) learn about their own (the brewer's own) contractual breach – because by doing so, they strengthen the credibility of their own promise not to breach. Bernstein (2015, 608) notes how Midwestern manufacturers construct networks among their suppliers through which each supplier can rapidly learn how the manufacturer has treated other suppliers. Miwa and Ramseyer (2000) detail the way Japanese car assemblers organize tight associations of their suppliers. And so too here: Brewers sometimes organize their contracting farmers into "study groups" where the farmers can meet each other and discuss the course of their work (Hayashi 2017, 56). The networks "increase the reputational harm and nonlegal sanctions

---

[49] Keiyaku (2018); see also Hirogaru (2018) and Miyajima (N.D.).

for misbehavior," observes Bernstein (2015, 604), and expand "the type of misbehavior that can be policed through multilateral nonlegal sanctions."

5. Summary. – For these brewers, the key to buying the rice that meets their desired level of quality is price. The brewer wants rice that meets not just the verifiable indices of quality that the cooperative can provide, but indices that are observable but non-verifiable (and therefore not contractible) as well. For that, the brewer wants to be able to work closely with the farmers. Toward that end, he (or she) wants to monitor the crop and intervene whenever he believes it helpful. Crucially, when he does so, he wants the farmer to welcome his intervention.

The contractual measure by which the brewers address this problem is simple: a one-year contract to buy all of the yield of a field at a high price, subject to renewal at the discretion of the two parties. In effect, the brewers pay the farmers "efficiency wages." The farmer could grow sake rice for the coop and receive a given price. Should he or she grow rice for the local brewery, he or she will receive a substantially higher price. In effect, that higher contractual price gives the farmer (even farmers who also care about factors other than money) an incentive to work closely with the brewer to grow a crop that more closely matches the (observable but not verifiable) attributes that the brewer so badly wants.

To induce their farmers to welcome this intervention, the brewers cultivate social capital. They spend time with each farmer – through which they learn to know their farmers and their farmers learn to know them. They encourage their farmers to spend time with each other – through which they learn to know each other. In effect, they build among themselves a web of networks through which their farmers can learn of any misbehavior on their own part. Through the networks, they increase the cost they would suffer should they cheat their farmers, and – thereby – the confidence that their farmers can hold about their (the brewers') own integrity.

F Leasing, Ownership, and Vertical Integration

1. Why do some breweries contract across the market?

(a) Introduction. For their best wines, many wineries do not use grapes they buy on the market. Instead, they use grapes they grow themselves. Sometimes, they grow them on land they hold under long-term leases. Usually, they grow them on land they own.

The question is obviously one of make or buy – the extent of vertical integration. A winery or sake brewer can integrate vertically into agriculture, or it can contract across the market to buy its agricultural supplies. High-end wineries in France tend to integrate vertically, while mass-market wineries buy their grapes on the market.[50] In the sake industry, even high-end breweries generally buy their rice on the market.

(b) The law. Until 2003, the explanation for the different patterns of integration between wine and sake was simple and legal. Japanese law banned rice farming by corporations. In the late 1940s, the occupation-dominated government had redistributed paddy land (see Chapter 5). It effectively took (the payment was trivial) land from its owners and gave (the price was trivial) it to those who had earlier leased the land. The government lowered the rate of growth in agricultural productivity in the process, but the occupation forced through the program in the name of "democratizing" rural society. Lest market participants transfer the land back to the earlier equilibrium, the occupation mandated a wide range of transfer restrictions. For the most part, it stopped people from taking land out of rice production. And relevant here, it banned corporations from owning or renting paddies.

During the first decade of the twenty-first century, the government changed the law. By the 1990s, farmers were abandoning their fields. Because agriculture now paid low returns to labor compared to other employment, young men and women were choosing not to farm at all. Those who owned paddy fields found that no one wanted to farm their land. Faced with increasing numbers of abandoned fields, the government finally loosened the restrictions on paddy transfers. It began to allow limited leasing of rice paddies by corporations in 2003 and further liberalized leasing in 2009. Subject to greater restrictions, it began to allow corporate ownership as well.[51]

(c) Relational specificity. – Sake brewers do have less reason to integrate than wineries. "Vines are perennials with a productive lifetime of more than 25 years," note Ashenfelter and Storchmann (2016, 26). As a result, they constitute substantial long-term investments. Because their value hinges in part on the relationship between the vineyard and the winery, they present the risk of holdups so famously explored by Williamson (1975, 1985), Klein, Crawford and Alchian (1978), Masten (1984), and others.[52]

---

[50] The contrast is less sharp in Napa, where Andrew Beckstoffer grows large quantities of high-end grapes.

[51] Shibuya (2016, 73; 2020, 89); Takayama and Nakatani (2017, 77–79). See government summaries of the statutory changes at www.maff.go.jp/j/keiei/koukai/pdf/hy.pdf; www.maff.go.jp/j/keiei/koukai/nouchi_seido/pdf/nouchi_taihi.pdf; www.nogyo-tetsuduki .com/corporation-yoken/

[52] Noted most recently in the Japanese context by Shishido (2019).

A rice farmer makes no such multi-year investment toward producing sake rice. He (or she) makes some, of course. Perhaps most notably, he invests in the knowledge and expertise he will need to grow the idiosyncratic varieties that the brewery wants and in the way that the brewery wants. But he will make few physical investments: A paddy to produce sake rice is little different from one to produce table rice. Should a brewery decide – however opportunistically – not to renew his contract, a farmer can safely return to table rice.

(d) And the theory of the firm. Recall that Hart (Grossman & Hart 1986; Hart & Moore 1990) suggested that assets should be owned by the institution whose involvement raises the value of the asset to its highest use. If the land is most valuable when used for the production of sake, it should be owned by the firm that best produces the sake. This would imply that since 2003 the premium breweries should be integrating vertically into farming on a massive scale. Some indeed are, but the shift is leisurely and modest. In turn, that relaxed pace reinforces the point made by many observers in other contexts: In a wide variety of situations, vertical integration and contracts are close substitutes. In a wide variety of situations, firms can replicate the incentives produced by vertical integration through contract.

2. Why do other breweries integrate?

(a) Aging farmers. And yet – leisurely as their pace may be – some breweries do integrate vertically into farming. Why? The breweries themselves suggest several reasons.

Often, the brewers explain that they started growing sake rice because the local farmers had grown so old. Their contracting partners were about to retire, and their partners' children were not staying on the farm. Their suppliers were about to disappear, and they needed to prepare.[53]

Young people are indeed leaving farming villages. Regional breweries that rely on farmers skilled enough to raise temperamental sake rice do indeed face the risk that their suppliers will die without a replacement. Take the Sekiya brewery in Aichi prefecture (Shibuya 2020, 95–98; Sekai 2019). After visiting European wineries, the firm's president decided to focus its production on local rice. Yet in his community, a sixty-year-old farmer was on the young side. "With another 10 years," explained the president, "I doubted there would be anyone around to farm for us." Nothing seemed feasible except to grow the rice himself. He asked the retiring farmers to teach him how to farm and by 2018 had 24 ha (hectare)[54] under cultivation.

[53] Niigata (2019); Nihonshu (2017); Shibuya (2020, 74, 94–96).
[54] 1 hectare (ha) = 100 ares (a) = 10,000 sq. meters = 2.47 US acres.

The Watanabe brewery in Nechi valley reached much the same conclusion (Shibuya 2020, 93–94; firm website). It wanted local sake rice, but the nearby farmers were growing old and had no successors in sight. The Watanabe family already owned a very small piece of land. The brewery rented another 15 ha and now grows its own rice. Its employees brew in the winter and farm in the summer.

(b) Seasonal work for employees. Like Watanabe, some breweries rent the farms to provide off-season employment for their own workers (Shibuya 2016, 76). Brewers traditionally made sake in the winter when the cold temperatures helped prevent spoilage, and hired their help on a seasonal basis. As long as the local community was agricultural, they could hire men and women in the winter and expect them to return to their own farms in the spring. With the agricultural industry in economic free fall and local farms no longer using young labor, that coordination became increasingly difficult. When breweries like the Watanabe terroir brewery raise the rice themselves, they assign their employees to make the sake in the winter and work the paddies in the summer (Shibuya 2020, 93–94; Watanabe N.D.).

(c) Contractual problems. Some breweries report that they started farming themselves because they could not convince independent farmers to cooperate. In the discussion above, I explain the logic by which breweries use contractual structures to induce farmers to grow the high-quality sake rice they need. If only life were so simple, these other breweries seem to imply. Some of them simply could not induce their supplying farmers to grow the high-quality rice they needed. Despairing of a contractual option, they integrated vertically into agriculture themselves.

The small Marumoto brewery in Okayama prefecture has fourteen employees and focuses on organic sake (Shibuya 2020, 92; Marumoto N.D.). The owner begged local farmers to supply him with low-fertilizer rice, but could not convince them to do so. Despairing of obtaining the rice any other way, he went into farming himself. His family had owned some land. He leased more, and by 2019, his firm was farming 18 ha. Again, his employees brewed sake in the winter and farmed the firm's paddies in the summer.

(d) The informational advantage. And some – perhaps most – of the brewers who integrate into farming do so to improve their ability to coach the farmers who still supply them with the rest of their rice under contract. Through contract, the brewers have negotiated the right to intervene in the farming. To intervene effectively, they need to understand farming itself. By tending even a modest-sized field, they acquire some of that essential technique.

Ichinokura is a large brewer in Miyagi prefecture. It farms some plots in order to test new varieties and farming methods. It still contracts extensively with local farmers, but grows rice itself to learn how better to advise those suppliers. "By cultivating sake rice and using abandoned fields," it explains, "we learn cultivation techniques, and become better able to convey that information to local farmers" (Shibuya 2020, 100; Ichinokura N.D.).

"The quality of sake rice and the quality of sake are inextricably intertwined," explained one group of partially vertically integrated brewers. "But there is not yet enough information flowing between farmers and brewers." The group turned to growing to obtain that information. They started growing some of their rice themselves in order first to acquire and then to "be able to convey the experience and skill" to others raising the temperamental sake rice (Sekai 2019; No to ieru shuzo no kai).

You learn as you farm, the Marumoto brewery in Okayama explained. The firm grows 18 ha itself and plans to expand. When you farm, you learn that "you can grow *koji mai* on this field. This other paddy would do better with *kakemai*." The brewery continued: "Each paddy has its own individuality." As a result, "we study the soil in each paddy." And "we study what rice works best in which field, match the field to our goals, and then proceed with the cultivation." Grow rice, and you come to appreciate more closely the connection between raising rice and brewing sake. "Rather than sake rice made by a farmer who doesn't brew sake," the firm explained, "we wanted a sake rice grown under the eye of a brewer."[55]

The Izumibashi brewery in Kanagawa prefecture both grows rice and buys rice. It uses five different kinds of rice and allocates the varieties among its supplying farmers according to farmer expertise and paddy suitability. It monitors rice growth with drones. And it ties that growth to paddy output and soil characteristics through computers. The firm grows some rice itself; it studies growth and outcomes scientifically; and it advises its contracting farmers. "Ultimately, we learn who, using which paddy with what kind of soil, grew a rice that upon brewing" produced what kind of sake.

VII Conclusions

For over a century now, Japanese consumers have been losing their taste for sake. But until the last few decades, sake brewers gave them little to taste. Stringent controls begun during the war drove a few producers in Kobe to

---

[55] Marumoto (N.D.); Denno (2018); Shibuya (2020, 93–94).

dominate the mass market through economies of sake. They flooded the country with mediocre but cheap drinks, and the regional brewers steadily went out of business.

Within this environment, desperate regional brewers began to explore whether they could create a market for unambiguously delicate and subtle high-end sake. A few of them succeeded spectacularly. Several more regional brewers then began to explore whether they could create a market for delicate sake that showcased environmental variation. By most measures, some of them seem to be succeeding as well.

In creating this new terroir sake, the regional brewers face a complex contracting problem. A few of them skirt the contracting process by vertically integrating into rice farming, but not many. Most of the new premium brewers contract with independent local farmers and pay them to grow the high-risk and high-cost varieties of rice optimized for their premium sake.

The brewers and farmers solve their information and incentive problems through deceptively simple arrangements. They virtually never conclude contracts with elaborate panoplies of verifiable terms. Instead, they deliberately cultivate a dense network of "closed" social capital. They then negotiate and enforce simple, short-term renewable (and hence terminable) contracts within it. The contracts provide a structure for their relationship. Through these contracts, they let the brewer monitor closely and let him intervene as necessary to maintain close control over the farming process. To induce the farmer to let the brewer do this, the brewers pay extremely high prices – prices high enough to convince the farmers to cooperate with the brewer's efforts to raise rice quality.

Most of the brewers do not vertically integrate, and none of them negotiate long-term, complex contracts. Instead, through short-term, terminable contracts paying high prices, they negotiate all the control they need. Through simple contracts embedded within dense networks of deliberately cultivated social capital, they obtain results that they could never generate through long-term complex terms, and duplicate instead the effects of vertical integration.

3

Contracting for Quality in Fish

Fishing was once a family operation in Japan, safely nestled within the larger hamlet enterprise. It had an "industrial organization" that mirrored the organization of rice growing. In both sectors, the families owned some equipment. They held a right (a legal property right) either (individually) to plant and harvest rice in a field or (collectively) to catch fish off the coast. They worked with their neighbors to accomplish tasks that involved substantial externalities or scale economies: maintaining the irrigation network, for example, or policing the bay against trespassing outsiders. And they sold their produce into a complex distribution network.

Technological and demographic changes have transformed that industrial organization. To both farming and fishing, the changes have increased the scale economies. Farmers now need more equipment to compete in the market for rice, and fishermen need more to compete in the market for fish. Larger-scale firms (still often family firms) can exploit those scale economies and undersell small-scale farmers and fishermen. In response, local farmers and fishermen have sometimes tried to find niche markets where they can compete despite their capital constraints.

The fishermen can position themselves in the industry by contract. But the political economy of democratic regimes being what it is, the Japanese government has subsidized small-scale fishing firms. And the industrial organization of criminal enterprises being what it is, those subsidies have drawn the mob into the industry. After the introductory Section I, I include a short diversion: the role – perverse in the extreme – played by the mob (Section II). That mob involvement reflects the fact that (and perhaps accelerates the way that) fishing in Japan is a rapidly disintegrating industry.

Contrarian optimists remain, however, and in the rest of this chapter, I explore the strategies by which they have worked to create a premium market niche. As in the other chapters, I begin by identifying the contractual problems at stake (Section I). After discussing the mob, I survey the legal regime (Section III), and then the industry (Section IV). Finally, in Section V, I turn to the focus of this chapter: the entrepreneurial strategies some fishermen have adopted in order to sell up-market. Some fishermen sell directly to consumers (Section V.B), while others sell through their fishing unions (Section V.C). In high-capital sectors, larger firms dominate the field through vertical integration. Local fishermen then compete in technologically simpler sub-sectors through contract (Section V.D).

I The Problem

In Chapter 2, I explore the contracts by which niche market sake producers and farmers contract for premium, specialized rice. I discuss the contracts they use, and the environment within which they use them. In fact, that environment is not exogenous: through their contracts, the brewers and farmers deliberately shape their own contracting environment. The brewers are gambling a year's worth of production on the rice. The farmers are gambling a year's harvest. Together, they use contract to structure a social context that will encourage them both to cooperate.

When fishermen and consumers trade with each other, they gamble less. On any given contract, the fisherman bets a few fish. At most, he bets a day's catch. His consumers bet a dinner. For both the fisherman and the consumer, the contract matters less than it did for the sake brewers and farmers in Chapter 2.

But that it matters less does not mean it does not matter at all. In this chapter, I examine the arrangements by which small-scale fishermen try to place their output in a similar premium niche. Toward that end, fishermen deliberately increase the stakes: they post their broader reputations on the line.

Sometimes, the fishermen sell directly to customers over the Internet. The human contact and potential for repeated transactions can enhance promissory credibility and encourage trust. Sometimes, the fishermen work together through their local fishing union; the union fosters trust by monitoring and certifying the quality of the members. The union places the community's collective reputation at stake. The union monitors its members to prevent free-riding.

Crucially, a consumer can attack the fisherman's (or fishing union's) reputation on the web. This dramatically raises the stake to the fisherman. In effect, he (or the union) has posted his reputation as a bond. In effect, he uses his contracts to create the network that sociologists call social capital: when selling publicly on the Internet, the fishermen enable their buyers to contact each other; in the process, they build a network that lets them more credibly promise high quality, precisely because their buyers can contact each other and learn how they have behaved in the past.

II A Diversion: Fishing Unions and the Mob

A The Kudokai[1]

In February 1998, a hitman shot and killed Tadayoshi Ueno, the seventy-year-old head of a local fishing union (Wakinoura) in the northern Kyushu city of Kitakyushu. In April 2012, a hitman shot a police officer investigating the senior members of the Kudokai. He survived. The Kudokai is not the largest of the Japanese organized crime syndicates, but it is the most brutal. It operates out of northern Kyushu, but with a national reach. With other crime syndicates, the police often maintain a delicate modus operandi: the syndicate limits its violence to occasional attacks on rival mobs; the police let it run its traditional businesses. The Kudokai has not constrained its violence to attacks against other syndicates, and the police have set out to shut it down.

In January 2013, a nurse at a cosmetic surgery clinic was stabbed. Kudokai chairman Satoru Nomura had visited the clinic for (unsatisfactory) penile enlargement surgery. "This can't hurt as much as your tattoos did," she had said – and Nomura had taken offense. She survived. In due course, the Wakinoura fishing union would merge into the larger Kitakyushu fishing union, and Tadayoshi Ueno's younger brother would become head of that Kitakyushu union. In December 2013, a hitman shot and killed the younger brother. And in early 2014, Ueno's grandson – a local dentist – found himself knifed in a parking lot. He survived.

The December 2013 murder remains officially unsolved, but for their role in the rest of these attacks, police arrested Nomura and Fumio Tanoue, respectively, chairman and president of the Kudokai mob. In August 2021, the Fukuoka District Court sentenced Nomura to death and Tanoue to life in prison. The presiding judge had been transferred to Tokyo in the spring of 2021, but returned to Fukuoka to announce the decision. He read the sentence.

---

[1] The following account of the Kudokai is based on Korede (2021); Kensatsu (2021), Kangoshi (2020), Kensatsu (2019), Gyokyo (2010), and Kudokai (2021); see generally Kuni v. [No name given], D1-law.com No. 28282033 (Fukuoka D. Ct. Mar. 28, 2019), aff'd, D1-law.com No. 28282035 (Fukuoka High Ct. June 25, 2020); Kuni v. [No name given], D1-com. No. 28260266 (Fukuoka D. Ct. Dec. 15, 2017), aff'd, D1-law.com No. 28263308 (Fukuoka High Ct. July 4, 2018).

"You'll regret this," declared Nomura. "I think you might have been lucky to be transferred to a Tokyo court," sneered Tanoue.

The northern Kyushu fishing union held long-standing rights to fish in the bay. It held these rights as property rights, and those rights gave it the ability to block any threat to fishing. Northern Kyushu is a heavily industrial area. Through those fishing rights, the union held an effective veto over the stream of large-scale construction projects in the bay. In turn, that veto also gave it the ability to allocate the subcontracting work involved. As one news account put it (Gyokyo 2010),

The city fishing union controls the decision about whether to go forward with the harbor-related public projects in Fukuoka. The power of the fishing union is that strong. It can stop construction before breakfast.

A senior official in the local fishing union explained (Gyokyo 2010):

They can live off of the land and the marina-related profits that they receive through the fishing subsidies. They apparently have fishing rights, but the only reason I can think of that they still hold them is to obtain the kickbacks. The majority of the union members aren't in fishing. They're in public sector construction.

At the turn of the twenty-first century, the government had been planning to expand the harbor. The work would cost 100 billion yen. The Kudokai wanted a bigger part in the construction projects, while members of the family controlling the fishing union wanted those projects for their own construction firms. For mob disputes, the attacks followed standard operating procedure.

B Nobeoka[2]

South of Kitakyushu city along the eastern coast of Kyushu island lies the modest city of Nobeoka. From Mt. Kirishima in the center of the island, the Gokase river flows eastward past Takachiho and through the city of Nobeoka to the Pacific. For years, the Gokase fishing union had controlled and allocated the right to fish in the river.

In time, one Masaru Kishimoto obtained a right to form a rival fishing union on the Gokase river. Kishimoto controlled the Nobeoka branch office of the Buraku Liberation League (BLL). The "burakumin" had ostensibly suffered discrimination, and the BLL served as the group's self-appointed human rights champion. In fact, BLL leadership could overlap heavily with

---

[2] See Osegawa gygyo kyodo kumiai v. Gokasegawa gyogyo kyodo kumiai, 1470 Hanrei jiho 121 (Miyazaki D. Ct. Mar. 25, 1992), and other sources on the Internet.

local organized crime syndicates, and the BLL could use those syndicate ties to extort massive subsidies from the local and national governments (Ramseyer & Rasmusen 2018; Ramseyer 2019).

Kishimoto knew nothing about fishing. In addition to heading the local BLL, however, he ran the Nobeoka mob. He also owned a construction form, and through the firm obtained large construction projects with the government.

Having licensed two fishing unions to the same river, the government tried to force the unions to merge. Kishimoto's union members were happy to oblige. They may have had that in mind all along. The legitimate Gokase union complained desperately. The men running Kishimoto's union had long criminal records in gambling, drugs, and weapons charges. The Gokase members could anticipate what would happen if the two groups merged. They sued, and successfully stopped the merger.

Kishimoto himself disappeared in 1985. He shot his lover that year, and ordered his subordinates to bury her body in the local beach. The police eventually found him, and the court convicted. He served time, and upon release returned to Nobeoka to run a construction firm (again).

C Other Unions

These examples generalize.[3] The Japanese shoreline is 35,000 km long. Of this, the government has designated 14,000 km for protection from erosion (Norin N.D.). It guards the coast by building dykes, retaining walls, and concrete barriers. Necessarily, these structures change local fishing patterns. Precisely because they do, the local fishing unions can veto their installation. The unions threaten to veto, and desist when the government pays. Extortion, in other words, is basic to a great many of the modern fishing unions.

When developers in Kuwana city in Mie prefecture (suburban Nagoya city) embarked on construction projects, the clerks in the city office told them to obtain the consent of the local fishing union.[4] Nominally, the clerks did this to protect the environment. In fact, the local union demanded a

---

[3] For litigation related to the distribution of subsidies paid to fishing unions over construction projects, see also, for example, [No names given] v. Kuni, 2102 Hanrei jiho 55 (Fukuoka High Ct. Dec. 6, 2010); Oita shi shiroki gyogyo kyodo kumiai v. Wakabayashi, 1323 Hanrei jiho 60 (Sup. Ct. July 13, 1989); Yamada v. Shimono isshiki gyogyo kyodo kumiai, 1133 Hanrei jiho 100 (Nagoya D. Ct. Oct. 17, 1983); Yorita v. Izumi otsu gyogyo kyodo kumiai, 865 Hanrei jiho 22 (Osaka D. Ct. June 3, 1977).

[4] See generally Gyokyo (2020); Kyokatsu (2020).

payoff, and work for its own subcontractors. Usually, it demanded 0.5 percent of any contract amount. For all this, in December 2020 the court convicted the head of the union of criminal extortion.

The subsidies and payoffs raise the value of fishing union membership, of course. One Kagoshima prefecture fisherman had routinely ignored his fishing union's ban on daytime net use. They quarreled, but the fisherman remained a member. In 1996, however, the prefecture agreed to pay the union subsidies of 2 billion yen. Together with another nine members, the fisherman sued the union over the distribution of the funds. The union responded by expelling eight of the dissidents. Nominally, it expelled them for violating fishing rules. The court found the reason pretextual and stopped the expulsion.[5]

The fishing unions could use their property rights over local waters to stop a wide variety of projects. They could, for example, use them to stop planned nuclear reactors. To permit the Fukushima reactors, the local fishing union had received amounts that dwarfed other extortion attempts. For letting Tokyo Electric build reactors number 7 and 8 at the Daiichi complex, in 2000 its members received 40–50 million yen per person (Tsukue 2012).

III The Legal Framework

A The Tokugawa Tradition

Extortion from the government is not what fishing unions had done traditionally, of course. Instead, the unions had carried on the control that the fishing hamlets had exercised over their members' collective work during the Tokugawa (1600–1867) period. Subject to enormous variation, the hamlets had classically claimed a collective property right to the adjacent coastal waters.[6] The line between the "coastal" waters and the more distant "offshore" seas could be hard to define, but beyond the coastal water, the hamlets held no claim.

Tokugawa fishing hamlets enforced property rights to the waters within and among themselves. They were customary rights and varied by location, by fish species, and by fishing technology.

As with other customary rights, the fishing customs at stake were not static. Instead, they stood perpetually in flux. They changed as the fishing

---

[5] [No names given], 2003 WLJPCA 03269016 (Kagoshima D. Ct. Mar. 26, 2003).
[6] See Kumamoto (1990, 37); Abe (2009, 6289); Okuda (2013, 83).

stock rose or fell. They changed as fishing technology evolved. They changed as the market for the catch grew. And they changed as hamlets aggressively cheated on the custom to subvert the property rights of their neighbors, and as those neighbors just as aggressively fought back.

Villagers within the coastal hamlets held their right to fish in their coastal waters in common. The people within the hamlet held their component rights by household unit. And should the hamlet wish to change those norms or otherwise act collectively, they acted by unanimous vote (see, e.g., Kumamoto 1990, 37).

Within their exclusive fishing zones, hamlets monitored usage closely. They could enforce starting and ending dates for the seasons for a given species. They could limit the hours during which their members could fish. They could allocate the right to fish to a limited number of their villagers. They could limit the nets and boats that their villagers could use.

Hamlets also varied widely in the extent to which they enforced egalitarian norms. Some hamlets were non-hierarchically structured and maintained egalitarian rules. At others, the fishing rights were essentially the exclusive rights of a few households. In either case, the hamlet often defined those rights precisely.

B The Meiji Transformation

The Meiji (1868–1912) regime maintained the local fishing rules as they were. Initially, it briefly tried to abrogate the customary fishing rights. All such rights, it announced, would revert to the government. It was the government's sea (kan'yu), just as so many mountains were the government's land. Should anyone wish to fish, he needed to pay the government for the right. The predictable outcry ensued, however, and the government promptly abandoned the idea.[7]

In 1896 (effective 1898), the regime enacted a variation on the German Civil Code. The statute did not itself address fishing rights. Given that those rights had turned on custom, one of the first statutes on point was instead the 1898 general choice-of-law statute (known as the Horei).[8] By Section 2 of the statute, in the absence of legislation "customs not contrary to the public order or good customs" had "the same effectiveness as statutes" (see also Kumamoto 1990, 39). The Diet had not legislated fishing rights. Ergo custom prevailed.

---

[7] See Kumamoto (1990, 37); Abe (2009, 6289).
[8] Horei [Choice of Law], Law No. 10 of 1898,

C The Fishing Acts

In fact, the government followed the Civil Code with specific fishing legislation almost immediately. In 1901, it passed the first Fisheries Act.[9] The statute authorized the government to issue licenses to fishing unions (rather than informal hamlet groups) for the exclusive right to fish in a given area (for what would be specified species).

The Diet amended the statute in 1910.[10] In the new form, the statute would govern the property rights within the fishing industry through the end of World War II. Closely echoing the framework it had created for rights in common to the forests, the Diet defined two forms of fishing rights.[11] The first gave a fishing union the chance to file for a license that gave it the exclusive right to fish (for what would be designated species) in a given area (Fishing Act, Sec. 5). Thereafter, the drafters intended that the hamlet would act through these newly formed fishing unions (Okuda 2013, 83).

The second right concerned any customary rights that a given group of fishermen might have to fish in an area otherwise under the control of another group (like the coastal waters of their adjacent hamlet; Fishing Act. Sec. 7). The first right paralleled the rights in common that members of a hamlet had to forests they jointly owned and was in rem (Civil Code, Sec. 263). The second paralleled the rights in common that they had to land owned by someone else and were in personam (Civil Code, Sec. 294). Readers from law will understand the implications of this very basic distinction; other readers may rest assured that for purposes of this chapter it does not matter.

D Fishing Rights in Practice

1. Introduction – The Meiji legislators saw themselves as enacting statutes and codes within a stable order governed by custom. In fact, however, the Tokugawa regime had not been stable. What the courts and legislators perceived as customary rules sometimes were not customary at all. Sometimes, they simply reflected the (precarious) situation at one

---

[9] Gyogyo ho [Fisheries Act], Law No. 34 of 1901.
[10] Gyogyo ho [Fisheries Act], Law No. 58 of 1910.
[11] 1910 Fisheries Act, supra note 10, Secs. 7, 13; see Abe (2009, 6290); Kumamoto (1990, 38).

arbitrary point in time. University of Tokyo legal sociologist Toshitaka Ushiomi put it this way (Ushiomi 1954, 106):

Let me state it more fully. At the base of the fishing right that can be asserted against the outside world lies a collection of fish, shellfish, and seaweed. But that is not all that lies at that base. The base also includes the exercise of power through violence. One would not think of this in the context of land ownership, but it is crucial to the field of fishing rights. Fishing takes place on the open sea. When control through actual power does not reach far enough, or when it is very weak, that open sea presents no boundaries. As a result, fishing communities face the constant threat of incursion from another village to take fish. When such incursions occur repeatedly, they become a customary right in common. Through the Fisheries Act, those repeated incursions have grown or can grow into the fishing rights that a group might hold in common. The factual relations are structured through violence, and those relations can then grow into a right in rem.

2. Hamanabuto – In the late 1940s, Ushiomi compiled a series of ethnographies across fishing villages (1954). One of the villages was Hamanabuto (now part of Kamogawa city) in Chiba prefecture near Tokyo (Ushiomi 1954, 80 et seq.). Hamanabuto juts into the sea, within sight of a modest island known as Niemon. For many generations, the Hirano house had controlled the island. Four kilometers in circumference, Niemon is now a quasi-national park. Legend has it that twelfth-century warlord Minamoto Yoritomo retreated here during Genpei war. Legend has it that the thirteenth-century priest Nichiren once worshipped on the island.

In 1948, the hamlet of Hamanabuto held 114 households, of which 53 fished. They had not enjoyed equal customary rights. Instead, various households had had rights to various fish, subject to a variety of limits (Ushiomi 1954, 84–85). Crucially, the Hirano house had held the exclusive right to fish for abalone in the waters surrounding the island. The house claimed to have held that control since the twelfth century. Perhaps it had indeed held that control during the twelfth century. Certainly, it had held it during the late Tokugawa period.

The Hamanabuto hamlet had no interest in preserving custom. Come the Meiji period, the hamlet demanded that the government give it – not the Hirano family – exclusive control over abalone fishing (Ushiomi 1954, 88–90). It lost, and the Hirano family retained control. Soon after this stage of the dispute ended, however, villagers found the leader of their litigation team dead in the local river. The leader's sons attacked Niemon island and killed several members of the Hirano household. The Hirano household and the hamlet then agreed to share the right to abalone equally (92–97).

In fact, the dispute continued. When the head of the Hirano house became ill and needed to be hospitalized, the hamlet refused to let his boat dock at the village (99). And when in 1909 the government issued the fishing licenses under the new statute, it did so on the basis of the negotiated equal split.

There was nothing customary about this arrangement. The equal split had merely represented the most recent stage in a long-standing, sometimes violent feud.

3. Tobishima – By way of contrast, take Tobishima off the coast of northeastern Japan. About 20 km out of Sakata harbor, 210 people now live on the island. Back in 1946, 1,500 people lived there. They comprised 186 households, of whom 174 were engaged in fishing (Ushiomi 1954, 66). They raised 60 percent of their revenue through squid.

Unlike Hamanabuto, Tobishima was decidedly non-hierarchical. It had no large landholders, no landless households, and no tenant farmers. Villagers did not use the polite variations on spoken Japanese, and for their children considered no marriage socially off-limits (Ushiomi 1954, 67–68).

Formally, the Tobishima fishing union held the rights over the island waters. That formality, however, disguised the actual custom. The legal village in fact contained three hamlets, and each controlled a distinct fishing area. Each hamlet considered the sea adjacent to it to be its own sea. Formally, fishermen from each hamlet assiduously stayed out of the waters of the other two hamlets. In fact, trespass claims recurred regularly (Ushiomi 1954, 69).

Octopuses live in underwater holes, of course. By custom, each household held title to its own holes. The hamlet itself held nothing. Instead, 42 of the households owned at least one hole. When someone located a new octopus hole, he (or she) obtained the title. Like other properties, the holes could be inherited. Subject to hamlet's consent, they could be transferred. They could be rented. A daughter might take one with her as dowry when she married (Ushiomi 1954, 71).

Cod (tara) fishing involved another set of customary rights. Villagers fish for cod from January through March, and in dangerous locations farther out to sea. They fish in different areas according to their hamlet, and each hamlet regulates the fishing heavily. Only 26 of the households held a right to fish for cod – indeed, the right was not so much the right of the local fishing union as much as the right of 26 specific households (Ushiomi 1954, 73).

As with the octopus holes, the 26 houses held the right subject to the hamlet's consent. In 1904, one house lost its right after it used it as security for a loan. Later, another family sold its right because it had no male heirs. In both cases, the transferring household obtained the consent of the hamlet (Ushiomi 1954, 74).

At least prior to the introduction of power boats, an owner staffed his cod-fishing boat with six other fishermen. They negotiated this staffing during the year. Of the revenue, the owner took 40 percent; each of the six other sailors took 10 percent. Despite these economics, however, Ushiomi insists in his ethnography that that the relationship was not socially hierarchical. Staff members did not use polite Japanese when they spoke with the owner. Occasionally, one might marry the owner's daughter (Ushiomi 1954, 73–74).

IV The Modern Fishing Industry

A The Industry

1. Coastal fishing – Fishermen today hold rights and arrangements that trace their roots to this customary and then statutory tradition. Informally, they divide the industry among "coastal," "offshore," and "deep-sea" fishing (see generally Table 3.1). Through the middle of the twentieth century, coastal fishermen had dominated the industry. The customary rights at stake in disputes, like Hamabuto and Tobishima, involved this section of the sea. After the end of the war, however, corporate firms began to use increasingly sophisticated long-range fishing vessels. They developed more effective fishing and storage techniques. They built bigger ships, stationed them at metropolitan harbors, and installed refrigeration facilities to flash-freeze the fish on board. They moved beyond the coastal seas. Instead, they ranged widely across the globe and soon came to dominate the industry.

The coastal, offshore, and deep-sea sectors differ by scale. Coastal fishermen primarily operate 5–10 ton boats out of local village harbors. They work in family firms, fish in the waters that had generated the customary property rights, and return before the end of the day. About 6,300 of these fishing villages dot the Japanese seacoast, about one fishing village every 5.5 km (Gyoson 2015, 1). A local harbor dots the coast about every 12 km (Gyoson 2015, 3). The offshore fishermen run larger ships (20–150 tons) out of the bigger metropolitan harbors (Yamauchi & Nagano 2014). They go as far as 200 nautical miles out, and stay away for 2–3 days. The deep-sea fishing firms operate ships as big as 500 tons. They sail beyond the 200-mile national zone and may be gone for a month or more.

Table 3.1 *Fishing industry production and employment*

	Total	Deep-Sea	Offshore	Coastal	Farmed	No. Employed
			Production			
1965	6,910,000	1,730,000	2,970,000	1,860,000	380,000	612,000
1970	9,310,000	3,430,000	3,280,000	1,890,000	550,000	569,800
1975	10,540,000	3,190,000	4,450,000	1,940,000	770,000	447,530
1980	11,121,800	2,167,200	5,704,700	2,036,700	991,800	457,370
1985	12,171,300	2,111,300	6,497,600	2,268,000	1,088,100	431,880
1990	11,051,800	1,496,400	6,081,100	1,992,400	1,272,900	370,530
1995	7,488,600	916,500	3,259,900	1,830,700	1,314,600	301,430
2000	6,384,100	854,800	2,590,600	1,576,100	1,230,800	260,200
2005	5,764,540	547,785	2,444,475	1,464,630	1,211,987	222,170
2010	5,312,687	480,074	2,356,340	1,285,688	1,111,338	184,220

Notes: Production in metric tons
Sources: Norin suisan sho. 2013. Nogyo yoshokugyo seisan tokei nenpo [Fishing and Fish Farming Industry Production Statistica Annual]. Available at: www.e-stat.go.jp/stat-search/files?page=1&dayout=datalist&toukei=00500216&tstat=000001015174&cycle=0&tclass1=000001034726. Gyogyo shugyo doko chosa. 2017. Heisei 29nen gyogyo shugyo doko chosa hokokusho. [Survey Report on the Direction in Employment in Fishing]

Throughout the postwar period, the coastal fishermen have harvested declining amounts. The fall has been gradual. From 2.3 million metric tons in 1985, it fell to 1.3 million tons in 2010 (Table 3.1). During the same period, total fishing production fell from 12.2 million to 5.3 million. Parallel to this fall in production, the number of workers in fishing fell from 432,000 to 184,000. Because of this decline in the number of fishermen, per capita production has stayed roughly constant: 28.2 tons per fisherman in 1985 and 28.9 tons per fisherman in 2010.

Fishing is unprofitable (Yamauchi & Nagano 2014). In 2017, the mean fishing household earned 2.2 million yen (Suisan cho 2018, tab. 4-4). During the same year, the mean (full-year) employee in Japan earned 4.3 million yen (Kokuzeicho 2020, tab. 1). Given these economics, young men and women tend to avoid the industry (Table 3.1). Roughly a third of the residents in the fishing villages are now 65 or older (Gyoson 2015, 11).

2. Offshore fishing – The Japanese offshore fishing firms venture farther out to sea than the coastal fishermen, but still stay within Japanese territorial waters. Through the 1970s, they focused on sardines. Much of it they did not catch for human consumption. Instead, they sold it as fertilizer or as feed for farmed species like tuna.

Curiously, after 1988 the sardine harvest plummeted. By 1996 it had almost entirely disappeared (Suisancho N.D.). Marine biologists suggest that the rise in ocean temperatures reduced the quantity of food available to the sardines. Whether overfishing played a part is unclear, though some scholars suggest that the fishermen may have aggravated the decline by catching sardines before they had reached reproductive age (Kaiyo 2008; Norin 2018b). Today, the remaining offshore fishermen focus on mackerel, sardines, and saury (Zenkoku N.D.).

3. Deep-sea fishing – The most ambitious and sophisticated of the three groups, Japanese deep-sea fishing firms grew rapidly and steadily through the 1960s. Then, in the 1970s, they ran afoul of what in 1983 would become the UN Convention on the Law of the Sea. Across the globe, the best areas to fish lie within 200 nautical miles of the coasts. Before the 1970s, Japanese deep-sea firms had focused on several regions adjacent to the various coasts around the Pacific.

The legal shift that would become the Law of the Sea began in the 1940s. Late that decade, Chile and Peru claimed exclusive fishing rights to their 200 nautical-mile coastal zones. The U.S. asserted exclusive control over its own 200 nautical-mile zone in 1976, and other countries soon followed.[12] In 1982, the U.N. finally wrote the emerging 200 nautical-mile "consensus" into the multilateral treaty.[13] Henceforth, Article 57 gave each state an "exclusive economic zone" over the 200 nautical miles.

The 200-mile limit devastated Japanese deep-sea fishing firms. The few such firms that remain focus primarily on deep-sea fish like bonito and bluefin tuna (Suisancho N.D.). To catch them, the firms need not worry about the 200-mile limit. That does not leave them free to fish, however. Instead, they now face increasingly stringent agreements focused expressly on the species.

V Contracting for Quality

A The "New" Arrangements

Within this nearly decimated industry, a few fishermen and fishing unions started to explore new approaches. One strategy involved building a credible reputation for quality and selling directly to their customers. To coordinate these efforts by their local fishermen to move up-market, some fishing

---

[12] See generally www.suisankai.or.jp/knowledge/enyou/enyou.html.
[13] U.N. Convention on the Law of the Sea of 10 Dec. 1982. Available at, for example, www.un.org/depts/los/convention_agreements/texts/unclos/unclos_e.pdf.

unions began to move beyond their traditional roles (police trespassers and prevent overfishing).

Both the fishermen and the unions undertook these efforts for reasons that track the concerns that drove the sake brewers and rice growers in Chapter 2. Recall the dynamic. Entrepreneurial brewers wanted to develop and sell a premium sake that captured something of the local terroir. Toward that end, they wanted farmers to raise a strain of rice that was hard to grow properly. They wanted to intervene in that farming, and wanted the local farmers to welcome their intervention. Rice farmers wanted the brewer to pay for the work they did and the risks they took. They wanted a brewer whose advice they could trust, who would buy what they produced, and who would not abandon them uncompensated for a failed crop.

Like the local sake brewers, coastal fishermen understand that they are battling economies of scale. The local breweries cannot outdo the Nada–Fushimi operations in the market for standardized mass-market alcohol. If they are to survive, they need a distinctive up-scale identity. Only with more delicate drinks that depend heavily on deliberate care and exhibit subtle variations will they be able to compete against Nada–Fushimi.

The same dynamic applies to fishing. The firms running large boats out of the metropolitan harbors with multi-person crews and massive nets can capture fish at a lower per-unit cost than any coastal family operation. If the family firm is to survive, it will need to focus on a sector where it can earn returns from a reputation for investing unusually high levels of care and attention.

A coastal fisherman cannot target this quality niche if he simply sells his catch to the local wholesaler. That dealer will mix the fisherman's catch with what he buys elsewhere, and sell the undifferentiated mass into the urban wholesale market. The fisherman will receive the price for average-quality fish, and lose any incentive to devote anything more than the average level of care.

Indeed, by Akerlof's (1970) classic logic, the fisherman may lose his incentive to invest even that average quality of care. If the wholesaler cannot cost-effectively assess quality, the fisherman receives the same price whether he invests average care or minimal care. He will take minimal care and so will all other coastal fishermen. In equilibrium, the fishermen will invest little care, the wholesaler will pay them all the same, lower price, and consumers will have no choice but low-quality fish. To earn a return for high quality, the coastal fisherman will need instead to distinguish his fish from others. He will then need a way to assure his customers – credibly – that his fish are uncommonly good. To achieve that goal, he will necessarily need something other than the standard undifferentiated distribution network.

Entrepreneurial fishermen in Japan have begun to take several new approaches. First, they use the Internet to sell their catch directly to their ultimate consumers. The fishermen build their own websites. They identify (sometimes with photographs) themselves, sometimes their families, their boats, and their pets. And they offer their catch for sale. To those who order, they use one of the Japanese FedEx equivalents and deliver the fish within a day. Through the Internet, in short, they cultivate a private reputation for quality and sell directly to consumers who order on the strength of that reputation (Section B).

Note that the Internet also allows customers to contact each other. By facilitating that communication, the fisherman builds a "closed" network of personal and social ties – he creates social capital. In turn, through that social capital, he increases his vulnerability to his customers – and thereby increases the credibility of his own promises about high quality.

Second, fishermen in a given area can work together through a local organization (usually their fishing union) to certify their collective quality. Together, they invest in a high level of care, and together they delegate to their local union the power to monitor and enforce that quality standard on each other. Working together, they economize on the cost of creating and maintaining a collective reputation for quality (Sections B, C). Again, they use the Internet to position themselves and their customers within a "closed" network of personal and social ties.

Third, the fishermen can join a vertically integrated operation. More realistically, national foodstuffs firms can integrate backward into fishing. They can then enter into contracts with fishermen, monitor their quality, certify that quality, and affix their own distinctive brand (Section C). By tying themselves to the well-established foodstuffs firms, the fishermen can exploit the firms' social capital networks to enhance their own (much newer) reputations.

B Direct Sales

1. Benkei-maru[14] – Nobuaki Kawanishi and his wife acted alone. Through their independent family firm, they created their own distribution system and positioned their fish up-market. An outsider with a university education, Kawanishi used technology to accomplish this end. Born in 1970 in Osaka, he had studied commerce at Kansai University and worked eight years in an Osaka white-collar job. In 2002, he decided he wanted a different

---

[14] The account below comes from Benkei-maru (2020).

life. He loved the ocean. He should move to rural Tottori prefecture along the Japan Sea, he thought, and fish.

Kawanishi's parents wondered why they had paid private university tuition for this, but his girlfriend agreed to the move. They married and moved to Tottori where he worked for two years as an apprentice. He and his wife then ordered a 4.9 ton boat for themselves – the Benkei-maru – and went into business. He fished, and she ran the family corporation.

The Kawanishi's encountered their share of cultural conflicts. They found it hard to understand the local dialect. In turn, their neighbors watched the new "oddballs from Osaka" around the clock. They "knew my schedule better than my wife," recalls Kawanishi. Compared to apprentices who had studied fishery in college, he felt a fool; "why wasn't there anything about fishing in Marx's *Das Kapital*," he asked himself. As apprentice, he sometimes fought with his master. When he went into business, he feuded with other local fishermen.

But Kawanishi and his wife maneuvered through the conflicts. As nosey as their neighbors were, he and his wife found them generous and helpful. He persevered, and – over time – learned the basics of the trade. He came to understand his master (the instructor in his apprenticeship). He negotiated his way through the local fishing community.

Kawanishi and his wife decided to sell directly to their ultimate customers. Fishermen did not earn high pay, and Kawanishi attributed it to Akerlof's lemons. He did not use the term expressly; after all, he had read Marx in his commerce department rather than Akerlof. But he realized that fishermen who sold their catch into the general market could not credibly commit to high quality. His plan: sell directly to the ultimate customers, and put his personal reputation at stake. He started in 2007, and by 2020 counted 680 regular customers.

"I put my face and my name on the line," writes Kawanishi on his website, "and send my fish to you directly." He offers only the best, he assures his readers: "I am selecting fish that I wouldn't be embarrassed to serve to my father and mother and children." He knows how to identify quality, he tells them: "the men who know which fish in the Japan Sea are most delicious in which season are the fishermen who actually go out and fish." And given his public reputation, he has the incentive to supply that quality: "because you are buying directly from the fisherman, you can see your supplier's face and feel secure."

Quality turns crucially on freshness, and Kawanishi promises that his fish will arrive in half the conventional time. Fishermen who sell their catch through traditional routes, he explains, sell it to the wholesalers at their own location. Those wholesalers then sell it to the wholesalers near the consumers; those wholesalers sell it to local retailers; and those retailers sell the catch to the ultimate consumers. Necessarily, writes Kawanishi, the fish take at least three days to go from the harbor to the dining table. By contrast, by selling direct on the Internet, he can (promises he) move fish from the harbor to the dining table in as few as 30 hours.

Kawanishi rhapsodizes about his work in nearly religious terms. As a fisherman:

[He] realized how [he had himself] been allowed to live ... within the great expanse of nature. [He] realized how petty and minor were the sufferings and anger of a single human being.

And through his work as a fisherman, he hoped:

to convey [his] sense of wonder at the vast expanse that is nature, and the blessings that can come from the sea.

His job is his mission:

In order to bring fresh, delicious fish to your table, we fishermen risk our existence every day. We cannot let go to waste those blessings of the sea which we have caught by gambling our safety, those lives that we have received from nature.

By selling his fish whole rather than fileted, he not only helps preserve its freshness but also provides customers a tangible sense that they are receiving life from the fish. When the fish arrives whole, parents can "teach their children about life, about the way they are receiving life from the fish." He quotes a grandparent:

When my grandchildren come over to play, I prepare the fish that I received from the Benkei-maru. At first, as they watched me prepare the fish in the kitchen, they were scared. But gradually they began to marvel at it. It gave me the perfect chance to convey to them the knowledge that to eat fish is "to receive life."

Another customer put it all in Confucian terms:

My mother likes fish, but in the big city there aren't a lot of varieties available in the store. It's hard to get really fresh and delicious fish. To my mother, the packages from Benkei-maru are "a special present." I serve her the food. As she eats it, she smiles. 'This is really delicious,' she exclaims. I'm so happy that I can practice this filial piety.

By providing the best fish, continues Kawanishi, he is helping to redeem the very institution of the family. "Human groups and organizations did not originate in the 'company.' They began with the 'family.'" By encouraging families to eat together, he is facilitating the return to that primeval family unit. "The mission of the Benkei-maru," he assures his customers, "is to renew the bonds of the family through the revival of the fish-diet culture in Japan."

2. The potential opposition – (a) Kawanishi. A fisherman will not find direct sales easy. When he started selling, recalls Kawanishi, only thirteen fishermen in the entire country sold their fish over the Internet. From time to time, other fishermen have visited him to learn how to start their own businesses, but most have found the process hard. Among his thirteen original compatriots, some found that direct sales caused conflicts with local colleagues. Some found they created conflicts with the fishing union. Among the fishermen who visited Kawanishi, some simply tried and failed.

(b) Takamori.[15] Yutaka Takamori illustrates some of the tensions. Takamori grew up in the tiny hamlet of Kanita in northern Aomori Prefecture. After university, he left for a Tokyo job in real estate sales. He returned home after two years. He would go into scallop farming, he decided.

Toward his scallop business, Takamori took a high-tech approach. He kept computerized daily records of water temperature and depth. He installed electronic monitors. He by-passed the usual community institutions to sell directly on the Internet. And in all this, he was fiercely successful.

Takamori also began to market the fish that other fishermen had abandoned. Some of this fish they abandoned because they had caught too few to market efficiently. Some they abandoned because the fish were wounded. Others they abandoned because the market price was too low. Takamori worked with the "Fair Trade Fishery" NPO to sell these fish directly to consumers.

Takamori made no pretense about being a team player. He had grown up in the town, and now he had returned. He knew better than the others, he was certain. He was doing extremely well.

Resenting his attitude and success, Takamori's colleagues collectively ostracized him. At one point, they even tried to rescind his fishing rights, but Takamori remains in business. He sells his catch on the Internet and maintains Twitter and Facebook accounts.[16] But his story illustrates how hard an innovating fisherman may find it to implement his plans.

---

[15] The account below comes from Moriyama (2017).
[16] Direct sales: https://poke-m.com/producers/54. Twitter: https://twitter.com/takamo riyutaka?ref_src=twsrc%5Egoogle%7Ctwcamp%5Eserp%7Ctwgr%5Eauthor. Facebook: www.facebook.com/yutaka.takamori.50/.

(c) Sassa.[17] Hirokazu Sassa faced less opposition. He too had enjoyed an elite white-collar job, his with a large consulting firm in Yokohama. Yet like Kawanishi and Takamori, he asked himself what he really wanted to do – and the answer was fish. He and his family left their condominium, steady incomes, and networks of friends, and moved to Kagoshima on the southern tip of Kyushu island. After three years in an apprenticeship, he set out on his own.

Like Kawanishi and Takamori, Sassa has worked to develop a distinctive brand. Toward that end, he posts his fish on the fresh-food website Pocket Marche (see Section III). He then sells it directly over the Internet.[18]

Unlike Takamori, however, Sassa collaborates with other young fishermen in the area. He is not developing the distinctive brand alone. Instead, he and several other young fishermen advertise together and sell through Pocket Marche together. Together, they cooperate to develop a collective brand.[19]

3. Possible mechanisms – (a) High-Speed Market. To sell their catch directly, entrepreneurial up-market fishermen can turn to a variety of Internet services. They need not write their own code. Most straightforwardly, they can sell on Rakuten, the Japanese analog to eBay. Alternatively, they can use services that more directly target high-quality fish. The "Fisherman's High-Speed Market" (Gyoshi san chokuso ichiba) lets participating fishermen load their catch onto its website each day (Gyoshi san N.D.). Started in 2014 by a former University of Tokyo graduate student, the website specializes in fish. Each day, participating fishermen enter their day's catch onto the High-Speed Market website. They give their names and locations. They can post a husband–wife team picture. They can post the name of their boat.

Across the High-Speed Market website, potential customers can chat with the fishermen. They can ask about quality. The fisherman can suggest ways to cook the fish. The consumer can ask about probable future catches.

Once a consumer decides to order an item on the High-Speed Market, he places the order on his cell phone. The Market then transfers his order to the fisherman involved, and sends a notice to Yamato delivery, one of the Japanese FedEx analogs. Yamato will arrive at the fisherman's warehouse with completed pick-up and delivery tickets, and the fisherman can hand the driver the fish. In general, Yamato promises one-day delivery.

---

[17]   The account below comes from Kaishain (2020).
[18]   https://poke-m.com/producers/53169.
[19]   See, for example, www.instagram.com/fukiage.fmg/.

The High-Speed Market need not eliminate the role of fishing unions. The unions had traditionally served many communities as wholesalers. By inspecting and certifying the catch besides, they can help promote a distinctive local brand. Should their members decide to develop an up-market reputation, they can then do so collectively by listing their union on the High-Speed Market and selling through its account.[20]

(b) Pocket-marche. "Pocket-marche" provides a similar service.[21] The mechanics track those of the High-Speed Market: consumers place their orders by cell phone; the orders go simultaneously to the fisherman and to Yamato shipping; the latter brings the completed address labels and picks up the fish from the seller. Hiroyuki Takahashi founded the service to enable consumers and producers to transact directly for premium vegetables and fish. He hoped that they could focus both on better-than-standard products generally, and on foodstuffs that reflected the place from which they came (their terroir).

C Local Collective Branding: Yellowtail

1. Himi Winter Yellowtail – Jutting from the backside of the island of Honshu, the rocky cliffs of the heavily forested Noto peninsula crash into the Japan Sea. Few people live on the peninsula. The largest city – Nanao – has fewer than 50,000 residents. The peninsula not only constitutes a "quasi-national park" but also sports a nuclear reactor.

At the base of the peninsula lies the modest city of Himi. Its residents once fished, but no more. As of 2018, barely 230 people still worked in the industry (Himi shi 2019). Yet over 2 million visit Himi in a typical year (Nihon 2021), and they visit it precisely because of the disappearing fishing industry. Large hotels and small inns dot the coastline, and promise visitors elaborate seafood dinners. A tourist willing to make do with a simple dinner could find a room with two meals for as little as $100. Add local marine delicacies, and the prices can soar to $400.[22]

The yellowtail (more precisely, the *buri*, or Japanese amberjack) live only in the waters of the northwestern Pacific. Mature, the fish can reach nearly

---

[20] See, for example, https://umai.fish/fisherman/ishikawa-prefecture-fishery-cooperative-saikai-branch; https://umai.fish/fisherman/misaki-fishery-cooperative; https://umai.fish/fisherman/kuishiooshiki-union.

[21] See generally https://poke-m.com/stories.

[22] See, for example, www.jalan.net/yad315952/?screenId=UWW3201&yadNo=315952&roomTypeCd=0501979&rootCd=2401&stayCountBkup=1&roomCountBkup=1&adultNumBkup=2&yadoDetailMode=1&dateUndecidedBkup=1&roomCrack=200000&roomCrackBkup=200000&stayCount=1&roomCount=1&adultNum=2.

a meter long and 8 to 10 kg., and the complexity of their flavor will rival that of the bluefin tuna. They migrate north in the spring and return in the winter. As they swim southward through the Japan Sea, some swim into the Himi bay at the base of the Noto peninsula. Coming from the icy winter waters near Hokkaido and Sakhalin, their rich concentration of oil makes them prime sashimi material.

The 200+ remaining Himi fishermen have transformed their winter yellowtail catch into an enormously popular – and profitable – brand. Every year, they organize a committee. They staff it with representatives of the fishermen (themselves), their fishing unions, and the wholesalers (Himi 2021). That committee determines the opening and closing of an official "Himi Winter Yellowtail" season. The local fishermen then sell the yellowtail they catch during this official season (that also meet other quality requirements) as certified "Himi winter yellowtail" (*Himi kanburi*). And for that certified quality, they earn a massive return. From 2015 to 2021, yellowtail generally sold for 248 yen to 301 yen per 100 g (Kouri 2021). In 2021, certified Himi Winter Yellowtail sold for as much as 1,500 yen per 100 g.[23]

2. Kagoshima's Yellowtail King[24] – Japanese fishermen farm an increasing fraction of their catch. By 2018, they farmed 1.0 million tons of their 4.4 million ton total (Miyazaki 2020, p. 11). In Shizuoka prefecture, they caught 195,300 tons (much of it bonito) in the wild and farmed only 2,400 tons. In Hiroshima, they caught 15,700 tons and farmed a 107,700 ton total (much of it oysters). Japanese fishermen first farmed yellowtail successfully in the 1920s. Today, about 90 percent of all yellowtail is farmed; of all farmed fish in Japan, about 40 percent is yellowtail.

Fishermen in southern Kagoshima prefecture have no access to the cold winter waters that produce the prime Himi Winter Yellowtail, but they do have access to infant yellowtail. As the yellowtail swim northward in the spring, they pass Kagoshima. When they do, they lay and fertilize eggs. These infants then swarm off the coast of Kagoshima.

Kagoshima fishermen catch these wild infant yellowtail for their farms. They feed them for three years and then sell them on the market. Scientists have been working on a closed-cycle farming process that would use eggs laid by yellowtail that themselves lived in captivity. But the technology remains difficult, and wild yellowtail are sufficiently plentiful that the industry faces no pressure to develop the process.

---

[23] Himi (or Nanao) kanburi. See, for example, https://item.rakuten.co.jp/nma-imonya/sg-buri-saku1100/.

[24] See generally www.azuma.or.jp/burioh/.

Fishermen in Kagoshima have been farming these yellowtail since 1958 (Kagoshima N.D.), but good prices have proven elusive. To increase those prices, the fisherman in Azuma village decided to develop a brand. Azuma lies on a small island off the western coast of Kyushu. Although yellowtail taste turns in part on water temperature – something Azuma fishermen can do nothing about – it also turns on the care that fishermen lavish on their fish.

Azuma fishermen decided to raise the level of that care. To maintain their standards, they bind themselves to rules established in their local fishing union. They inspect each fish they sell. They keep daily records of the fish environment, of the feed they use, and so forth. And they sell their certified fish through their fishing union under a distinct brand: "Yellowtail King" (*buri-o*) (Seesaa N.D.). For their care, the Azuma fishermen receive a premium. As of late 2021, Yellowtail King sold for as much as 954 yen per 100 g. – less than Himi Winter Yellowtail, but treble the price of generic yellowtail.[25]

D Entrepreneurial Intermediaries

Kawanishi, Takamori, and Sassa developed their own internet mechanisms to sell to consumers. Through those direct sales, they built and maintained a personal reputation for quality that supported premium prices. The fishermen in Himi and Azuma worked through their fishing unions. They delegated to their unions the task of monitoring each other and maintaining premium quality. They, too, built a collective reputation for quality.

Ryohei Nomoto offers something of a "market alternative": a third-party intermediary that facilitates premium pricing by creating and maintaining its own independent reputation for premium quality. Born in 1965 to a family in the food distribution industry, Nomoto lived a substantial block of his childhood in poverty. He took a job after high school, and (like his father) worked several positions in the food distribution business (Katayama 2016; Nomoto 2015).

Nomoto understood that the buyers who would pay the best prices for good fish were the consumers in Tokyo (Sunaga 2016): "The people who'll pay the highest price for the morning's catch are the metropolitan consumers." He also understood that fish quality turns heavily on freshness, and that the existing distribution channels took several days to move fish from fishermen to consumers.

---

[25] See, for example, https://search.rakuten.co.jp/search/mall/鰤王/

Nomoto set out to provide same-day delivery. To ensure that speed, he established a central clearing house at the domestic Tokyo airport (Haneda), and put his plan in operation in September 2015. Under his arrangement, participating retailers would order fish directly on Nomoto's website from participating fishermen. Those fishermen would then load their catch on the first flight out of their city (Nomoto 2017, 37). Once those planes arrived in Haneda, Nomoto would route the fish to the retailers who placed the order.

Within the Tokyo metropolitan area, Nomoto promised delivery in time for dinner: hence, restaurants and consumers could both serve the morning's catch. For retailers outside of the Tokyo area, he immediately transferred the fish to relevant flight to the destination – in some cases still in time for same-day delivery (Katayama 2016; Nomoto 2017, 36). As of late 2016, he held contracts with about 700 fishermen across Japan (Katayama 2016; Anon 2016). He had contracts with 3,000 retail stores, and on a given day supplied fish to about 500–600 stores (Nomoto 2017, 36).

Nomoto's strategy involves several components. First, he actively recruits the most talented fishermen. One writer describes the process (Sunaga 2016):

First, he decides what kind of seafood he needs. He might, for example, decide that "I'd like some live shrimp." There are a variety of recruiting tactics, but he might go to the local fishing union and ask to be introduced to the most skilled fisherman. "I drink sake with the fishermen, and help them handle the fish they've caught. In the process, I obtain their trust."

Second, Nomoto imposes quality standards on all the fishermen who supply him. Most importantly, he requires that they follow special instructions about gutting and packing the fish (Nomoto 2017, 37). Regularly, he travels the country to meet with his contracting partners and make certain that they understand these procedures (Anon 2016). How, and how soon, a fisherman guts his catch dramatically changes the price Nomoto can charge.

Third, Nomoto pays his suppliers a quality surcharge. Consider this the fishing analogue to "efficiency wages." Because he requires his contracting fishermen to gut the fish by his own procedures, he pays extra. In exchange for their following his standards, he pays them at least 10 percent more than his rivals (Sunaga 2016).

Fourth, Nomoto maintains a website – Haneda Market (Haneda ichiba) – on which registered fishermen and retailers can contract. Like Kawanishi, some of the fishermen post pictures of themselves (Katayama 2016;

Nomoto 2017, 37). Like Kawanishi, they stress individualized exchange: Nomoto deliberately encourages them to establish human contact with their buyers. Nomoto (2015) writes:

Because I got rid of the distribution [network], [buyers] could safely purchase from people whose faces they could see.

Obviously, their visibility also enables Nomoto's contracting fishermen to contact each other as well. Among farmers supplying sake rice to an entrepreneurial brewer, the contacts among the farmers helped make credible the brewer's promises not to cheat. Among fishermen selling fish to Nomoto, their public presence on his website makes credible Nomoto's own promises not to cheat.

E Vertical Integration

1. Farming the bluefin tuna – The bluefin tuna is the king of the sea. It can live 35 years (Tell NOAA). It can grow 4.6 meters long and weigh 900 kg (Oceana). It can swim 40 miles per hour, and dive to 3000 feet.

The bluefin is also the king of the Japanese plate.[26] Over the course of the last half-century, it has become one of the most popular fish in sushi and sashimi. Prime fatty tuna can sell for 1,500 yen per 100 g in department stores. In high-end Tokyo restaurants, it can sell for multiples of that figure.

Most tuna is not bluefin. Of the 7.3 million metric tons of tuna caught in 2019, about half (3.4 million) is skipjack tuna destined for cans (Atuna N.D.). That year, fishing firms caught only 30,700 metric tons of Atlantic bluefin, 16,200 tons of Pacific bluefin, and 16,800 tons of Southern bluefin.

Increasingly, fishing companies raise bluefin on farms. The practice began in 1996 in Croatia, and has since spread to Italy, Turkey, and Spain (Facts 2012). Typically, these Mediterranean farmers buy juvenile tuna old enough that they need only feed them another four to eight months. Japanese farmers buy their bluefin younger, and feed them for two to three years before selling them on the market. (Karakulak, et al. 2016, 66; Buentello, 2016, 192–93). In 2014, Mediterranean farmers raised 14,500 metric tons of bluefin tuna. Japanese farmers raised 9,000 metric tons, Australians 8,400 tons, and Mexicans 4,500 (Benetti, et al. 2016, 4).

The farmers do not promote bluefin survival. The bluefin are not (yet) endangered, but their stock is low. By one account, they number only 30 percent of their 1970 levels and 3 percent of their peak (Aquaculture 2019;

[26] Nicely explored in Feldman (2006) and Bestor (2004).

Yamaguchi & Slobig 2011). Yet although the farms lower the cost of bringing mature bluefin to the market, they do not promote the species' long-term viability. Because fishermen remove the fish from the wild before reproductive age, they actually reduce the likelihood that any one tuna will reproduce.

Relatedly, as the global catch declines, it increasingly includes very young fish (International 2016, 4–6). Many caught bluefin are small. Necessarily, a given tonnage will include more fish than the same tonnage several decades ago.

2. Closed-cycle farming – (a) The process. To stabilize the bluefin population, the industry will need to turn to closed-cycle farming: fish raised to maturity from the eggs of tuna that were themselves raised in captivity. It thus made news in 2002 when Kinki University successfully fertilized eggs taken from tuna grown in captivity and raised the offspring to adulthood. Since then, the tuna-farming industry has begun to migrate from using wild-caught juveniles to relying on the full closed-cycle practice (in part because of government pressure; Fujii 2015, 46). Of the 590,000 young tuna used for farming in 2019, 233,000 came from closed-cycle hatcheries (Reiwa 2019, 2020).

Closed-cycle tuna farming in Japan includes three distinct phases. First, a hatchery takes bluefin eggs, fertilizes them, and raises the embryo to about 5 cm. Second, an intermediate farm takes the 5 cm embryos and grows them to 30 cm (300 g) juveniles. The tuna face extremely high mortality rates in both of these phases. Young tuna are notoriously sensitive creatures. When surprised, they swim into walls or netting and die. They eat each other. They have weak skin and can die if touched by humans (e.g., Maguro 2015; Yoshoku 2020; Benetti, et al 2016, 7).

Necessarily, a tuna farmer who hopes to overcome these difficulties will need a large capital investment (Torii 2005, 197). Kinki University pioneered the process and is a private university. Throughout, however, it relied on government grants.

Finally, a more traditional tuna farm will take the 300 g juveniles and raise them to maturity. This process takes about three years. At that point, the adult tuna will be about 1 meter long and weigh 30 kg.

(b) Kinki University. Since pioneering the technology, Kinki University has both operated its own firms and licensed others. By 2014, it ran two restaurants, one in the hyper-posh Ginza district. Call it science, or call it the macabre: the restaurant told its customers the day the fish they ate had been born, the day it had died, the "types of food it had been fed, and the chemicals it had been given" (Hayashi 2014). "Traceability," the promoters call it.

Simultaneously, Kinki University entered into a licensing agreement with the Toyota Trading (Toyota tsusho) firm (affiliated with the automobile company). Toyota Trading had entered the tuna-farming industry with technological help from Kinki University. It began with the second stage of tuna farming: raising the embryo to juvenile size. It started with a facility off the shores of Kyushu in 2010 and expanded back to the first stage in 2014. Toyota Trading now handles the entire closed cycle, but still markets its fish under the Kinki University Tuna brand (Toyota 2020; Goto 2015; Tsuna 2015).

(c) Vertical integration. Besides Toyota Trading, several other private firms have entered the closed-cycle tuna farming market. Maruha nichiro, Kyokuyo, and Nihon suisan have all integrated vertically into closed-cycle production. Maruha nichiro was the first of these to succeed in closed-cycle tuna farming (Morikuni 2017; Maruha 2019). It began shipping its tuna in 2015. Kyokuyo and Nihon suisan followed soon thereafter (Morikuni 2017, Kanzen 2018). All three firms are large marine-product firms that date from the pre-war period (Maruha Nichiro began in 1880). All three list their stock on the Tokyo Stock Exchange, and all were involved heavily in whaling at one point.

3. Fishing unions – Although competing in the first two stages of tuna farming requires massive capital investments, the third (raising juveniles to adulthood) requires much less. Indeed, of the 104 firms engaged in tuna farming in Japan in 2012, 45 were individual fishermen (Kitano & Yamamoto 2013, 330, tab 2). Should a fisherman want to enter the closed-cycle tuna-farming industry on a modest outlay, he could (even if none seems yet to have done so) enter it through contract: he could simply buy his juveniles from Kinki University or one of the vertically integrated firms.

On the one hand, take the massive Sojitsu (Sojitz) trading company. It went into tuna farming in 2008. It could have tried to engineer the entire three-stage closed-cycle process. It did not. Instead, it defers to Kinki University for the first two stages. It obtains some of the juvenile tuna for its farms in the wild. The rest it buys directly from Kinki University (Bluefin 2021).

On the other hand, even small fishing unions could (and perhaps will soon) follow the Sojitsu strategy. After all, tuna-farming fishermen who do not use Kinki juveniles can successfully work through their union. Tsushima island, for example, is midway between Kyushu and South Korea. Because infant tuna travel near the island, local fishermen have turned to tuna farming (Fujii 2015).

To build their own reputation for quality, in 2002 the Tsushima tuna farmers together organized the "Toro no hana" (The Flower of the Tuna) fishing union. The firms had been farming tuna since the 1990s, and had long cooperated. They had bought equipment together and shipped their produce together (Torii 2005, N.D.; Fujii 2015).

Through their union, the Tsushima tuna farmers now worked together to improve their fish and establish their brand. They ran taste tests and cooperated toward identifying the right feed for the fish. They then trademarked "Toro no hana," standardized production, and shipped their tuna together (Torii 2005, 198–99).

VI Conclusion

To enter the premium fish market, a fisherman must be able credibly to promise his customers high quality. A fisherman who sells his catch to the local wholesaler cannot do so. The wholesaler will simply pool the fish with the rest.

Some fishermen commit to high quality by selling their fish directly. They operate a website on the Internet and promise one-day delivery to customers who order. No longer are customers buying whatever the local supermarket might have. They are negotiating directly with the seller who caught the fish and can easily contact others who have bought from him in the past.

Some fishermen commit to high quality by acting together. Toward that end, the fishermen might appoint their local fishing union as their agent for enforcing quality standards upon each of them. That collective agent can then brand their fish and market the catch. Together, the fishermen are economizing on the costs of creating a reputation for quality.

Fishermen can also commit to quality by integrating vertically. In sectors (like closed-cycle tuna farming) with high capital costs, they can contract with a vertically integrated firm. That firm, in turn, will monitor and certify the quality of their fish.

In these processes, the fishermen are not simply contracting to buy and sell. In contracting, they are not taking their environment as a given. Instead, they are using their contracts to create a relationship – ideally, a continuing relationship. The fisherman will sell directly to an urban consumer; he will provide high quality in hopes that the consumer will continue to buy from him; knowing that he has that incentive to provide quality, the consumer in turn continues to buy.

And when possible, the fishermen use their contracts to create a network. Within a hamlet, they contract with their fishing union and with each other. Through the union, they monitor each other. When selling publicly on the Internet, they potentially enable their buyers to contact each other. In the process, they build social capital – they build a network that allows them more credibly to promise high quality, precisely because their buyers can contact each other, and learn how they have behaved in the past.

4

Contracting for Geothermal in Hot Springs

As the train pulled out of the tunnel dividing the two worlds, the base of the night turned white.

From Nobel laureate Yasunari Kawabata's Snow Country, the sentence is one of those opening lines every literate Japanese knows. Think of it as the Japanese equivalent to "It is a truth universally acknowledged," or "Happy families are all alike."

Kawabata set his 1930s elegy to time, transience, and the fading beauty of age in what was then the small hot springs village of Yuzawa. Located in Niigata prefecture (see Figure 2.1), Yuzawa lies along the Japan Sea coast. It is a 240 km drive to the Himi yellowtail fishermen of Chapter 3. It is a 90 km drive from the Takahashi brewery of Chapter 2. And it is a 90 km drive from Kashiwazaki city, home to the largest nuclear power complex in the world.

Yuzawa is no longer quite a small town. Instead, it has grown into a booming hot springs and skiing resort. It has over 30 hotels and inns, and maybe more. Yet despite the abundant steam underground, it does not host a geothermal plant.

Japan is itself a chain of 100 active volcanos. Hot molten rock sits just below the surface. In turn, that heat has given rise to a thriving hot springs hotel industry. It is an industry that has effectively kept the geothermal program at bay. Until the 2011 Fukushima meltdown, nuclear development had thrived. Geothermal development had stalled.

Hot springs hotel owners worry that geothermal plants will run their wells dry. The geothermal developers argue that this cannot (or at least usually will not) happen, and can point to some solid science behind their claims. By Japanese law, the hot springs owners often have the power to enjoin a geothermal plant. Yet if geothermal energy generates larger returns than the risk it poses to hot springs, the two groups ought to be able to negotiate a set of prices and terms that would let the developers proceed.

"Ought to," but the two groups usually do not. After identifying the contracting problem (Section I), I turn to the lack of geothermal development in Japan. I explain the technology behind geothermal energy (Section II), trace the property law of hot springs (Section III), and summarize the measures the government has taken to promote the geothermal industry (Section IV). Finally, I explore the contractual difficulties behind the slow pace of geothermal growth (Section V).

I The Problem

In towns like Yuzawa, a wide assortment of firms rely on the hot springs for their revenue. Hotels offer visitors lavish and sometimes medicinal baths. Restaurants provide gourmet meals. Back in Kawabata's 1930s, geisha entertained the men who came alone.

The same molten rock that heats the baths might potentially power geothermal generators. Scientists often assure local residents that the generators would not imperil the baths. They explain that the geothermal plants tap a different layer underground than the rocks that drive the hot springs. And if the geothermal plants generated electricity more valuable than the quaint hot springs, the two sectors ought to be able to negotiate indemnity agreements that raise the welfare of the parties both.

In fact, several contracting problems have plagued geothermal development. The stakes are high. The breweries and farmers in Chapter 2 staked a year's production. The fishermen and consumers in Chapter 3 staked the day's catch. The hotel and restaurants in the hot springs towns stake their entire business.

The geothermal firm could promise to indemnify local residents for any harms it causes, but should a resident believe it? The hot springs industry is overdeveloped in Japan, and existing wells randomly go dry on a regular basis. Given this random failure of the wells (as well as the potential moral hazard), geothermal developers will not want to agree to compensate hotels for all wells that go dry. Yet because of the resulting "noise," owners know that if a geothermal developer were to harm a well, they would find it hard to prove causation in court.

And can the geothermal firm trust local residents not to demand more? Even if every hotel owner wanted to negotiate a deal with a geothermal developer, no one owner can credibly promise that all subsequent owners will also negotiate in good faith. Japanese hot springs owners do not just have a right to damages. In many communities, they have a customary right to enjoin a firm that exhausts their steam. Because each owner has this potential right to hold up the entire project, the geothermal developer effectively faces sequential negotiations, each of them a bilateral monopoly, and each of them a potential hold-up.

II The Geothermal Industry

A The Potential

As the first decade of the twenty-first century closed, Japan generated about a quarter of its electricity each from coal (27.8 percent, in 2010), natural gas (29.0), and nuclear power (25.1; METI 2019, Fig. 214-1-6). That situation stopped abruptly, of course. In March 2011, a magnitude 9.0 earthquake hit the northeast. It battered the coast with a 38.9-meter-high tsunami, destroyed the coastal Fukushima nuclear complex, and shocked three reactors into meltdown mode.

The Japanese government had turned to nuclear power in the wake of the 1973 OPEC embargo. That year, mid-eastern oil-producing nations decided to boycott countries that supported Israel. The group included Japan. Because it produces almost no oil itself, Japan had relied instead on OPEC oil, and the boycott now slammed GDP growth into negative territory (Ramseyer 2012).

Rather than let OPEC dictate its foreign policy, the Japanese government moved quickly to diversify its energy sources away from petroleum. It had long since tapped out its rivers for hydroelectric power. It had exhausted its coal mines decades earlier. That left nuclear power.

The 2011 tsunami crashed this policy and forced Japan to shut down its nuclear plants. By 2017, the country had slashed electricity use by about a tenth, and nuclear power constituted only 3.1 percent of the remainder. Coal produced 32.3 percent of its electricity, and natural gas 39.8 percent (METI 2019, fig. 214-1-6; Kankyo 2020).

Could Japan produce its electricity from geothermal sources? Iceland famously does, but only 364,000 people live there. Japan has 126 million. With its long chain of volcanos, Japan (with 23,000 MW) has geothermal potential third only to the United States (39,000 MW) and Indonesia (27,000 MW).[1] Yet the United States has installed geothermal capacity of 2,511 MW, the Philippines has 1,916 MW, and Indonesia 1,534 MW. Iceland has 665 MW, while Japan ranks 10th in the world with only 533 MW (Table 4.1 Panel A; IRENA 2017). Those 533 MW barely produce 0.2 percent of its electricity (Table 4.1 Panel B).

The question is why Japan does not produce more.

---

[1] Nagashima (2018); Geothermal (2014); Yamazaki (2019).

Table 4.1 *Geothermal production*

A. Geothermal installed capacity and aggregate production

	MW	GWh
1975	52	379
1980	161	1,091
1985	214	1,493
1990	270	1,724
1995	504	3,109
2000	533	3,349
2005	534	3,228
2010	540	2,652
2011	540	2,689
2012	515	2,609
2013	515	2,570
2014	520	2,591
2015	525	2,567
2016	530	2,250

B. All renewable energy

	2010	2011	2012	2013	2014	2015	2016
Solar	0.4%	0.5%	0.7%	1.4%	2.1%	3.3%	4.8%
Wind	0.4	0.4	0.4	0.5	0.5	0.5	0.6
Geothermal	0.2	0.2	0.2	0.2	0.2	0.2	0.2
Biomass	1.0	1.1	1.1	1.1	1.5	1.6	1.7
Hydro (small-scale)	1.5	1.6	1.6	1.6	1.7	1.7	1.7
Hydro (large-scale)	6.3	6.7	6.0	6.2	6.5	7.1	5.8
All renewable	9.8	10.5	10.1	11.0	12.5	14.5	14.8
Nuclear	24.8	9.1	1.5	0.9	0.0	0.9	1.7
Total electricity (indexed at 2010)	100	96	95	95	92	89	90

Sources: ISEP, Shizen enerugii hakusho [Natural Energy Whitepaper] Sec. 4.5 (2017), available at: www.isep.or.jp/jsr/2017report/chapter4/4-5

B The Plants[2]

1. General – Geothermal plants tap the energy radiating from the core of the earth. That core lies 2,900 km below the crust. It has a temperature of some 5,000°C, primarily generated by radioactive decay. When rocks reach temperatures of 700°C to 1,300°C, they melt and form magna. That magna

----

[2] See generally Kondo (2015); National (2020); IRENA (2017); U.S. Dept. Energy (2008).

heats other rocks and aquifers. And when magna surfaces during a volcanic eruption, it takes the form of lava.

2. Steam – The most (conceptually) straightforward way to transform underground heat into electricity is through a "dry-steam" plant. Under this approach, a developer drills a set of wells into an underground steam deposit. He pipes the steam to a turbine, generates electricity, and returns the condensed steam into the ground through a second set of wells. If straightforward in theory, the method is also rare. In the United States, only the Geysers (in California) and Yellowstone National Park (in Wyoming) have the deposits necessary to support dry steam plants. In Japan, the Matsukawa plant in Iwate prefecture runs on dry steam (Science 2012).

3. Flash – More commonly, geothermal engineers turn to underground deposits of pressurized high-temperature (over 182°C) water. Through one set of wells, they pump the high-pressure water to the surface. Once that water enters a lower-pressure container, it evaporates (it "flashes"). The engineers separate the steam from the remaining water and drive a turbine.

In pumping the water out of the underground cavity, geothermal engineers lower the pressure of the water that remains; with its mix of arsenic, fluoride, boron, and heavy metals, the pumped water is itself something of a biohazard. For both reasons, after generating the electricity engineers pump the water back into the earth. The process is not simple. They use a second set of wells for this, but the silica and calcite in the water can precipitate and easily clog the pipes. In turn, to prevent this from happening the geothermal plants typically mix sulfuric acid – a deadly risk in its own right – into the already toxic water they pump into the earth.[3]

4. Enhanced Geothermal Systems (EGS). – Most areas underground do not contain the accessible layers of the water and steam necessary to transport the underground energy to the surface. To extract that heat anyway, geothermal engineers turn to the new "enhanced geothermal" technique. They first fracture the underground rock by pumping high-pressure liquid into the dry, hot rock. Sometimes, they use explosives as well. After the rocks crack, they pump in additional water to absorb the heat. Through a set of extraction wells, they bring the heated water back to the surface and drive a turbine (NEDO 2014, ch. 7; Shin 2016).

The EGS fracturing technique closely resembles the "fracking" used to extract natural gas. Necessarily, it creates analogous environmental risks (Kondo 2015). Sometimes, EGS causes earthquakes. Sometimes, it can

---

[3] Wanner, et al. (2017); Rajvanshi (2018); Gunnlaugsson, et al. (2014).

cause land to sink. In the process, it sometimes damages highways, pipe-lines, and so forth.

5. Binary. – Even when water underground is too cool for flash, modern geothermal developers can sometimes still generate electricity by piping it past a second liquid flowing in a closed loop. For that second liquid, they use something with a lower boiling point than water (e.g., ammonia–water mixtures, or a butane or pentane hydrocarbon). The heat in the extracted water causes the second liquid to evaporate and drive a turbine. As with flash and EGS, the developers then pipe the cooled water back underground.[4]

C The Welfare Caveat

Table for purposes of this chapter whether geothermal plants advance social welfare. They may, but scientists disagree and for these purposes the question does not matter. Hydrocarbon emissions harm the environment, but how much they harm it remains a scientifically contested question. Nuclear power poses small risks of extraordinarily large harm, but the size of the small risk remains similarly contested.

Geothermal plants may not be as clean as its proponents have hoped. The massive plants straightforwardly degrade national parks. They may (or may not) threaten the centuries-old hot springs industry in Japan. And EGS plants bring all the (scientifically contested) risks associated with the fracking industry. For the rest of this chapter, however, I assume that geo-thermal development does raise net public welfare, and explore the con-tracting problems that have plagued developers in Japan.

D The Cost

Geothermal plants are expensive to build. Glacier Partners (2009) special-izes in geothermal consulting. In 2009, it concluded that a 35 MW binary plant in Nevada would cost $161 million. It would provide electricity for about 44,000 households (see Ishida 2015c; Nihon 2019).

To estimate drilling costs, Glacier Partners posited a cost per well of $4.5 million. If each well produced 4.5 MW, a 35 MW capacity plant would need eight production wells. It would need another seven injection wells to pump the water back into the ground after running the turbine. Given that about a fifth of drilled wells are unusable, it reasoned that the developer

---

[4] NEDO (2014, ch. 7); Kondo (2015); Baba (2015); Kawanami (2013).

would need to drill eighteen wells. At \$4.5 million per well, it calculated a drilling cost of \$81 million.

Glacier Partners (2009) estimated that the plant itself would cost \$2.0 million per installed MW. Given a 35 MW plant, it calculated a \$70 million cost. Glacier Partners budgeted another \$5 million for the transmission lines necessary to connect the plant to the grid. Located as they are in volcanic areas, some Japanese geothermal plants will require long transmission lines and access roads.

Note that this estimate excludes costs and subsidies specific to a given political and geographic environment. Glacier Partners excludes the cost of exploring for the wells, for example, the cost of the environmental assessments, the costs of negotiating with the community, and the costs of any other regulatory restrictions. One Japanese consulting firm estimates that the early exploratory wells have a success rate of about 20 percent (Deloitte 2016).

Geothermal plants do not last forever. Almost inevitably, they instead lose pressure and temperature.[5] In Table 4.2, I give the decline over time in energy production at the major Japanese geothermal plants. From 1997 to 2010 only one plant continued to generate water at the rate at which it had initially produced; only one produced water as hot as it had initially produced. Half of the plants produced less than two-thirds of what they had initially produced. At three of the plants, water temperature had fallen more than 10°C.

III The Rival Industry

A Hot Springs

Hot springs resorts are a booming business in Japan. In 1962, there were 1,500 hot springs resorts, with 9,200 hotels and inns. By 2011, there were 3,100 hot spring resorts with 13,800 hotels and inns. In 1962, about 500,000 people worked in the industry. By 2011 about 1.4 million did. In a given year, Japanese make about 120 million overnight visits to the hot springs resorts (this in a country with a population of 126.5 million). They make another 10 million one-day visits (Nihon onsen, N.D.).

B The Conflict

The trade association of hot springs hotels vehemently opposes new geothermal plants. Allow the plants, it argues, and their springs may lose

---

[5] Oyama (2014, 346); Kankyo (2017, ch. 4.5); Ehara & Noda (2014, 314).

Table 4.2 *Geothermal electrical generating plants with capacity >10 MW*

Plant	Prefec.	PIS	Installed capacity MW	2010/ 1997 pdtn	2010–1997 Temp. ch °C	Park
Matsukawa	Iwate	1966	23.5	57.6%	+49	Yes
Otake	Oita	1967	12.5	82.0	-56	Yes
Onikobe	Miyagi	1975	15	77.7	-25	Yes
Hacchobara	Oita	1977	112	85.9	-5	Yes
Kakkonda	Iwate	1978	80	54.0	-1	Yes
Mori	Hokkaido	1982	25	59.6	-3.6	No
Uenotai	Akita	1994	28.8	20.4	-11.7	Yes
Sumikawa	Akita	1995	50	77.2	-7	Yes
Yanaizu NY	Fukushima	1995	65	48.7	-1.1	Yes
Yamakawa	Kagoshima	1995	26	62.5	-7.8	No
Ogiri	Kagoshima	1996	30	99.9	-4.1	Yes
Takigami	Oita	1996	27.5	100.5	-3.2	No
Wasabisawa	Akita	2019	46	–	–	No

Notes: Park – whether the plant is located in a national, quasi-national, or prefectural park.
Sources: Kaori Kondo, Jinetsu hatsuden no genjo to kadai [The Current State of and Issues Relating to Geothermal Electrical Generation], [National Diet Library] Issue Brief, 837: 5–6 (2015); Masao Oyama, Jinetsu hatsuden to onsen no kyozon no mondai [Problems in the Coexistence of Geothermal Electrical Generation and Hot Springs], Onsen kagaku, 63: 341–52 (2014); NEDO, Saisei kano enerugii gijutsu hakusho [Renewable Energy Technology White Paper] 2d ed. (N.D.).

temperature, lose volume, and possibly even run dry. The Ebino plateau in Kyushu straddles the line between Kagoshima (of Chapter 3's Yellowtail King brand) and Miyazaki (home to Chapter 3's Gokase River fishing union) prefectures. Near Mt. Kirishima and several other active volcanos, Ebino had been home to many geysers and an outdoor bath that attracted 39,000 people a year. In 1996, Kyushu Electric built a 30 MW flash plant nearby. Soon, the geysers started to wilt, and the water to the bath cooled and receded. Over time, the geysers in one field stopped entirely, and in 2006 the famous outdoor bath permanently closed its doors (Jinetsu 2012; Kondo 2012). Nor is it only Ebino. Hot springs operators tie geothermal plants to lower water volume or temperature in Fukushima prefecture, in Oita, in Iwate, in Akita, in Miyagi.[6]

Geothermal developers insist this cannot happen. Hot springs wells go 100 to 200 meters below the surface. Geothermal wells extend 1 to 3 km

---

[6]   Oyama (2014); Matsuzaki (2016); Endo (2016); Kondo (2012).

below the surface, and a non-permeable "caplock" membrane separates the two deposits (Oyama 2014, 344; Kondo 2015). Industry spokesmen quote scholars like Kyushu University professor Sachio Ebara:[7]

Despite more than 40 years of geothermal electrical generation, no geothermal project has ever so harmed a hot springs firm as to drive it out of business.

The Environmental Ministry routinely claims the same (Zenkoku 2013, 242). Nonetheless, when they choose places to drill, developers tend to avoid areas with an extensive hot springs industry anyway (Hymans & Uchikoshi 2022).

From time to time, hot springs wells run dry. In 1977, the Environmental Ministry found that 3,800 of the country's 22,000 hot springs no longer produced water. When a well stops producing, hotels and bath operators usually just drill a new one (Jinetsu N.D.). About Ebino and the other springs that went dry when a geothermal plant opened, geothermal developers simply assert coincidence: the geothermal plant could not have caused the hot springs to go dry, because the two underground deposits simply do not connect (Zenkoku 2013, 247).

Japanese have heard this all before. Prior to 2011, the government had adamantly insisted that the nuclear reactors were safe too. A large corps of scholars did the same. So predictably enthusiastic about nuclear development were these scholars that the press took to calling them the "nuclear power tribe." Scientists did not all back the nuclear tribe before 2011. And scientists are not all as certain as the industry and the government that the hot springs and geothermal deposits never connect.

C The Law

1. Early common law – The late nineteenth-century Japanese Civil Code[8] said little about water. It said even less about underground hot springs. It did provide that fee simple ownership extended below the surface (Sec. 207). From that premise, the Supreme Court declared in 1896 that fee simple owners held an absolute right to percolating water: own the land and the owner could use the percolating water as he pleased.[9] The plaintiffs in the case were farmers who had been using water from the defendant's land to irrigate their rice paddies. When the defendant built new paddies, he

---

[7]   Kondo (2012); see also Science (2012) (quoting Hirosaki Univ. professor).
[8]   Minpo [Civil Code], Law No. 89 of 1896 and Law No. 9 of 1898.
[9]   Nakanobo v. Yoneda, 2 Daihan minroku 3-1111 (Sup. Ct. Mar. 27, 1896).

left them insufficient water to farm as they had been doing. The plaintiffs claimed a customary right to the water, and the defendant claimed a fee simple interest in his land. The court held for the defendant: title to land extends to water flowing under the land.

That very year, however, the Supreme Court made clear that the rule applied only to percolating water: disputes over water flowing above ground it would decide according to a rule that resembles a "prior appropriation" regime: riparian farmers had a right to use water only to the extent of custom.[10] "By ancient custom," the court explained, the downstream farmers had a right to continue to use the water. An upstream riparian owner could increase the water he used only to the extent that he did not interfere with downstream customary use. Three years later, the court explained:[11]

By established national custom, [riparian owners] may not use [flowing] water freely if other established users already use that water to irrigate rice paddies. On the contrary, they may use it to develop new paddies only if they do not thereby damage the existing use of the downstream riparian users. This custom is one we recognize in this court.

About percolating hot springs, the courts enforced a customary prior appropriation regime close to the rule it used for riparian rights. To be sure, they did not reach the rule immediately. In 1905, the Supreme Court instead held that Section 207 of the Civil Code gave fee simple owners a right to exploit any underground steam. Yet even there, it left room for contrary custom. Landowners held that right to underground steam, it noted carefully, only "absent any custom to the contrary."[12]

The Tokyo High Court explained the logic in 1935:[13]

Cold water that percolates from the ground is attached to the ownership of that land. It is rare that the right to that water is treated as a right separate from that of the land. Hot springs water, however, is much more economically valuable than cold water. Hence it is often transferred independently of the land from which it flows.

The court seemed almost to anticipate Harold Demsetz (1967): the more valuable the resource, the more likely people will develop clearly enforceable private rights to it.

Whether custom required the prior appropriation regime turned on local facts. The village of Kinosaki lay on the Japan Sea coast of Hyogo

[10] Yoshida v. Komori, 2 Daihan minroku 9-19 (Sup. Ct. Oct. 7, 1896).
[11] Kasuga v. Miyahara, 5 Daihan minroku 2-1 (Sup. Ct. Feb. 1, 1899).
[12] Kiyono v. Takauchi, 11 Daihan minroku 1703 (Sup. Ct. Dec. 20, 1905).
[13] Furihata v. Okamura, 3873 Horitsu shimbun 5, 6 (Tokyo High Ct. July 17, 1935).

prefecture, on the other side of the mountains from the Nada breweries. It touted six outdoor medicinal baths.[14] To cater to the visitors, residents operated over sixty bathless inns. Visitors would stay at an inn, and rest in the public baths. It was a quiet town. Novelist Shiga Naoya stayed there to write.

In 1910, the railroad arrived. Increasingly, it brought vacationers from metropolitan Kobe, Kyoto, and Osaka. The wealthier of the new visitors wanted hot springs baths in their villas. They wanted hot springs baths in their hotels. And to cater to the new demand, entrepreneurs began to build hotels with indoor baths.

The new indoor facilities threatened to run the public baths dry, and the sixty bathless inns out of business. Local residents ostracized the owner of one of the new hotels. They boycotted merchants who did business with him. Their children harassed his children. They cut the electricity to the town and used the chaos to storm his hotel.

And the villagers also sued. By custom, they argued, no one could pump the hot water indoors. They lost: whatever the custom in the distant past, the town no longer had such a custom. By the time the inn-keepers sued, reasoned the court, so many residents had pumped water indoor that any customary ban had long since vanished.

Yet if Kinosaki had no longer given prior users a customary right to the hot springs, many of the most prominent resort towns did. If they had that custom, the courts enforced it. Wrote the Supreme Court:[15]

Owners may use underground water that flows through the land they use. They may use that underground water even if it is part of a hot springs. This right, however, is conditional: it holds only when there is no law to the contrary. And [in the presence of such a custom,] it gives the land owner usage rights only to the extent that his use does not infringe the rights of others to use the water.

About the hot springs in Matsumoto, a few-hour train ride from Tokyo, the Tokyo High Court explained in 1939:[16]

The rights to the hot springs in the Matsumoto area of Nagano prefecture constitute a type of real rights. They are independent of the ownership rights to the land from which they flow. By the customary law of the area, parties may transfer these rights to hot springs through a simple meeting of the minds.

[14] Ramseyer (1989, 63–64); Kinosaki Village v. Kataoka, 4249 Horitsu shimbun 5 (Kobe D. Ct. Feb. 7, 1938); Kawashima, Shiomi & Watanabe (1964).
[15] Japan v. Masaki, 3453 Horitsu shimbun 15 (Sup. Ct. Aug. 10, 1932).
[16] Nagano shogyo K.K. v. K.K. Nihon kangyo ginko, 4517 Horitsu shimbun 12, 13 (Tokyo High Ct. Oct. 16, 1939).

2. Post-war – (a) The statutory overlay. On this common law of property, the Japanese government added an administrative overlay in 1948.[17] The new statute – the Hot Springs Act – added a requirement that one who would dig a well obtain an advance permit from the prefectural government (Sec. 3). The governor was to deny the permit if the existing well would interfere with existing hot springs or otherwise with the "public welfare" (Sec. 4). Absent such interference, he was to approve the application.[18] He was to maintain a hot springs council and consult with it about any drilling application he might receive (Kondo 2015, 9; Kawanami 2013, 51).

Some prominent hot springs communities did not trust their governor. Rather than take the legal regime as given, they added regulations of their own. The Oita town of Kokonoe, for example, required applicants to obtain the approval of the village mayor, and to take any steps necessary to avoid harm specifically to the local hot springs resources and more generally to the local environment. The town also required potential geothermal developers to consult with a specifically geothermal committee (Kokonoe 2015, sec. 5, 6). The larger Oita city of Beppu deliberately introduced municipal requirements so onerous that it hoped developers would decide to dig elsewhere just to avoid the paperwork (Yamane 2018).

(b) The common law, again. The post-war courts continued the earlier common law of hot springs. "Absent a special rule or custom to the contrary," wrote one district court in 2002, title to land carried with it the right to exploit hot water underground.[19] With that custom to the contrary, however, ownership of the surface land was separate from ownership of the hot water below.[20] When a developer petitioned for a drilling permit under the Hot Springs Act, the outcome turned in part on the presence or absence of such a custom. Wrote the Fukuoka District Court:[21]

When we consider the import of Section 4 of the Hot Springs Act regarding the drilling permit, in some areas, by long years of custom, the owner of a hot springs

[17] As Smith (2008, 455) notes has happened with the prior appropriation regime in the U.S. Onsen ho: Law No. 125 of 1948. See generally Onsen ho seko kisoku [Implementation Rule for the Hot Springs Act], Rei. No. 35 of 1948 (general implementation order).
[18] See Ishikawa ken v. Onsen kaihatsu K.K., 1311 Hanrei taimuzu 104 (Kanazawa D. Ct. Nov. 28, 2008), aff'd, 1311 Hanrei taimuzu 95 (Nagoya High Ct. Aug. 19, 2009) (reversing a denial of a permit on grounds that evidence was too vague).
[19] [No names given], 2002 WLJPCA 10319014 (Gifu D. Ct. Oct. 31, 2002).
[20] Kigyo kumiai Higashiyama onsen v. Sako, 888 Hanrei jiho 107 (Kochi D. Ct. Jan. 26, 1978), aff'd, 1044 Hanrei jiho 383 (Takamatsu High Ct. Dec. 7, 1981).
[21] Kokusai baiyaa shitei hoteru v. Shizuoka ken chiji, 5 Gyoshu 1482 (Fukuoka D. Ct. June 2, 1954), aff'd 113 Hanrei jiho 10 (Fukuoka High Ct. Nov. 8, 1956), aff'd, 157 Hanrei jiho 14 (Sup. Ct. July 1, 1958).

has the exclusive right to the water at stake. In these areas, the rights relating to the hot springs are separate from the ownership rights in the land. The right to use the hot springs is itself a distinct form of customary real rights.

Major hot springs resorts often maintained exactly that custom. Take the city of Beppu (within Oita prefecture). Of the 27,400 hot springs in the country, Oita has 4,381, and Beppu has 2,291. Of the 2.63 million liter/minute produced in Japan, Oita produces 279,000, and Beppu produces 87,360. Crucially, Beppu has a customary tradition that treats the underground steam and hot water as an interest separate from the land.[22]

Typically, courts treated the customary hot springs right as an in rem "property right." Accordingly, the holder held both (a) a right to specific performance as appropriate, and (b) a right that he could enforce against a good-faith purchaser of the land from which the hot water flowed. The plaintiff in one 1968 case had contracted for hot springs water from a landowner. The local real estate registry did not formally record such contracts, but the plaintiff did report his arrangement to the prefectural health agency, and the pipes were easily visible on the land. When the defendant bought the source land and refused to deliver the hot water, the plaintiff sued. The court ordered specific performance.[23]

IV Geothermal Promotional Policy

A Early Development

Japanese utilities began developing commercial scale geothermal generators in the 1960s. In northeastern Iwate prefecture, Tohoku Natural Energy placed the 25 MW Matsukawa dry steam generator in service in 1966 (see Tables 4.1 and 4.2). In southern Oita prefecture, Kyushu Electric placed the 12.5 MW Otake flash generator in service in 1967. Development continued, and by the end of the century Japanese utilities ran geothermal plants with a combined capacity of 530 MW.

And there in 1996 it stopped. Geothermal plants were expensive and produced only these trivial amounts of electricity. Together, all geothermal plants in the country produced that 530 MW. By contrast, the nuclear reactors at Fukushima alone produced 9,200 MW.

[22] Goto v. Horikawa, 5 Kamin 985 (Oita D. Ct. June 28, 1954); Inoue v. Hadano, 7 Kamin 2151 (Oita D. Ct. Aug. 9, 1956).

[23] Kokka komuin kyuzai kumiai rengokai v. Hayama onsen kanko K.K., 543 Hanrei jiho 70 (Yamagata D. Ct. Nov. 25, 1968).

B Post-Fukushima

The 2011 meltdown changed this government policy, of course. The Japanese government returned almost immediately to the geothermal project. To promote the technology, it faced several straightforward problems. First, over 80 percent of Japanese geothermal potential lay in national, quasi-national, or prefectural parks (Nihon onsen N.D) and geothermal plants are massive eye-sores. The Hacchobara complex in Oita covers 20 million square meters. The plants present an unsightly maze of pipes, tubes, and cooling towers. They emit constant flumes of steam.

Notwithstanding what might otherwise seem environmental obstacles, the Japanese government moved quickly. In 2012, the Environmental Ministry liberalized the standards for approving projects. These new liberalized rules applied specifically to national parks.[24]

Second, geothermal plants are expensive. To encourage their development, the government announced a portfolio of subsidies. The amounts vary by the size of the plant, and so forth. In general, however, the government will pay two-thirds of the cost of surveying an area, and up to three-fourths of the cost of any exploratory drilling. It will subsidize the cost of negotiating with local residents (Yamazaki 2019). It will provide equity investment and guarantee debt (Yamazaki 2019). In the case of the 46 MW Wasabisawa plant, the loan guarantees reached 21 billion yen (about $210 million; Keizai 2020).

Third, energy prices fluctuate wildly. To placate potential investors, the government instituted a "feed-in tariff" (FIT) program to provide high fixed electricity prices. Under FIT, it required utilities to buy specified amounts of electricity from approved renewable suppliers at specified prices. In effect, it guaranteed geothermal producers steady demand at high prices.

Under the post-Fukushima FIT program, the government guaranteed geothermal prices of 26 yen/kWh for plants with capacity of 15 MW or more, and 40 yen for smaller plants (Table 4.3).[25] The FIT supports applied to other renewable energy sources as well. Of the FIT-approved capacity in 2017, 78.5 percent went to solar energy (Kankyo 2017, 1.3).

---

[24] Kankyo sho (2012); see Shin (2016); Kawanami (2013, 49–50); Yamazaki (2019); Kankyo (2017, ch. 3.4.1); Kondo (2015, 8).

[25] Yamazaki (2019); Kondo (2015, 4); Denki jigyosha ni yoru shin enerugii to noriyo ni kansuru tokubetsu sochi ho [Special Measures Act Regarding the Use of New Energies, Etc. by Electrical Industry Firms], Law No. 62 of 2002. This set up the Renewable Portfolio Standard (RPS), and would later be amended to cover geothermal plants. The Denki jigyo sha ni yoru saisei kano enerugii denkino chotatsu ni kansuru tokubetsu sochi ho [Special Measures Act Regadrding the Raising of Renewable Energy Electricity by Electrical Industry Firms], Law No. 108 of 2011, creates the FIT scheme.

Table 4.3 *FIT guaranteed prices, 2017*

Solar		
	x < 10 kW	28 yen
	10 kW < x < 2 MW	21
	x > 2 MW	Auction
Wind (land)		
	x < 20 kW	55
	x > 20 kW	21
Wind (sea)		
		36
Geothermal		
	x < 15 MW	40
	x > 15 MW	26
Small-scale hydroelectric		
	5 MW < x < 30 MW	20
	1 MW < x < 5 MW	27
	200 kW < x < 1 MW	29
	x < 200 kW	34

Notes: Separate prices given for replacement facilities in some cases.
Sources: ISEP, Shizen enerugii hakusho [Natural Energy Whitepaper] Sec. 2.6 (2017), available at: www.isep.or.jp/jsr/2017report.

For locations that accepted nuclear power plants, the government had provided elaborate subsidies directly to the communities themselves (as distinct from the developers; Ramseyer 2012). The same programs nominally apply to communities that accept geothermal plants. Because the programs key the amount of the subsidies to the power capacity of the plants, however, to communities accepting geothermal plants, the government pays only trivial amounts.

C Minor and Well-Less Plants

Since 2011, entrepreneurs have mostly built geothermal plants that are small or which require no new wells. Between 2011 and September 2017, Japanese developers built thirty-three binary plants (see Table 4.5). Most were extremely small. A 100 kW plant produces electricity for about 125 households (Ishida 2015; Nihon 2019). Of the 33 plants, 24 are smaller than 100 kW. Only three are larger than 1 MW, and one of those was an in-house generator for a large medical facility.

Many of the plants did not involve new wells. Recall that binary plants can use cooler water than that required for the large flash plants. With

Table 4.4 *Binary plants with capacity >100 kW, placed in service 2011–2017*

Name	Location	Installed capacity	PIS
Takigami	Oita pref, Kokonoe	5,050 kW	2017
Sugawara	Oita pref, Kokonoe	4,400 kW	2015
Medipolis	Kagoshima pref, Ibusuki	1,410 kW	2015
Tsuchiyu onsen	Fukushima pref, Fukushima	440 kW	2016
Cosmo Tech	Oita pref, Beppu	400 kW	2014
Okujiri	Hokkaido pref, Okujiri	250 kW	2017
Beppu Spa Service	Oita pref, Beppu	125 kW	2016
Obama onsen	Nagasaki pref, Unzen	115 kW	2016
Setouchi Nat Energy	Oita pref, Beppu	110 kW	2015

Sources: Tadahiko Okamura, Zenkoku no nessui katsuyo oyobi bainarii hatsuden no jirei [The Hot Water and Binary Generators in the Country], Sept. 27, 2017; Kankyo enerugii seisaku kenkyu jo, Shizen enerugii hakusho [Natural Energy White Paper] 4.1, 4.5 (2017), available at www.isep.or.jp/jsr/2017report

binary technology, an entrepreneur can even use water below 100°C to power a turbine. It will use that water to heat a liquid with a lower boiling temperature and power a generator with the gas from that second liquid.

With binary technology, the hot springs hotels could use their own water to power the hotel. If their water were 90°C, for example, they would need to cool that water to 50°C anyway before they could pipe it into their baths. With a binary generator, they could use the energy released in the cooling to power a turbine generator.

Even some of the larger binaries did not involve new wells. Take the 5.05 MW Takigami plant (see Table 4.4). As Table 4.2 shows, Takigami already had 27.5 MW flash capacity. The water emitted from this plant was still hot, even if not hot enough to power a flash generator. With the addition of a binary generator in 2017, the firm was able to use the water from the flash plant to generate still more electricity (Kamitaki 2017, 2).

Similarly, the Yamakawa flash plant in Kagoshima prefecture has a 26 MW capacity (Table 4.2). Like Takigami, it emitted hot water. In 2017, it installed a binary plant. With the water left from the flash plant, it powered the new binary turbine and generated another 5.0 MW (Shin 2018).

D The Overbuilt Hot Springs Industry

Unfortunately for the government's geothermal drive, by 2010 hot springs hotels realized that their industry was badly overbuilt. Over the course of

Table 4.5 *Hot springs production (liter/minute)*

A. Major producer prefectures:

Total	1998	2003	2008	2013	2018
Hokkaido	305,381	261,822	267,397	243,192	198,022
Aomori	162,812	149,080	171,961	140,537	147,259
Iwate	159,338	113,174	113,224	107,977	113,077
Nagano	128,391	134,622	121,734	118,858	113,400
Shizuoka	127,581	119,810	119,672	123,009	116,004
Kumamoto	119,822	149,595	132,084	135,730	133,158
Oita	261,804	267,434	295,740	285,553	279,253
Kagoshima	196,777	200,804	200,694	186,824	160,132

B. Change over time:

1963	930,110
1968	1,258,138
1973	1,348,554
1978	1,557,303
1983	1,846,090
1988	2,037,301
1993	2,375,503
1998	2,638,980
2003	2,681,178
2007	2,799,418*
2008	2,772,022
2013	2,642,705
2018	2,546,813

Note: *peak.

Source: Ministry of Environment, Onsen riyo jokyo [Hot Springs Usage] (2010), available at: www
.env.go.jp/nature/onsen/data/index.html

the second half of the twentieth century, hotel owners had sunk massive numbers of wells. They had turned small rural villages into tourist retreats, and small retreats into massive entertainment centers.

From 1973 to 1998, hot springs developers had doubled productive capacity: from 1,258,000 liters/minute to 2,639,000 (Table 4.5). Then, around 2007 output began to fall: from 2,799,000 l/min (2007) to 2,772,000 (2008), to 2,643,000 (2013), to 2,547,000 (2018). The decline hit the biggest resort communities hardest. The northern island of Hokkaido promised visitors both hot springs and lavish skiing. From 1998 to 2018, total hot springs output in the prefecture fell 35 percent. The central Japanese mountain ranges in Nagano (home to the Takahashi sake brewer of Chapter 2) promised hot springs and fresh powder too: from 2003 to 2018, hot springs output fell 16 percent. Output in the deep northern prefectures of Aomori and Iwate fell 15 percent (2008–2018) and 29 percent (1998–2018). Output in Kagoshima, home to the spectacular Mt. Kirishima volcano, fell 20 percent (2003–2018).

In the wake of the Fukushima meltdown, the Japanese government proposed to drill massively for geothermal. It did this just as firms in the hot springs industry were coming to realize how far they had already passed the level of energy they could safely extract from the ground. They had created a massive industry: 13,800 hot spring inns in 2011, and 1.4 million workers. And that industry was now in peril.

V Contracting for Geothermal

A Introduction

Disproportionately, the few geothermal plants in operation involve cases where the developer and the hotel owners were able successfully to solve the contractual problems that have plagued the industry everywhere else in Japan. Sometimes, they solved it by engineering. The geothermal developer piped hot water directly from its plant to the hot springs hotels. Unfortunately, many (if not most) geothermal projects lack the volume of hot water to cut this deal.

Sometimes, the geothermal developer and the hotels could solve the contracting problems because a local firm already integrated into the community's social capital network undertook the geothermal development itself. A developer outside that network would find it hard to draw on any reservoir of trust to make its promises credible. It would also find it hard to enforce principles of integrity and good faith on the hot springs hotels. The contractual problems that an outsider could not solve, an insider – tied to the community through dense networks of social and economic ties – could sometimes successfully maneuver.

And sometimes, the hotels solved their collective action problem by negotiating through their trade association or town government. Even in tight communities, an entrepreneurial hotel might find it profitable to refuse to join a collective contract. By contracting through their common trade association or town government, sometimes the hotels could prevent even this deviation.

B The Problem

1. Introduction – By 1996, Japanese utility companies had built a solid start in geothermal. A 10 MW capacity plant provides electricity for about 12,500 households (Nihon 2019; Ishida 2015). By 1996, the utilities had placed twelve 10+ MW plants in service. And then, they stopped.

After the 2011 meltdown, the Japanese government tried to restart the geothermal project. As noted earlier, it eased the regulatory restrictions in the national parks. It subsidized development. It guaranteed high prices. It successfully convinced hot springs hotel owners to install small binary generators. And in May 2019, Mitsubishi Materials, Mitsubishi Gas Chemicals, and a privatized government agency together opened a 46 MW plant in northern Akita prefecture. The new Wasabisawa plant was the first 10+ MW plant since the 27.5 MW Takigami plant opened in southern Oita prefecture in 1996 (Yamazaki 2019).

Eight years after the meltdown, the utilities had finally built a large geothermal plant. The question is why it took so long, and why they still find it so hard.

2. The solvable hurdle – The 1948 Hot Springs Act presents one obvious problem. The Act requires a geothermal developer to obtain clearance from the prefectural governor before he drills. The governor must consult his hot springs committee before issuing that clearance. And by most accounts, incumbent hot springs hotels and inns dominate the committees. As political scientist Jacques E.C. Hymans (2020) put it, the "Hot Springs Law hands a virtual veto to local onsen [hot springs] businesses to block any unwanted drilling in their vicinity."

This may be a problem, but it is a legally solvable problem. Should the government want to do so, it could amend the statute to lower the influence of industry incumbents. It could even repeal it.

More fundamentally, if the geothermal plant were indeed social welfare increasing (as posited in this chapter, see Section. II.A.6.), a geothermal developer should be able to buy the approval of any local hot springs committee. The developer earns a return from his investment, but imposes a risk of loss on the hotel owners on the committee. It follows from the definition of welfare increasing that the developer's return should exceed the risk-adjusted loss to the committee members. Absent contracting problems, he should be able to purchase their approval.

But of course there are indeed contracting problems.

C The Reciprocal Contracting Problems

1. Ex post: the developer's promissory credibility – The private-law obstacles to geothermal development are less obvious but potentially cut more deeply. The problems are twofold. First, the geothermal developers cannot credibly promise to compensate a hot springs hotel for harm ex post. No rational hotel or inn keeper would fight a geothermal project if the developer coupled substantial compensation ex ante with a credible promise to pay damages for harm ex post.

Yet although a developer can promise those damages, he will find credibility elusive. Obviously, he can promise a hot springs hotel not to lower the volume of steam or hot water. He can promise to compensate the hotel if he does. But given that hot springs routinely go dry for no apparent reason, he will rarely find it profitable to compensate the hotels for all wells that go dry. The hotel owner himself knows hot springs randomly go dry. He also knows that for decades now, the hotels and inns have been extracting steam and hot water at rates the local sources cannot sustain. And he knows that many geologists and most government officials insist (and would testify in court) that 1- to 3-km-deep geothermal wells would never affect the amount or temperature of the water in the separate hot springs cavities 100 to 300 meters below the surface.

As a result, each hot springs hotel owner knows that even if a geothermal plant were to cause its spring to go dry, he could find judicial recovery problematic. The owners reason, writers one observer, that "you can't see underground" (Uechi 2016, 51). "Even if a geothermal plant exhausted" their hot water source, "we'd never be able to prove causation." Complained the village council chair in one hot springs community (Jinetsu 2011), even if a geothermal plant were to damage their source, "it'd be nearly impossible for us to prove in court that the plant had caused the harm."

The question then turns on whether a developer can credibly promise to negotiate honestly and fairly if a spring goes dry. Most large-scale developers come from outside the community. They stand outside the network of ties that general social capital. Like a promise to deliver 800 pounds of soybeans on September 1, some promises are easy to verify and enforce. Like a promise to negotiate honestly and fairly, other promises are impossible to verify. Only if a promisor can tap a large and longstanding reservoir of trust would he be able to contract, and most geothermal developers stand outside that reservoir of community trust.

2. Ex ante: the hotel owner's promissory credibility – Second, absent a tight network of social capital, any individual hotel owner will find it hard

credibly to promise that his competitors will negotiate in good faith. By Japanese common law (see Section III.C), hot springs users in many of the most popular resort areas have a customary property right to the continued use of the steam and hot water that they currently use. That right includes the right to enforce their continued use against good-faith third-party transferees. And it includes the right to enforce the continued use through injunctions.

By common law, in other words, a Japanese hot springs hotel owner may have a right to hold up an electrical plant. Absent an injunctive right, if electrical generation constituted a more efficient use of the underground steam and water than the local hot springs hotels, the utility could simply ignore the hotels. It would build the generating plant. Maybe it would harm the local hotels, and maybe not. But if it did, the utility would let the hotels sue. After all, it could make them whole through expectation damages and still make a profit.

With the injunctive right, however, the hotel owner (in many resort communities) may have a right to shut down the plant. He does not necessarily have that right. The geothermal plant will not necessarily affect hot springs water flow. Even if it did, the hotel owner would find it hard to prove his claim in court. But potentially he has that right.

Should the plant and the hotels try to negotiate a solution to this problem ex ante, they face a collective action problem. If a geothermal plant is indeed welfare enhancing, it would benefit the developer and incumbent hotel owners both: it would pay the developer returns high enough to more than compensate each hotel owner for the risk of harm. Should the developer try to negotiate such an arrangement ex ante, however, he must negotiate with each hotel seriatim – yet no hotel owner can credibly promise him that each succeeding owner will agree to terms that will leave him a market return on his investment.

D Successful New Plants

Hence, the twin reciprocal problems: the developer cannot credibly promise local hotel owners that they can successfully collect ex post the damages he might cause; in turn, should a developer try to negotiate a deal – any deal – with all hotel owners ex ante, he faces a sequence of bilateral monopoly negotiations that could potentially leave him no return on his investments.

Geothermal developers and hot springs hotels cannot necessarily solve these problems. But some do. And among the geothermal plants that one observes, the instances where the parties did solve these problems obviously predominate.

1. Solving the problem through engineering – Some parties solve the problem of developer liability through engineering: the geothermal plants pipe steam and hot water to the hotels directly. Recall the problem: a geothermal plant would like to promise hot springs hotels that if it caused their wells to go dry, it would pay them expectation damages in the courts; yet the plant and the hotels both know that the hotels would find causation hard to prove. By piping steam and hot water directly to the hotels, a developer can go a long way toward mitigating the question.

The first plant to pipe water directly to nearby hotels was the very first modern geothermal plant of them all: the Matsukawa plant in Iwate prefecture. Matsukawa opened in 1966 with a 23.5 MW capacity. From the beginning, it piped hot water, free, to all 38 local hotels and inns.[26]

Kyushu Electric followed the same practice at Hacchobara, the largest geothermal operation in the country. The plant covers 20 million square meters in the Oita mountains of central Kyushu – within the Aso kuju National Park, no less. The complex includes three geothermal plants: a 55 MW double flash plant from 1977, a second 55 MW double flash plant from 1990, and a 2 MW binary plant from 2006. The first two plants rely on 30 wells (as of 2008); the binary plant uses the emissions from the two flash plants.[27]

Like Matsukawa, the Hacchobara plant pipes steam and hot water, free, to all local hotels and inns. When the plant opened in 1977, seven hotels and inns operated in the area. Attracted by the prospect of free hot water from Hacchobara, the local village now houses twenty-nine hotels and inns (Kirishima 2015). Given that the plant pipes distilled hot water, the hotels and inns add minerals as necessary to replicate the water they would obtain directly from the ground (Kirishima 2015).

Geothermal developers have continued to pipe hot water to local hotels and inns in a variety of projects. They cannot do it always. Only if their wells yield a sufficient volume can they safely commit to supplying hot water to the hotels, and many wells do not yield that volume. Some hotels and inns would probably find it unsatisfactory anyway. Although many do use pumped hot water, others rely on naturally percolating hot springs. For them, water piped from a utility may lack the "natural" cache their customers demand.

---

[26] Jinetsu (2011); Ministry of Environment (2015). Nihon (2010, 42–3) writes that Matsukawa charges for the water.

[27] Jinetsu (2011); Abe (2012); Kirishima (2015).

Other geothermal plants piping steam and hot water to local hotels and inns include:[28]

Otake, Oita prefecture, 12.5 MW flash unit placed in service 1967.
Onuma, Akita prefecture, flash, 9.5 MW flash unit placed in service 1974.
Yanaizu Nishiyama, Fukushima prefecture, 65 MW flash unit placed in service 1995.
Waita, Kumamoto prefecture, 2 MW flash unit placed in service 2014.
Sugawara, Oita prefecture, 4.4 MW binary unit placed in service, 2015.
Tsuchiyu, Fukushima prefecture, 440 kW binary unit placed in service 2016.

2. Local initiative – Turn to the second problem: unless the hot springs hotels and inns agree to waive their hold-up rights simultaneously, the geothermal plant faces a sequential set of contractual negotiations, each of them a bilateral monopoly. Although all hotels and inns would do better if they all agreed ex ante to limit their demands, no hotel can legally speak for any other hotel. Unable collectively to limit the demands they each will make, they leave the developer at risk of not earning a positive return.

Disproportionately, the plants we observe are plants where the hotels and inns seem to have solved this collective action problem before negotiating with the geothermal developer. A plant might – conceivably – make a conditional offer: we will pay x to each hotel if they all agree to waive later claims. Instead, disproportionately the plants we observe seem to be those in which the hotels solved their own collective action problem first.

"Seem to be" – because the apparent solution is informal and not visible. Many of the hotels and inns recruited local social capital to organize themselves first. They formed an association (or recruited the town government), and then negotiated through that association. Apparently, they then enforced their collective norms on each other through the informal sanctions that the social capital made possible.

The Tsuchiyu hamlet in suburban Fukushima had once thrived. Throughout the 1980s, it had served as a popular hot springs destination for tourists, but then had fallen on hard times. After the 2011 nuclear meltdown, tourism plummeted still further. To earn local revenue, several residents urged the community to accept a geothermal plant. They (and a local cooperative) formed the K.K. Genki Appu Tsuchiya (Invigorate Tsuchiya!) firm, and opted for a 440 kW binary plant – enough for 720 households.

---

[28] Abe (2012); Ministry of Environment (2015); Yamazaki (2019); Risoteki (2018).

They built it on land provided by the city and used a well provided by the hot springs association.[29]

The small hamlet of Waita in Kumamoto had faced a geothermal developer in 1996. The developer had presented a plan, but the proposal had split the community, and the opposition killed the proposal. Like many rural Japanese villages, however, the hamlet continued to lose population. The average age of those who remained steadily climbed.

In 2011, several of the more entrepreneurial Waita citizens revisited the idea of a geothermal plant. They organized residents into an LLC. They obtained government subsidies for the development. They negotiated a contract with an electrical firm to build and operate the plant. The modest 2 MW flash plant opened for business in 2015 (electricity sufficient for 3,900 households).[30]

Several years ago, geothermal developers decided to expand the 26 MW Yamakawa plant. To facilitate the expansion, the city government negotiated with the developer itself. The city rented a 3,500 square meter piece of land to supply to the plant. From the plant, it contracted to buy 30 tons/hour of pressurized water at least 120°C (Ibusuki 2019; Sasaki 2019).

In Yuzawa village of Akita prefecture (not the Niigata Yuzawa mentioned in the introduction), the developer for the Wasabizawa plant gave the town several 1000-meter-class wells. In turn, the town pipes hot water from the wells to local inns. Not only did this eliminate opposition to the Wasabizawa plant, it actually brought new hot springs inns to the community (Akitaken N.D.).

To build the Sugawara binary plant in Kokonoe village, the geothermal developer similarly negotiated with the village. It rents the requisite well from the village (METI 2020; Ministry of Environment 2015).

VI Conclusions

Japan has no oil, no coal, and an understandably vehement public opposition to nuclear power. It does have the third largest deposit of geothermal energy in the world. Yet its total installed geothermal generating capacity remains a paltry 533 MW, tenth in international rankings.

In part, contractual problems of promissory credibility have stymied the geothermal development. First, by the common law of property, hot springs hotels in many communities can potentially shut down geothermal

---

[29] Onsen (2018); Ito (N.D.); Moriya (2016); Ishida (2015a); METI (2020).
[30] Ishida (2015b); Waita (N.D.); Nihon (2019).

plants. Geothermal developers could promise to compensate the hotels for any damages they cause, but – coming as they do from outside the community – cannot necessarily make that assurance credible. The hot springs industry is badly overdeveloped in Japan, and existing wells randomly go dry on a regular basis. Whatever a developer may say, owners know that if a geothermal plant were to damage a well, they would find it hard to prove causation in court.

Second, hot springs hotels cannot necessarily promise that their competitors will negotiate in good faith. Because each hot springs owner may have a right to the continued use of steam and hot water enforceable through injunctions, each can potentially hold up the entire geothermal project. The developer faces sequential negotiations, each of them a bilateral monopoly, and no one owner can credibly promise the developer that all subsequent owners will negotiate in good faith.

The few geothermal plants that one observes are disproportionately those where the hot springs owners and geothermal developer did solve these contractual problems. Some developers found an engineering solution to their contracting problem: they piped hot water to the hotels directly. Some of the more successful developers were home grown: they came from the local community itself. Already integrated into a dense network of social and economic ties, they were able to employ the community social capital to make their own promises more credible. They were able leverage their access to that social capital in order to enforce principles of good faith and integrity on the hotels. Negotiating from within the network of community ties, insiders could sometimes succeed where outsiders could not.

5

Contracting for Credit in Agriculture

Villages in pre-war Japan presented a contracting problem common to a wide variety of newly developing societies. Some people wanted to farm and knew how to do it – but lacked the capital to buy a working farm or to transform undeveloped land into a viable farm. Some local people with money understood which of the would-be farmers presented the best bets, and which of the would-be farmers most faithfully followed community norms of honesty and industry – but lacked any expertise in formal legal procedures. Some non-local institutions with money had that legal expertise – but lacked local information or ties to local social and economic networks.

Take a talented young man in a rural village. He is smart. He is willing to work hard. But he does not have money to buy a farm. He could move to the city and find a good job, but he likes the comfort of his home village and enjoys farm work. Many of his friends have moved to the city, so he does know what he would earn there.

The local sake brewer has funds to invest. In the 1930s, he has yet to face the brutal competition from beer factories or massive Nada-Fushimi breweries (Chapter 2). Having lived his life in the village, he knows the local families and most of the young men. He knows local geography and the productivity of the local farms. Like most people in the village, he attended school for six years. He can read and calculate. As a member of the local community, he is part of the network of social and economic ties by which members enforce their collective norms on each other.

The local banker is talented too. He runs the village branch of a major national bank. He grew up in a city 100 km away, however, and attended university in Tokyo. Like many young bankers, he studied in the law faculty. This assignment is his third posting. He expects (and hopes) that his supervisors will transfer him to a branch in a major city within three or four years.

He knows nothing about the character of local farmers and has no ties by which to invoke informal social and communal sanctions.

In other words, would-be farmers in pre-war Japan faced two potential sources of funds: local elites and banks. Of these, the local elites had the better information. They had the easier access to informal social sanctions against non-performance. They knew the potential borrowers, the land, the weather, and the agricultural technology.

In 1947–48, however, the American-dominated military occupation effectively banned this local source of credit through a draconian "land reform" program. In 1941, Japanese farmers had cultivated 5.81 million hectares (1 hectare = 10,000 square meters, or 2.47 acres).[1] Of that amount, they had owned 3.13 million hectares (54 percent) and rented 2.68 million (Teruoka, 2003, 133; Nochi, 1957, 647). They had farmed 3.17 million hectares of irrigated rice paddies. Of that, they had owned 1.48 million hectares (47 percent) and rented 1.69 million (Nochi 1957, 647).

Through the land reform, the American-dominated occupation (governing through the Japanese government) effectively expropriated 1.76 million hectares (66 percent) of the rented land from its owners and gave it to its renters. Of the rented paddies, it expropriated 996 thousand hectares (59 percent). Nominally, the Japanese government paid for the land and resold it to the renters. In truth, it paid so little that it effectively "took" the land. It charged so little that it effectively gave it away.

Lest the lessors and lessees restructure the earlier equilibrium, the occupation simultaneously crippled the market for agricultural real estate. Through a brutal set of legal restrictions, it effectively banned the rental of farm land. It also effectively banned the use of farm land as security for a loan.

Post-land-reform, farmers owned almost all the land, but lost their access to the local capital market. Post-reform, they were richer than they had been, but no longer had access to investors who knew the local community and could tap the social capital network for informal enforcement mechanisms.

Cited regularly as an example of the way redistribution can increase the rate of productivity growth, the Japanese land reform program did nothing of the sort. It did not accelerate the pace of growth. Instead, it slowed the rate of productivity growth.

In the chapter that follows, I describe the way in which farmers and investors used leasing as a mutually advantageous, cost-effective credit mechanism in pre-war Japan. I do this by exploring the effect of the land

---

[1] The traditional Japanese measure for area is one "cho," which in turn is 10 "tan." Because 1 cho is 0.9917 hectare, I treat cho and hectare interchangeably.

reform program that effectively banned it. Using prefecture level data on productivity, I find that the land reform program effectively slashed the pace of productivity growth.

After stating the contracting program (Section I), I summarize the literature on land reform (Section II). I survey the agricultural industry in Japan (Section III) and the land reform program (Section IV). I then study the effect of the program on agricultural productivity (Sections V–VII).

I The Contracting Problem

Many young men knew how to farm, wanted to farm, but lacked the money to buy a farm. To obtain those funds, they could turn to two broad categories of investors: local elites and banks. Local elites (think sake brewers) knew the local would-be farmers. They had lived in the same community. They had attended village schools. They were part of the network of social and economic ties (call it social capital) by which members of the local community enforced their norms on each other.

What the local elites lacked was expertise in the formal legal mechanisms by which to mitigate default risk. Our hypothetical local sake brewer could lend our young would-be farmer money directly as a loan, but then would need to create a security interest in the land that the farmer bought with it. Literate and numerate as he assuredly was, he lacked the university education necessary to manipulate the legal procedures involved in creating security interests.

Banks had the university-trained officers who could create the security interests, but they were not local. As outsiders, they lacked the informational edge in the local credit market that the village elites enjoyed, and access to the network of social connections by which to police norms of honesty. Our hypothetical banker knew how to create security interests, but had no idea which young man was most talented or which land would prove most productive, and had no ties to the others in the community who might help convince a farmer to pay his bills on time.

Leases gave local investors a simple but effective way to protect their funds. Rather than lend would-be farmers the money directly, they bought (or developed) farms with the funds, and leased the land to the would-be farmer. If a farmer defaulted on the rent, they evicted him and moved on. The process was easy to understand and relatively simple to enforce. Through it, the funds moved to those farmers who presented the best projects, and farmers and investors jointly economized on the transaction costs inherent in legal mechanisms anywhere.

Because leases constituted a form of credit extension (and put the investor at risk), investors more readily leased farmland in areas with high levels of social capital than low. Where that level was high, people more readily followed community norms about appropriate behavior: they stayed married, they bore their children within marriage, and they paid their bills. Leasing (tenancy) was not a reflection of poverty. Instead, it was a reflection of a tightly bound, coherent community, where members generally lived by widely held social norms.

Over the course of 1947–48, the American-controlled occupation would effectively (not formally, to be sure) ban farm leases. Working through the Japanese government, it took from lessors and gave to lessees, but – in the process – effectively ensured that local elites would no longer fund local agricultural projects.

After 1947–48, farmers had more land. But for additional funds, they no longer had access to investors with local knowledge. They no longer had access to investors who could enforce agreements through the informal sanctions that the local social capital made possible. Given that the occupation government also (almost) banned the use of farm land as security, they had only limited access to banks besides.

II The Fable

A Development Economics

1. Land tenure – Scholars in the development economics tradition focus primarily on the under-developed third world. There, they purport to find that productivity falls with farm size (e.g., Binswanger, Deininger & Feder 1995, 2693–94). This apparent negative correlation raises several obvious questions.

Most obviously, why? Why should agriculture show diseconomies of scale? Within this tradition, scholars often imply that farmers invest greater effort and care in farms they own. Sometimes, they attribute this differential in effort to "imperfections in labor, credit, and land markets" (Binswanger, et al. 1995, 2700). But perhaps instead farmers select different types of land for small farms than they do for large? For the most part, scholars claim that they adequately control for land quality in their productivity regressions, though they do identify problems in the empirical estimates (id., at 2702–04).

And why would the owners of the large farms not divide them into smaller units and sell them to landless farmers (Ghatak & Roy, 2007, 254)? By hypothesis, the new owners could farm the land more productively than the old.

Necessarily, the two groups of farmers should be able to negotiate a mutually beneficial transfer. As with the question of farmer effort, the reply seems to turn on non-clearing markets. The credit market does not clear, scholars claim, and landless peasants consequently cannot raise the funds they need to buy the land.

2. Land reform – Within this tradition, the need for coercive land reform follows straightforwardly. Posit that (A) land currently farmed in large-scale units would be more productive if distributed among landless peasants in smaller units, but (B) problems in the credit (and other) markets prevent those peasants from buying the land. If the government forcibly divided the larger farms and distributed the land among the landless, it would not just produce a more egalitarian world but it would also create a more productive one. As Binswanger, et al. (1995, 2644–45) put it:

Because land ownership distribution has often been determined by power relationships and distortions, and because land sales markets do not distribute land to the poor …, land reform has often been necessary to get land into the hands of efficient small family farmers ….

And scholars in this tradition assert that land reform programs have indeed raised productivity (id., 2685):

Since the end of World War II, landlord estates in Bolivia, large areas of China, Eastern India, Ethiopia, Iran, Japan, Korea, and Taiwan have been transferred to tenants in the course of successful land reforms. Theoretically, the productivity gains associated with such reforms come about because of improved work and investment incentives associated with increased security of tenure.… Empirical evidence shows that the reform of landlord estates led to considerable investment, adoption of new technology and increases in productivity ….

"Theory and empirical evidence," write World Bank officers (1993, 160), "suggest that widespread ownership of land not only improves equity but also improves land productivity." United Nations studies make much the same claim (Ghai, et al., 1979, 9; see United Nations, 1976): "radical land reform can, at a stroke, remove the deadweight of landlordism and install a system of egalitarian peasant farming which ensures growth without mass destitution." As an example, they cite Japan (Berry & Cline, 1979): "land reform in the early 1950s proved extremely successful in Japan, Taiwan, and Korea."

B Scholars of Japan

Scholars of Japan have often supported these claims about productivity. Farmers who own rather than rent have stronger incentives to boost production, they explain.[2] For instance, economic historian Ryoichi Miwa (2012, 164–65) reasons that:

Because land reform dissolved the landlord system, farmers were able to keep all of the income from the land that they now owned. This increased their incentive to work and improve their lands. By giving them the resources to invest in agriculture, it also raised their ability radically to increase agricultural productivity.

Similarly, prominent University of Tokyo scholar, Takafusa Nakamura (1995, 29–30), writes:

[T]his stringent reform had the effect of rapidly increasing the productive capacity of rice-growing land in such areas as Hokkaido, Tohoku, Hokuriku, and Tozan – generally the northeast half of Japan – where large landlords had been especially powerful …. After the transfer of property rights, land improvements were carried out on a large scale and combined with the introduction of new rice-growing technology to raise the level of agricultural productivity.

In the most careful study of the Japanese program in English, however, sociologist Ronald Dore reported a curious puzzle. The reforms *must* have raised productivity, Dore reasoned. By the late 1950s, Japanese farms had grown more productive, and "land reform must be given considerable credit" (Dore, 1959, 216). After all, he mused, the program let renters avoid landlords who might have fought change. It gave renters "greater incentive to carry out improvements on, and to maintain the fertility of, the land" (id., 216). It offered them the "psychological" benefit of believing that "their future [was] in their hands" (id., 217). And it supplied them with the capital they would need for any improvements.

Given all this, in Dore's mind, the reform *had* to have increased productivity. Yet the data left him puzzled. The evidence simply was not there. Dore worried that it showed no sign that the reform had raised productivity, and scrupulously reported the puzzle to his readers. Productivity must have increased, he wrote, but the evidence did not show it (id., 217).

C Tenancy as a Credit Market

1. Fixed-rent contracts and sharecropping – Outside of the development economics tradition, scholars have explored the effect that the *type* of rental contract might have on agriculture. Coase (1960) of course showed that, absent transaction costs, the initial allocation of property rights would

---

[2] The claims that land reform increased the farmer's incentive to raise production are extremely common: e.g., Shimizu (2007, 345); Takagi (2008, 42); Moehwald (2004, 264); Kosai (1986, 22); Teruoka (2003, 138); Minami (1986, 70); and Isobe (1979, 4).

not affect the way people used resources. Adam Smith (1992 [1776], 376), however, had claimed that sharecropping caused inefficient farming by slashing a farmer's incentives. In a world with positive monitoring and enforcement costs, it might indeed have that effect. Steven N.S. Cheung (1969) concluded that farmers nevertheless chose sharecropping contracts because they let the farmers share the risk of harvest variability with their owners.

Yet the argument that risk-sharing might explain sharecropping contracts presented an empirical problem: the evidence is not there. In a careful study of 3,000 contracts among American farmers and micro-level information on another 1,000 farms and 2,500 pieces of land, Allen & Lueck (2002) found no evidence that farmers use sharecropping contracts to spread risk. Rather than risk-aversion, the choice between sharecropping and fixed-rent contracts turned on "measurement costs" and other facets of transaction costs more generally.[3]

2. Leasing and credit – (a) Functional equivalence To focus on when farmers choose one land-rental contract over another ignores the preliminary question: whether to rent at all (Allen & Lueck, 2002, 139). Sometimes, the choice between leasing and buying (with borrowed money) turns instead on transaction costs specific to credit markets. Leases and loans both represent ways for investors to extend credit. As such, a lease is not an alternative to the credit market, and neither is it a contract that investors and farmers adopt only when forced to adopt because of imperfections in the credit market. Instead, investors can extend credit to farmers through either a loan or a lease, and they choose the latter when it more efficiently economizes on the transaction costs inherent in any credit market: on the cost of information about borrower quality and on the cost of creating and protecting the investor's interest in the funds conveyed.[4]

In developing economies like pre-war Japan, banks and local elites (think successful farmers, sake brewers, or factory owners) tend to extend credit through different means. Banks lend money directly; they protect their interest in the funds through court-enforceable security interests. Local elites lend money indirectly by buying land in their own name and leasing it to a farmer; they protect their interest in the land by retaining a right to evict.

---

[3] Others who have explored the risk-sharing hypothesis include Ackerberg & Botticini (2000, 2002) and Eswaran & Kotwal (1985).

[4] For modern US farmers, the choice between leasing and buying often turns on tax considerations. See Ford & Musser (1994). The lease–loan equivalence was central to "safe-harbor leasing" under Reagan-era tax reforms. See Chiorazzi (1985).

The logic is simple. Take two parties, investor I and farmer F. I has capital; and F runs a business. F has a profitable use for an asset in his business; and I either owns the asset or can readily buy it. I expects to earn a return on his money (or on the asset he buys with the money); and F is willing to pay for the use of the money (or asset). I and F could structure a mutually beneficial arrangement in two formally different ways: (i) I could buy the asset (if he does not already own it) and lease it to F or (ii) I could lend F the money and let him buy the asset himself. Add the appropriate contractual detail, and the two arrangements generate functionally identical results.

For example, if I rents (leases) F an asset (like land), F will obtain the right to use it, and for that use will make regular rental payments to I. If I lends money to F, F will buy the asset, and for the use of the money will make regular interest payments to I. In either case, I will earn a market return on his money and F will obtain the use of the asset. In the first case, F becomes a "tenant," and in the second he becomes an "owner." In either case, however, F obtains the right to use the asset, and I earns a return that reflects the time value of money and the risk of F's nonperformance.

(b) Protection. In agricultural markets, leases present two transaction-cost advantages over bank loans. First, investors (particularly investors with less formal education) can more easily protect themselves through a lease. If I and F use a lease to convey the funds, they will negotiate the amount of the rent, and perhaps a few other terms like the maintenance of irrigation facilities. If F defaults, I will throw him off the land and rent to someone else.[5]

If I and F use a loan, I will need to take and record a security interest in the land F buys with the money. Pre-war Japan did offer this option; in some less-developed countries, investors cannot obtain readily enforceable security interests even if they wish. Although a university-educated bank officer in pre-war Japan would not have found the process hard, few local elites had a university education. Most had attended only elementary school. They were literate and numerate, but would have found the

---

[5] The power to evict depended in part on whether the investor and farmer negotiated their agreement as a contractual right (*saiken*) or a property right (*bukken*). If a property right, the renter could claim a minimum 20-year term (Minpo, Sec. 278), could assert his interest against a later buyer of the farm, and could sell his leasehold (Sec. 272). The landlord could evict him only if he failed to pay rent for two years (Sec. 276). If the lease was a contractual right, the tenant had less power, but 1924 legislation did give him some leverage. See Adachi (1959, 81–82); Tanabe (1974, 603–21). In some areas of the country, an owner could not evict a renter without paying a substantial eviction fee (Norin sho, 1928). Given this security, tenants could (and did) sell their leasehold.

procedures for taking and recording security interests hard to master. For them, a lease provided the same security at lower cost.

(c) Information. Second, these less-well educated local elites had (i) better information about the potential borrowers than bank officers and (ii) better access to the informal network (social capital) by which community members enforced their social norms on each other. After all, they were local, and many of them farmed themselves. They knew the potential farmers, the local paddies, the local variations in micro-climates, and the relevant farming technology. They were part of the network of overlapping social and economic ties by which local residents enforced their normative expectations on each other.

By contrast, banks recruited most of their officers from outside a community. They understood the value of local information, but they needed university-educated officers. Few students from farming villages in pre-war Japan attended universities, and if they did attend they did not return to their village upon graduation. To recruit trained officers who could document, record, and enforce a security interest in a loan, a bank had little choice but to hire from outside a farming village.

In short, in developing economies like pre-war Japan, agricultural leases potentially dominate bank loans. Local elites have better information about the borrower pool than banks. They are tied to the local social and economic networks by which residents enforce their norms on each other. And they could as effectively protect their investment through a lease as through a security interest.

In communities like these, leases need not represent "second-best" alternatives to bank loans. Neither need leases reflect any problem in the credit market. Instead, the lease is itself a credit extension: investors and farmers choose leases rather than loans when leases – in their world – better economize on standard credit-market transaction costs.

III Japanese Agriculture at Mid-Century

A Wet Rice Farming

Rice lies at the core of the Japanese diet. People eat less rice now than they did in mid-century, but they still eat much. In 1965, the typical Japanese obtained over 40 percent of his calories from rice; by 2006, he still took over 20 (Takagi, 2008, 31). In 1957, he ate 88 kg of rice a year; by 2000, he still ate 59 kg (Sato, 2002). To this rice, he traditionally added wheat, barley, soybeans, eggs, vegetables, and fish. In 2010, Japanese farmers grew

571 thousand tons of wheat, 148 thousand tons of barley, 223 thousand tons of soybeans, and 13.4 million tons of vegetables. They grew 8.48 million tons of rice (Norin sho, 2012, 196).

Farmers raise this rice in meticulously irrigated paddies. Each field represents a major capital investment. For most crops, farmers anywhere will need to plow, fertilize, weed, and harvest their field. To grow rice in Japan, they will need to build a clay base, level it, add topsoil, encircle the field with waterproof dikes, and connect it to the vast network of communal irrigation sluices that traverse the village fields (Ramseyer, 1989). They will plant their seeds in one flooded field, transplant the seedlings to a bigger flooded paddy, and then drain the field as the plants mature. Their capital investment is massive and front-loaded: on the rocky, dry, hillside, they must create the paddy. But it is also on-going: against the perpetual depredations of the weather, they must maintain the soil, the dikes, and the irrigation canals.

B Land Tenure in Pre-War Japan

1. Owned and leased – Japanese farms have long been small. Pre-land reform, those who owned farmland owned a mean 1.16 hectare (1935 figures; Nochi, 1957, 598). In 1940, of the 5.00 million owners, only 2,941 owned 50 hectares (123 acres, US) or more. Of that number, 1,199 owned the land in the far northern island of Hokkaido. Nearly half (47.6 percent) owned less than half a hectare, and only 7.5 percent owned more than 3 hectares (Nochi, 1951, 599). Small-scale farming in Japan did not begin with land reform. Farms were small before.[6]

In 1941, farmers owned 54 percent (3.13 million hectares) of their 5.81 million hectares of farmland. They owned 47 percent (1.48 million hectares) of their 3.17 million hectares of irrigated paddies. Everything else they rented.

Of their rented land, farmers obtained 26 percent (695 thousand hectares) from "absentee" owners – men and women who lived outside the area. The rest of their rented land they obtained from local owners (Nochi, 1957, 647, 624). In significant part, absentee landownership was a creature of the

---

[6] The OECD (2009, 31) states that land reform shifted "the landholding structure away from large landlords towards smaller farmer-owned operations. The trade-off in any such reform is between larger, more economically efficient operations and the greater social equality and security that come from creating a new land-holding class." In fact, however, this is incorrect. Farms were not substantially larger before the land reform took effect.

far northern island of Hokkaido and the urban centers. After Hokkaido, the three prefectures with the largest fraction of farmland (not just leased farmland) held by absentee landlords in 1945 were Tokyo (11.7 percent), Osaka (10.6 percent), and Miyagi (9.0 percent; seat of the city of Sendai). Hyogo (7.3 percent; seat of Kobe) and Fukuoka (6.1 percent) followed not far behind (calculated from Norin sho, 1956).

Like modern American farmers (see Allen & Lueck, 2002: 11), pre-war Japanese farmers mixed ownership and rental. Some cultivators farmed both land they owned and land they rented. Some farmed some of the land they owned, but rented some of their land to others. And some simultaneously farmed some of their own land, farmed some land they rented from others, and rented out some of their land. As of 1941, 28 percent (1.52 million households) of the 5.41 million farm households owned no land. Another 28 percent (1.49 million) farmed only the land they owned. The rest farmed their own land and rented fields besides (Nochi, 1957, 646).

2. Rented and sharecropped – Japanese farmers leased most of their rented land under fixed price contracts. Sometimes, these contracts required them to pay the rent in cash and sometimes in kind, but they almost always required a fixed amount. The alternative – sharecropping contracts – was rarely used by Japanese farmers. According to economists Yutaka Arimoto, Tetsuji Okazaki, and Masaki Nakabayashi (2010, 295, 298), they primarily sharecropped only their least productive fields. Everywhere else, they negotiated fixed rent terms.

Generally, Japanese farmers paid about half of the harvest in rent. This should not surprise – agricultural rents average half the expected harvest in a wide range of societies (Basu, 1984, 130). Consider one 1928 study from the Ministry of Agriculture and Forestry (Norin sho, 1928). As a fraction of the 1928 yield, the prefectural average contractual rent ranged from 0.33 to 0.61. The contracts did not specify a rent of half the crop – after all, they did not use share contracts. Instead, they specified a fixed amount that approximated half the crop that year.

Fixed rent contracts did place the risk of harvest failure on the farmer. Modern scholars have suggested a variety of reasons for sharecropping contracts – including screening farmers and land in the presence of asymmetric information, and compensating owners for managerial and entrepreneurial expertise. As noted earlier, however, Cheung (1969) began the inquiry by noting that sharecropping let renters and owners split the risk that the harvest might fail. A fixed wage contract placed all risk on the owner, while a fixed rent contract placed it on the renter. The sharecropping contract let the owner and renter split the risk.

Bearing that risk of crop failure, Japanese farmers reduced it through several means. First, they farmed scattered plots of land (Beardsley, et al., 1959, 124; Smith, 1978, 75). Like their counterparts in pre-enclosure England, they tilled a portfolio of small fields dispersed across the community. Given the wide variation in microclimates over a village from year to year, the scattering let them reduce the risk of a failed harvest (McCloskey, 1991).

Second, farm households pooled their agricultural incomes with non-agricultural earnings from unrelated by-employment (Smethurst, 1986, 21–22). Household members took a wide range of jobs, a mixture that varied from region to region and family to family. In some families, for example, one member (often the wife) might spin silk thread through putting-out arrangements (Miwa & Ramseyer, 2006). In others, a member might run a small store or work as a carpenter.

And in many families, young, unmarried sons and daughters left for several years to work in a city. In the mid-1930s, between 5 and 6 million households farmed (Norin suisan sho, 2003, 12–17), but over a million young men and women (603 thousand men, 407 thousand women) left those homes for a job in another prefecture. Many others left their village, but stayed within their prefecture. Of those who crossed prefectural lines, 347,000 worked in factories, 173,000 worked in homes as hired help, and 131,000 worked in commercial establishments. Among the factory workers, 127,000 went to a textile firm (Okawa, 1979, 52).

Third, farmers usually negotiated a fixed rent contract that was not quite fixed. Instead, they negotiated a contract that required the owner to reduce the rent if the harvest turned unusually bad. Indeed, even when they did not put the term in the contract, courts sometimes enforced a local custom to that effect anyway.[7] Effectively, in Cheung's (1969, 32) words, the owner bundled an insurance contract with the land. He agreed to bear part of the risk that the crop might fail, and in exchange collected a higher rent.[8]

Consider the agricultural ministry's data from 1928. The harvest that year had been good. From 1921 to 1925, the rice harvest in one year had fallen as low as 8.06 thousand tons. Thereafter, it reached 8.15 thousand tons (1926), 9.08 thousand tons (1927), and 8.81 thousand (1928). Nevertheless, the prefecture-wide ratios of mean rent paid to mean contractually specified

[7] [No names given], 4019 Horitsu shimbun 39 (Sup. Ct. Apr. 9, 1936); [No names given], 16 Horitsu gakusetsu hanrei hyoron keiho 112 (Sup. Ct. Oct. 5, 1926).

[8] Arimoto, et al. (2010, 294, 298) describe this as "a unique contractual form," a "unique characteristic of the Japanese fixed-rent contract." In fact, Cheung (1969, 31) describes it as a contract that was common in China.

rent in 1928 ranged from 0.8 to 1.1. Those means themselves averaged 0.92. Even in good years, many farmers apparently negotiated rent reductions.[9]

IV The Land Reform Program

A The Early Occupation

During its first years, the occupation (known as SCAP, for Supreme Commander for the Allied Powers) ran a brutal regime. Although celebrated by western historians as "idealist" (e.g., Dower, 2003a, 2003c), Douglas MacArthur's early team enforced a ruthlessly punitive series of policies. It purged 200,000 government leaders (Takemae, 2002, 269). In the name of reparations, it choreographed a massive plan to ship overseas most of Japan's most sophisticated manufacturing infrastructure. The plants stayed in Japan only because MacArthur himself thought the plan a bad idea and stalled. It decided to liquidate the largest 500 Japanese corporations for the simple sin of being too big. It shuttered two, and stopped only because Washington thought the plan preposterous and intervened (Miwa & Ramseyer, 2005, 27–28). It decided to dissolve the family-owned "zaibatsu" conglomerates on the (largely incorrect) theory that they had promoted the war. Before Washington had time to notice, it had finished the dissolution.

B The Land Reform

1. The terms – Almost immediately, this "idealist" team at SCAP decided to confiscate land from its owners and distribute it to its renters. The Japanese government had enacted a modest "land reform" program in 1946, but SCAP's team declared it too timid. They drafted a more draconian program, presented it to the Japanese government, and the government enacted it in late 1946.[10]

By 1949, SCAP had forced the Japanese government to redistribute about 2 million hectare of farmland, and 1 million hectares of irrigated paddies. As of 1941, farmers had rented 46 percent of their land. After the SCAP-mandated transfers, they rented only 10 percent.[11]

---

[9] Norin sho (1928); Norin suisan sho (2012, 198).

[10] Jisaku no sosetsu tokubetsu sochi ho [Special Measures law Concerning the Establishment of Owner Farmers], Law No. 43 of Oct. 21, 1946 (hereinafter SML); Nochi chosei ho [Agricultural Land Adjustment Act], Law No. 67 of Apr. 2, 1938, as amended by Law No. 64 of Dec. 28, 1945 and Law No. 42 of Oct. 21, 1946 (hereinafter ALAA).

[11] See Teruoka (2003, 133); Takemae (2002, 344); Sasaki (2005, 737).

By the terms of this program:[12]

a. Local owners (residents of the village in which the land was located) of leased land could keep 1 hectare (4 hectares in Hokkaido) to lease out. The rest they sold to the government, which in turn resold it to their lessees.
b. Absentee owners could keep nothing.
c. No farmer could own more than 3 hectares of farmland (12 hectares in the northern prefecture of Hokkaido). All land beyond that amount he sold to the government.
d. Lessors could charge no more than 25 percent of the harvest for paddy fields, and no more than 15 percent for dry fields.
e. The government would base prices on the capitalized value of the rental rates used for tax purposes in 1938. It could pay the owners in 30-year bonds.

2. Implementation – MacArthur's team could not take 2 million hectares from large-scale absentee landlords. Large-scale landlords did not own anything close to 2 million hectares. At a time when the Japanese population numbered 80 million (Sasaki et al., 2005, 737), they took land from 2.4 million owners. They distributed it to 4.3 million renters.[13] They did not just take from the rich, because the rich did not own that much land. They reached far into the middle class, and took from anyone who happened to have invested his savings in farmland.[14]

For "take" the team did. Nominally, the Japanese government bought from landlords and offered tenants the option to buy. It bought and offered, however, at prices the team had deliberately keyed to 1938 values. Given the intervening hyperinflation, this let it acquire the land for trivial amounts. From 1939 to 1949, nominal prices had jumped 150-fold (Flath, 2000, 74). One historian (Takemae, 2002, 344) wrote, "tillers of

---

[12] See SML, supra note 10, at Secs. 3, 6, 43 as supplemented by land reform committee decisions; ALAA, supra note 10, at Sec. 9 8; see Takagi (2008, 214); Hara (2007, 288); Hewes (1950, 29–33).

[13] Nochi (1957, 619, 632); Nochi (1980, 38, 40, 43).

[14] Flath (2000, 75). Studying a village in the early 1950s, sociologist Ronald Dore recalls two families who had left their small farms with tenants when they left for the colonies as government officials. They returned impoverished, and found themselves categorized as "absentee landlords." A young mother of four children could not farm her 2-1/2 acres herself when her husband was drafted, so she rented 2 acres to her neighbors. She was now a "landlord" subject to the confiscatory program. Although the law required all three families to forfeit their land, Dore (1978, 59) writes that the local villagers manipulated the facts to let them keep their fields.

soil acquired property rights for what amounted to the cost of one salted salmon per 0.1 hectare." Explained another, at 760 yen, that 0.1 hectare of paddy land cost a bit less than a pair of rubber boots (842 yen; Sasaki, 2005, 738).

Predictably, the owners of the land fought the "reform." If they sabotaged the actual process, however, little record of it remains. Instead, Dore (1959, 172) describes the transfers as primarily "peaceful and orderly." Plausibly enough, he attributes the order to "the overwhelming power" of occupation military force (1959, 172–173). During 1947–48, writes Dore (1959, 173), observers reported "only 110 incidents between owners and renters involving physical violence."

The SCAP staff feared that the beneficiaries of their program would promptly unwind it. They could take from the owners and give to the cultivators, but worried that the cultivators would sell the land back and pocket the cash. They seem not to have understood quite why investors and cultivators pre-war had negotiated the arrangements that they had. Yet they did apparently sense that those underlying dynamics (whatever they might have been) might drive the two sides back to their earlier equilibrium.

To forestall such a return, SCAP staff mandated a stringent set of rules over transactions in agricultural real estate. By 1952, these rules would become part of the basic Agricultural Act[15] and govern the field for several decades (and influence the arrangements between sake brewers and their suppliers, see Chapter 2). No one could own more than 3 hectares of paddy land under these rules. And no one could buy paddy land without first clearing his purchase with a local agricultural land committee.

3. Litigation – When MacArthur's team decamped in 1952, it left the Japanese government with a legal problem. In 1947, it had told the government to adopt a constitution that protected property rights. The government had duly complied and through Article 29 declared private property "inviolable." It could take that property only by paying "just compensation." Simultaneously, MacArthur's team had told the government to expropriate rental farmland and give it to the cultivators. Straightforwardly, the occupation-imposed land reform program violated the occupation-imposed constitution.

Dispossessed landowners sued, and by 1953 their case reached the Supreme Court. Tetsu Katayama of the Japan Socialist Party had briefly

[15] Nochi ho [Agricultural Land Act], Law No. 229 of 1952; see generally Tanabe (1974, 1036–61).

run the government in 1947–48. As Prime Minister he had named the first 15 justices of the new Supreme Court, and in 1953, ten of his appointees still served on the Court. The intervening conservative Prime Minister Shigeru Yoshida had appointed the rest (Zen saibankan, 2010, 407).

The justices upheld the program. The price that the government pays should "promote the public welfare," the majority explained, and need "not always match the price based on current economic revenue. Certainly, it need not match the price that might arise in a free-market transaction."[16] Four of socialist Katayama's appointees dissented on the ground that the compensation was inadequate. All conservative Yoshida appointees voted to uphold the program.

The land reform program obviously fit the left's agenda, and the left did well among some farm communities in the early elections. Politicians need not be socialist, however, to realize the electoral potential to redistributive politics. Conservative politicians quickly catered to the new owners, and the farm vote soon shifted dramatically to the right. There it would stay for decades to come (Babb, 2005).

V Preliminary Questions

A Immiseration

1. The claim – SCAP described the world on which it imposed its land reform as positively Dickensian. To the Japanese government, it (1945) declared that the country needed "to destroy the economic bondage which [had] enslaved the Japanese farmer for centuries of feudal oppression." Those farmers had lived within "an archaic, oppressive, and entrenched system of tenancy," explained one SCAP official (Hewes, 1950, 11). Desperately, they needed it gone.

Archaic, oppressive – and "exploitative." Much recent scholarship repeats the claims. According to one historian (Fukui, 2011, 56):

The social relations between the landlord and the tenant remained feudal, and the democratization of the villages stalled. The tenancy contract was not a modern contract. Instead, the landlord exploited his tenants as much as he wished. Because he charged such a high fee, his tenants lost their will to work, and production stagnated.

As MIT historian John Dower (1993, 112) put it, the arrangement "often involv[ed] exploitive rents."

---

[16] Hoshina v. Koku, 7 Saihan minshu 1523 (S. Ct. Dec. 23, 1953) (en banc).

Hand-in-glove with claims of exploitation have come dismissals of the landlords as "parasitic."[17] Quite which landlords historians consider "parasitic" is less than clear, but at least the absentee owners seem to have qualified. Nakamura (1983, 57) recounts "parasitic" landlords who ran urban businesses and rented farmland on the side. By the late-nineteenth century, he writes, Japan had become the site of "[c]omprehensive parasitism." Economist Yutaka Kosai (1986, 21) describes non-"entrepreneurial" landlords as "parasitic." And several years earlier, T.A. Bisson of the SCAP staff (1941, 43; see also Bisson, 1944, 152) had dismissed Japanese landlords as "parasites ... intent only on drawing high rents – often as much as 60 percent."

Some landowners also lent money, and by the standard accounts they lent money as exploitatively as they rented land. Historian Mikiso Hane (1982, 23) captures the flavor of this approach. "[M]ost moneylenders charged usurious rates," he reports. They "were merciless in collecting what was due."

Extortionate rents, usurious interest – given the economic pressure they faced, farmers who owned land lost it, and those without land struggled simply to survive. "Farm owners continued to lose their land and the rate of tenancy steadily increased," explains Hane (1982, 27, 23). Landless farmers "in 'underdeveloped' areas, in particular, lived on the razor's edge," both "because of the constant threat of crop failure caused by bad weather," and because landlords were so "rapacious." "Crop failures, illness, a fall in the price of rice coinciding with the expense of a wedding or a funeral where social custom would permit of no stinting – the factors leading to the sale of land recurred," writes sociologist Ronald Dore (1959, 19). "Owner-cultivators became tenants as they lost their land plot by plot."

2. Initial doubts. – But did "owner-cultivators" lose their land "plot by plot"? Some did, of course. Some firms go bankrupt in any competitive industry, and agriculture is famously competitive everywhere. The tenancy rate did rise during the first half of the century. In Table 5.1, I include the numbers Nakamura (1983, 56) cites (and they are indeed the standard numbers): from 1887 to 1932, the tenancy rate climbed steadily.

But did the tenancy rate rise because market competition and "rapacious" lenders caused farmers to lose their land? Next to Nakamura's tenancy figures, I add the amount of land under cultivation (Umemura, 1966, 226–27). Although the tenancy rate rose at the turn of the century, so did the amount of land farmers cultivate. By simple arithmetic, one can back

[17] E.g., Nakamura (1983, 50, 57); Kosai (1986, 22).

Table 5.1 *Tenancy Rates and Total Farm Land*

	Tenancy %	Farm Land	Owner Cultivated Farm Land
1887	39.5	49,007	29,649
1892	40.0	50,051	30,031
1897	41.2	51,396	30,221
1903	43.9	53,026	29,748
1908	45.4	55,029	30,046
1912	45.4	57,110	31,182
1917	46.2	59,243	31,873
1922	46.4	60,185	32,259
1927	46.1	59,798	32,231
1932	47.5	60,789	31,914
1937	46.8	61,694	32,821
1940	45.9	61,548	33,297

Notes: Tenancy percentage gives the percentage of farm land subject to tenancy contracts. The area of farm land is in 100 cho. Amount of owner cultivated farm land is calculated from first two columns.

Sources: Mataji Umemura, et al., Noringyo [Agriculture and Forestries] (Tokyo: Toyo keizai shimpo sha, 1966)(Hitotsubashi Long-term Economic Statistics series, vol. 9); Takafusa Nakamura, Economic Growth in Prewar Japan (New Haven: Yale University Press, 1971) (transl. Robert A. Feldman).

out of these columns the amount of land farmed by the "owner-cultivators" who Dore believes lost their land "plot by plot." The result appears in the third column of Table 5.1.

The message is stark: other than two dips (one at the turn of the century, the second at 1930), the amount of owner-cultivated land rose steadily and dramatically for half a century. Tenancy rates did not rise because the amount of land cultivated by owners fell – because the amount of land cultivated by owners did not fall. Instead, the amount of owner-cultivated land rose.

3. The Smethurst imbroglio – Why then did tenancy rates rise? In the mid-1980s, historian Richard Smethurst (1986) advanced a very different hypothesis. Over the decades surrounding the turn of the century, he noted, wealthy merchants and industrialists invested in large-scale land reclamation projects. As they created new tracts, they leased them to local farmers. Those farmers rented them, reasoned Smethurst, because with extra acreage they could raise (and sell) more crops.

Tenancy increased, in other words, because investors built new paddies and leased them to farmers who used the land to raise their incomes

(Smethurst, 1986, 61–62). As Smethurst (1989, 419) phrased the hypothesis, "the primary cause of the spread of tenancy was land reclamation." The growth in tenancy rates did "not reflect differentiation and the pauperization of small-scale farmers" (1986, 66–67). Instead, it reflected the "improved opportunities for the rural poor." Wealthy investors used their resources to create additional paddies; farmers rented the new land to farm more area and earn more money.

Historians responded brutally. One journal published two separate hostile essays on Smethurst's book. Reviewers laced their critiques with ad hominem attacks. And one writer (in time, he would become president of SUNY New Paltz) added what he obviously thought the ultimate insult (Bowen, 1988, 828): Smethurst's book was positively "Reaganesque."

Smethurst's sin had been to suggest that farmers might have used the market to improve their lives. In the course of his research he had found, as he later put it (Smethurst, 1989, 418):

evidence for steadily rising agricultural productivity and disposable income ...; improving health, nutritional, and educational levels; higher expenditures on food and clothing; and increased use of modern facilities such as medical and dental clinics, trains, bicycles, telegraph and postal systems, electricity, and even entertainment forms such as motion pictures.

Like humans everywhere, Smethurst's farmers chose among alternative strategies to maximize their welfare. They used the markets to sell their harvest to a broad swath of buyers, and to borrow from a broad swath of lenders. They sold as high as they could, and borrowed as low as they could. As Smethurst (1989, 435) summarized it all:

[T]he growth of a market economy brought better and better living standards to Japanese farmers as a whole between 1870 and 1940.... [I]n this process of becoming better off, Japanese tenant and owner-tenant farmers became better educated, more cosmopolitan, more powerful politically, more independent of their landlords, better able to control their own destinies, and more aware of that ability.

4. The shadow urban labor market – Even without Smethurst's pivotal study, the immiseration story should puzzle. Any notion that Japanese farmers as a whole (not farmers here and there, but systematically across whole prefectures) might have let "parasitic" landlords "exploit" them is obviously implausible on its face. Granted, farmers were not rich. Japan in 1940 was not yet the wealthy country it would become by 1970.

But even in 1940, farmers should not have lived lives worse than the lives their peers in the factories lived. After all, a farmer could always move to the city and take that factory job. What he could earn at that factory placed a floor under his long-term agricultural income. In part, this is precisely why the market economy benefited the farmers. If his owner tried to charge a rent that left him with less than he could earn in a factory (adjusted for amenities), he could simply quit. He could take the factory job, and earn the higher income.[18]

Information was not an issue. Farmers knew what they could earn in non-farm employment. Many of them diversified their household income by adding other jobs like silk spinning. Many sent their sons and daughters to work several years in the city before they returned to marry. Farmers knew what factories paid.

And neither was quitting agriculture an issue. Farmers abandoned the industry regularly. From 1912 to the late 1940s, the Japanese population grew 60 percent – from 50 million to 80 million (Takagi, 2008, 28). Over the same period, however, the number of farm families grew only 15 percent – from 5.4 million to 6.2 (Norin, 2003, 12–17). Given that farm couples raised large families, a majority of their children must have quit the farm. A farmer knew what he made on his paddies, and knew what he could make at a factory if he left. He knew, because his brothers, sisters, and children did leave.

Given that farmers knew what the industrial sector paid and could abandon the farm at any time, the wage they would earn in industry provided a floor under their agricultural income. To be sure, life on the farm brought with it a variety of amenities that factory life did not. If they stayed on the farm, they paid lower housing costs. They could grow vegetables on marginal lands. They could work flexible hours. But the amenities were not infinitely valuable. If a local industrialist financed a new paddy, he needed to find a farmer willing to cultivate it. To locate that renter, he could not charge a rent that left the renter with less (adjusted for the amenities) than he could earn at a factory. If he tried, the farmers simply would not come.

B Productivity

1. Marginal calculations   The notion that redistributing land could have raised productivity should puzzle just as much. After all, the redistribution did not give farmers stronger incentives. Pre-land-reform, they had leased their land on fixed rent contracts. Post-land-reform, they owned

---

[18] Ironically, this is subject to the caveat that some farmers had paid money for the lease upfront. They had done so because courts took such a "protective" approach toward tenants that leases acquired value as capital assets.

their land outright and captured all of the marginal gains to any productivity improvement they made. Yet they captured no larger a share of those
improvements than they had captured before. When they rented their
land on a fixed rent contract, they captured all the marginal improvements
already.

2. Funds for improvements. – Neither did the land reform program
increase a farmer's access to the capital necessary to make the improvements. Pre-land-reform, suppose a renter found a way to increase productivity in a cost-effective fashion but lacked the funds. He could have
approached a bank – banks were common throughout mid-twentieth
century Japan. If his plans were cost-effective, he could (by definition)
have paid the bank market interest and still earned a positive return
himself.

Or the renter could have approached the owner of his land. After all (as
discussed above), the owner had much better information than the bank. If
the renter could cost-effectively raise productivity, then (again, by definition) he could pay his landlord market interest and still earn a return himself. If he worried that his landlord might expropriate the improvements
by evicting him after he invested the money, he could demand a longer
contractual term. Given that his improvement earned positive returns, he
could profitably have paid his landlord for the longer term.

Suppose that, for whatever reason, a renter refused to make a cost-
effective improvement. The landowner could take the initiative himself. He
could buy the technology. He could invest the capital. He could obtain the
engineering expertise. And he could charge a new rent that earned him a
return on the improvements but still left his renter with at least as much as
he had before.

In fact, landowners did make improvements. In his study of large landowners, historian Hiroki Ikeda (2008) confirms Smethurst's instinct that
they acquired their farms by creating them. Building irrigated paddies
involves a massive capital outlay, and many of the large landlords had
made those outlays. Often, they came to agriculture from other industries.
Some had been sake-brewers who vertically integrated into rice production (Ikeda, 2008, 144–45, 188). Some had been wholesale merchants who
vertically integrated into their supply source (Ikeda, 2008, 160). Some were
simply wealthy families looking to diversify their investments beyond their
securities portfolios (Ikeda, 2008, 56–64).

3. Access to information – For the most part, renters and owners both
would have had the knowledge they needed to incorporate the available productivity-enhancing improvements. Renters obviously knew

the conditions in their local community. Like peasants in pre-enclosure England, they each farmed plots scattered around the entire village. Necessarily, everyone walked past everyone else's fields. Landowners knew the relative ability of potential renters. Renters knew the relative quality of the various farms. And any time anyone introduced a new technology, everyone else would have watched what happened.

The owners knew the community too. Half of the owners (i.e., 45 percent of those who lost land in the reform; Nochi, 1957, 632) lived in the area themselves, and many of the others used local agents who did. They sent their children to the same schools as the renters. They shopped at the same stores. They drank at the same bars. They talked with each other, with the other local landowners, and with the other local renters.

Owners and renters lived and worked within the same (generally closed) network of social and economic ties. Within the villages, they lived in a world where residents could draw on that network of social capital to enforce on each other the social norms by which they expected each other to live. The owners were subject to the social sanctions of the community; the renters were subject as well.

Renters and owners also had access to scientific and engineering expertise. By the 1920s, nearly everyone attended elementary school (see Table 5.2, Panel B). The owners could read, and so could the renters. The owners could handle basic arithmetic, and so could the renters.

Renters and owners had access to modern technology besides. Farmers had their news, and they could act on the news. From virtually any village, they could travel to the city. Over nearly all of the country, bus routes and railroads tied the farms to the urban centers. In 1975, Japanese could travel on 26,900 km of railroad track. In 1940, they could actually travel on more: 27,300 km (Ando, 1979, 12).

4. The expected result – (a) Productivity increases? If most farmers had information about productivity-enhancing improvements, access to the capital necessary to acquire them, and the incentive to put them in place, then most would have operated near their production-possibility frontier. They would have operated there whether they owned their land or rented. If so, then transferring title from landowners to renters would not have raised output. As agricultural technology improved, productivity would have risen. But the productivity would have risen at all farms, whether owned by the cultivator or no.

Take a manufacturing firm. Some firms own the land and factories they use, while others rent their facilities instead. The former are not more productive than the latter. So too modern agriculture. Some successful farmers own the land they cultivate, but other successful farmers choose to rent instead. Land will sell for the capitalized value of its expected rental stream. As a result, agency costs aside (at times non-trivial, to be sure), a successful farmer will not earn more by purchasing his farm than by investing his money elsewhere. Given the risks inherent in agriculture, a successful farmer could rationally choose to cut his exposure by farming rented land and investing his savings in the stock of the local cotton-spinning firm instead.

Recognizing this logic, economist David Flath (2000, 74) writes in his text on the Japanese economy that the land reform program "almost certainly did not" increase productivity. It "may have transferred wealth from landlords to cultivators, but it did not stimulate agricultural production, or eliminate wastes and inefficiencies."

Flath shows exactly the right instinct, but at the time he wrote his book the evidence was not there. The best test at the time had appeared in Toshihiko Kawagoe's article in the Hitotsubashi University economics journal, *Keizai kenkyu*.[19] Kawagoe proposes a simple correlation. He first measures the productivity increase in the 46 Japanese prefectures from 1923 to 1959. He then asks whether that increase correlates with the fraction of rented paddies in each prefecture in 1923. He finds no statistically significant correlation, whether positive or negative.

Kawagoe reasons that his test shows that land reform could not have raised productivity. Plausible as his no-positive-effect claim assuredly is, however, his exercise does not actually show it. After all, the orthodox claim is that tenancy prevented communities from improving productivity. Those areas with high-tenancy rates would have had lower productivity growth pre-reform, and higher growth thereafter. Kawagoe compares 1923 tenancy rates against productivity growth rates over the entire 1923–59 period. By the orthodox account, those communities with high tenancy would have had lower growth rates from 1923 to 1949, and higher rates from 1949 to 1959. Because Kawagoe conflates the two periods, if the orthodox accounts were right his exercise might not show it.

(b) Productivity *decreases* In fact, the land reform program may have hurt agricultural productivity – but if it did Kawagoe's exercise might not have shown this either. Suppose land owners in pre-war Japan disproportionately provided the capital to build paddies, improve fields, and modernize

---

[19] Kawagoe (1995). More tentative studies, suggesting (but not showing) the lack of any boost to productivity include Kawano (1969), Kaneda (1980), Kawagoe (1993), Hayami & Yamada (1991), and Hayami (1988, 45; 1991, 85).

agricultural technology. They focused on raising capital and coordinating reclamation and improvement efforts. Others leased the improved land from them and focused on cultivating it.

By expropriating the landowners' assets and effectively banning future rentals, the land reform program radically disrupted this process. More specifically, it disrupted the market through which the many participants in agriculture had coordinated their efforts to improve productivity. If so, then some high-tenancy prefectures with productivity increases from 1923 to 1949 might also have seen the lowest productivity increases from 1949 to 1959. By combining the two periods, Kawagoe's exercise would miss this possible effect as well.

VI The Empirical Inquiry

A The Exercise

To test whether land reform raised productivity, I break productivity measurements at the point of the reform, and ask whether prefectures with the largest transfers saw the fastest productivity growth after the reform. I take as my main independent variable the fraction of paddy land transferred under the land reform program. As additional independent variables, I add pre-war productivity measures, characteristics of the lease contract, demographic controls, and measures of credit availability.

Given the straightforward nature of this exercise, I do not outline a formal model. Instead, I refer interested readers to Allen & Lueck's (2002: 142) clear model and discussion. In exploring a farmer's decision to buy or lease, Allen & Lueck model his production as a function of his effort, the contractually specified qualities of his land, the unspecified and thus unpriced qualities of his land, and a randomized component reflecting the weather. They treat the marginal product of effort and land quality as positive and diminishing, and each variable as independent of the others.

Crucially, although development economists generally argue that many of the factor markets do not clear, Allen & Lueck (2002: 142, 6) present a model where "competitive rental markets exist for all inputs":

> Competition among farmers for land, and among landowners for rents, and competition between on- and off-farm opportunities generally determine the returns to individual factors of production within narrow bounds.

Like Allen & Lueck (2002), I hypothesize that agricultural factor markets in pre-war Japan did indeed clear. Local elites and banks competed to offer enterprising farmers credit. Agricultural and non-agricultural employers competed for workers. Wholesalers and retailers competed to buy agricultural produce. And a wide variety of firms competed to sell fertilizer and other supplies. If these markets cleared, then the leasing arrangements in place would have represented a competitive equilibrium, and the government would not have raised productivity by redistributing land and limiting contractual choice. In this chapter, I ask whether productivity did indeed rise.

B Did Land Reform Raise Productivity?

1. Introduction – If land reform in occupied Japan raised productivity, then the prefectures where the program transferred the largest fraction of land should have seen the fastest productivity increases. They did not. Instead, the communities where the program redistributed the most land saw the slowest increases in productivity.

2. Data and variables. – I begin by collecting and creating the following data and variables. I include selected summary statistics in Table 5.2 Panel A. Although I would have preferred data partitioned at a more micro-level than prefectures, the data for many of these variables are available only at the prefectural level.

Fraction paddies purchased: Total paddy land bought under the land reform program by July 1950, divided by the total area of paddy land in 1941. Calculated from Nochi (1957).

Productivity, 1940: The amount of rice produced (in *koku*), divided by the area of paddy fields (in *cho*) (1 *koku* = 180 liters; 1 *cho* = .992 hectare). Calculated from Norin sho (tokei hyo; various years).

Productivity, 1950: Calculated analogously.

Productivity, 1955: Calculated analogously.

Productivity, 1960: Calculated analogously.

Productivity growth, 1935–40: (1940 productivity – 1935 productivity)/ 1935 productivity.

Productivity growth, 1950–55: Calculated analogously.

Productivity growth, 1955–60: Calculated analogously.

Absentee paddy ratio: Fraction of paddy land owned by landlords not living either in the town in which their land was located or in an adjacent town in 1945. Calculated from Norin sho (1956; kaiho jisseki).

Absentee household ratio: Number of landlords not living either in the town in which their land was located or in an adjacent town in 1945, divided by the total number of farm households in 1947. Calculated from Nochi (1957).

Table 5.2 *Selected summary statistics (I)*

	Min	Median	Mean	Max.
A. Did Land Reform Raise Productivity?				
Fraction paddies purchased	.232	.315	.318	.485
Productivity, 1940	9.586	20.095	19.478	26.859
Productivity, 1950	16.026	22.237	22.551	31.508
Productivity, 1955	11.290	27.013	26.152	32.117
Productivity, 1960	22.111	28.000	28.619	35.624
Productivity growth, 1935–40	−.354	.052	.077	1.191
Productivity growth, 1950–55	−.500	.212	.181	.712
Productivity growth, 1955–60	−.124	.074	.120	1.740
Absentee paddy ratio	.023	..042	..057	.203
Absentee household ratio	.107	.195	.198	.291
Land-rent ratio	28.3	37.2	41.7	93.3
Rent-paid ratio	.800	.941	.929	1.101
B. Where Did Tenancy Contracts Thrive?				
Tenancy area	.333	.447	.457	.589
Tenant households	.341	.694	.688	.822
Girls height, age 7	103.4	107.5	107.4	109.1
Boys height, age 7	104.7	108.6	108.6	110.1
Emigration rate	.0009	.004	.011	.126
Divorce rate	.047	.074	.079	.303
Illegitimacy rate	.012	.026	.028	.063
Young wife rate	.008	.019	.025	.094
Elem. school attendance	92.6	96.4	96.2	98.1
C. Did Land Reform Promote Civic Engagement?				
Voter turnout, 1947	.573	.668	.669	.773
Voter turnout, 1952	.538	.771	.757	.854
Voter turnout, 1958	.641	.790	.783	.868
Voter TO change, 1947–52	−.158	.143	.133	.271
Voter TO change, 1947–58	.003	.169	.172	.336

Sources: See notes to Tables 5.4, 5.7, 5.8.

Land-rent ratio: Mean sales price of one hectare of paddy in 1939, divided by mean rental price of one hectare in 1939. Calculated from Nochi (1981, v. 13; shiryo shusei).

Rent-paid ratio: The mean rent actually paid for paddy land in 1928, divided by the mean contractually specified rent for paddy land in 1928. Calculated from Norin sho (1928; kosaku jijo).

Population density: Population in 1950/land area in 1950. Calculated from Sorifu (1952).

Fraction population rural: Non-urban population in 1950/total population in 1950. Urban areas are municipalities with population of at least 100,000. Calculated from Sorifu (1952).

Bank branches per capita: (Number of bank branches in prefecture in 1925)/population in 1925. Calculated from Okura sho (1926); Fukumi (1928).

Paddy area growth, 1920–25: (1925 paddy area – 1920 paddy area)/1920 paddy area. Calculated from Norin sho (tokei hyo; various years).

Paddy area growth, 1925–30: Calculated analogously.

Paddy area growth, 1930–35: Calculated analogously.

Paddy area growth, 1935–40: Calculated analogously.

Paddy area growth, 1950–55: Calculated analogously.

Paddy area growth, 1955–60: Calculated analogously.

3. Productivity growth. – (a) Basic results. Consider first the simple statistics in Table 5.3 Panel A. At the half of the prefectures where the land reform program transferred the largest fraction of paddy land during 1947–50, productivity in rice production rose 14.3 percent over 1950–55. At the half where it transferred the least land, it rose 22.0 percent. Productivity climbed 65 percent slower at the prefectures where the government expropriated the most land.

In Table 5.4 Panel A, I regress (OLS, prefecture-level data) productivity growth in rice from 1950 to 1955 against the fraction of paddy field purchased under land reform during 1947–50. Consistently, the effect is negative: those prefectures where SCAP redistributed the largest fraction of paddies showed the slowest productivity growth in the succeeding half-decade.

I include several specifications. In Regression (1) of Table 5.4 Panel A, I use no controls. In Reg. (2), I introduce the prefecture-level productivity of paddy fields in 1940, and in Reg. (3) I use the prefecture-level change in productivity over 1935 to 1940. In the remaining specifications, I add several other independent variables.

The land reform program has a consistently negative effect on productivity growth in all specifications. The effect is statistically significant at the 10 percent level in Reg. (2), at the 5 percent level in five of the other Panel A regressions, and at the 1 percent level in two.

The effect of the program on productivity is also economically substantial. Between 1950 and 1955, the median prefecture showed a productivity gain of .212. Given the magnitude of the coefficient in the first specification,

Table 5.3 *Selected summary statistics (II)*

A.	Productivity growth, 1950–55	
	Above median Frac paddies purch'd	.143
	Below median Frac paddies purch'd	.220
B.	Prefectural income	
	Girls height	
	Above median tenant households	107.64
	Below median tenant households	107.10
	Boys height	
	Above median tenant households	108.64
	Below median tenant households	108.42
	Emigration rate	
	Above median tenant households	.077
	Below median tenant households	.087
C.	Social capital	
	Divorce rate	
	Above median tenant households	.073
	Below median tenant households	.086
	Illegitimacy rate	
	Above median tenant households	.024
	Below median tenant households	.032
	Young wife rate	
	Above median tenant households	.024
	Below median tenant households	.028
	Elementary school attendance	
	Above median tenant households	96.51
	Below median tenant households	95.86

Sources: See notes to Tables 5.4, 5.7, 5.8.

a one standard deviation increase in the fraction of paddy confiscated lowered that productivity gain by .064. On a median gain of .212, this is a 30 percent cut.

(b) Type of tenancy. In Regressions (4) and (5) of Table 5.4 Panel A, I ask whether the type of landlord affected post-reform productivity. Recall that some historians call absentee landlords "parasitic." In Reg. (4), I add the fraction of the *area* of tenanted land owned by absentee landlords; in Reg. (5), I add the ratio of the number of absentee landlords to all farm *households*. Both resulting coefficients are insignificant. The presence of absentee – "parasitic" – landlords did not affect later productivity growth.

In Regressions (6) and (7), I ask whether the relative power of renters and landowners affected post-reform productivity growth. To the extent that courts enforced renter perquisites against a landowner, land would

Table 5.4 *Land reform and productivity growth*

A. Determinants of Productivity Growth (I)
Dependent variable: Productivity growth, 1950–55

	(1)	(2)	(3)	(4)	(5)	(6)	(7)	(8)
Frac paddies purch'd	-1.045**	-1.001*	-1.161**	-1.327**	-1.497**	-1.257**	-1.387***	-1.874***
	(2.15)	(1.96)	(2.35)	(2.48)	(2.34)	(2.53)	(2.74)	(2.79)
Productivity 1940		-.003						
		(0.31)						
Prod'y growth, 35–40			.146	.143	.155	.134	.198	.197
			(1.15)	(1.12)	(1.22)	(1.06)	(1.54)	(1.50)
Absent paddy ratio				.894				.226
				(0.82)				(0.20)
Absent h-h ratio					.729			.820
					(0.83)			(0.92)
Land-rent ratio						.004		.003
						(1.24)		(0.93)
Rent-paid ratio							-.723	-.702
							(1.61)	(1.51)
Adj. R2	.07		.08	.07	.07	.09	.11	.09
N	46	46	46	46	46	46	46	46

B. Determinants of Productivity Growth (II)
Dependent variable: Productivity growth, 1950–55

	(1)	(2)	(3)	(4)	(5)	(6)	(7)	(8)
Frac paddies purch'd	-.563	-.673	-1.023*	-1.081**	-.543	-.474	-.717	-.573
	(0.93)	(1.03)	(1.90)	(2.26)	(0.92)	(0.79)	(1.14)	(0.91)
Prod'y growth, 35–40	.067	.057	.125	.159	.087	.081	.096	.079
	(0.50)	(0.39)	(0.95)	(1.30)	(0.67)	(0.62)	(0.68)	(0.56)
Pop density	-.115	-.266			-.105	-.156	-.170	-.294
	(1.62)	(0.82)			(1.52)	(1.55)	(0.54)	(0.91)
Frac pop rural			.119			-.169		-.405
			(0.68)			(0.69)		(1.47)
Bank branch, PC				1.434**	1.353*	1.338*	1.444*	1.456**
				(2.08)	(1.98)	(1.95)	(2.02)	(2.07)
Adj R2	.12	-.01	.07	.15	.17	.16	.07	.10
n	46	40	46	46	46	46	40	40
Prefectures	All	Non-urban	All	All	All	All	Non-urban	Non-urban

Notes: All regressions are OLS. The table gives the coefficient, followed by the absolute value of the t-statistic in parenthesis. ***,**,*: statistically significant at the 1 percent, 5 percent, and 10 percent levels. n = 46.

Sources: Norin sho, ed., Norin sho tokei hyo [Ministry of Agriculture Statistical Tables] (Tokyo: Norin sho, various years); Norin sho, ed., Nochito kaiho jisseki chosa [Survey of Performance of Agricultural Land Liberation] (Tokyo: Norin sho, 1956); Nochi kaikaku kiroku iinkai, ed., Nochi kaikaku tenmatsu gaiyo [Summary Account of Land Reform] (Tokyo: Nosei chosa kai, 1957); Nochi kaikaku shiryo hensan iinkai, ed., Nochi kaikakushiryo shusei [Compilation of Material on Agricultural Land Reform], vol. 13 (Tokyo: Nosei chosa kai, 1981); Norin sho, ed., Kosaku jijo chosa [Survey of Tenancy Circumstances] (Tokyo: Norin sho, 1928).

sell for a smaller multiple of the rental stream. In Reg. (6), I introduce the ratio of sales price to rental price. To the extent that courts refused to enforce contractual terms against tenants, landowners would collect a smaller fraction of the contractually specified rent. In Reg. (7), I introduce the ratio of the rent actually paid to the contractually specified rent. Both calculated coefficients are insignificant. To the extent that these variables capture tenant power, that power did not affect productivity growth in the early 1950s.[20]

(c) Urbanization. Much changed in Japan during the late 1940s. Between 1 and 2 million Japanese young men died in battle. They would never return. US bombers destroyed half the housing stock in Tokyo, and a quarter of all housing in the country (McClain, 2002, 506–07). Many Japanese died in the bombing; some rebuilt on the ruins; and some moved far away. Seven million Japanese streamed home from Manchuria, Taiwan, and Korea (Gordon, 2003, 229). Some returned to their ancestral villages; others settled in the cities.

Conceivably, the fraction of land redistributed under the land reform program could have coincided with the impact of some of these demographic shifts. Many of the changes did correlate with the degree of urbanization. In several respects, so did some farming practices and some of the impact of the land reform program itself.

First, the land reform program redistributed all absentee-owned land, and absentee owners tended to hold land near urban centers. Absentee rates were 7.6 percent at the six prefectures with the largest cities (Tokyo, Osaka, Nagoya, Yokohama, Fukuoka, Kobe), but only 5.4 percent elsewhere. The difference is significant at the 10 percent level.

Second, in part because the government confiscated all land held by absentee owners, it confiscated more land near these urban centers. At the six municipal prefectures, it confiscated 36.5 percent of the paddies. Elsewhere, it confiscated 31.1 percent. The difference is significant at the 5 percent level.

Third, cultivators obtained higher productivity levels from urban farms than from farms elsewhere. Although most of Japan is mountainous, the cities are located on the coastal plains. Necessarily, cultivators found economies of scale easier to exploit on those plains, and the productivity figures

---

[20] Given that investment decisions are endogenous to expected court outcomes, arguably these variables will *not* reflect tenure power at all. To the extent that courts are pro-tenant, for example, investors will rent out fewer fields. Among the fields that they do rent out, however, we have no reason to expect either a higher or lower price/rent ratio or actual/contractual rent ratio.

reflect that difference. At the close of the land reform (1950), paddies at the six urban prefectures produced 25.7 koku/cho (see Section V.B.2. for units), while those elsewhere produced 19.3. The difference is significant at the 5 percent level.

Last, an owner faced higher-valued alternative uses for his farmland near the urban centers. Given the post-reform controls on land use, he could not necessarily take his farm out of agricultural production. He first would need to maneuver through the local agricultural land committee (see Section III.B.2.). He had stronger incentives to try in suburban Tokyo, however, than in the mountains of Nagano.

Whatever the reason, cultivators increased rice productivity more slowly at the urban prefectures. At the 40 non-urban prefectures, they raised productivity (yield/area) 20.7 percent over 1950–55. At the six urban prefectures, they hardly raised it at all: an increase of 1.0 percent.

The first three specifications of Table 5.4 Panel B track this informal discussion. The discussion suggests that productivity at the most urban prefectures grew more slowly in the early 1950s than elsewhere. According to Reg. (1), productivity did indeed grow most slowly at the prefectures with the highest population density, though the effect is not statistically significant. Simultaneously, the variable reduces the magnitude of the land reform coefficient – though it does remain negative.

The apparent association between population density and slower productivity growth is not an artifact of the largest metropolitan centers. In Reg. (2), I drop the six most urban prefectures, and run the regression on the remaining 40. Population density remains negatively associated with productivity growth, even if only insignificantly so. The coefficient on the land reform program remains roughly unchanged.

In Reg. (3), I introduce a variable capturing the fraction of the population living outside urban areas (defined as cities with at least 100,000 population). The coefficient is positive – suggesting again that productivity grew most slowly in the urban areas. Importantly, the negative coefficient on the fraction of land purchased through the land reform program remains negative and statistically significant.

Crucially, the land reform program never *raises* the pace of productivity growth. By some specifications, it has a significantly negative effect on growth; by others, it has a negative but statistically insignificant effect. The conventional account, however, is that it caused growth rates to rise. For that, the data offer no support at all.

4. *1955–60.* – The land reform program did not retard productivity growth indefinitely. Instead, it slowed it (see Table 5.4 Pan. A) only during

the initial reform years. More specifically, it slowed productivity growth at the prefectures most subject to its terms during the first half of the 1950s. In Table 5.4 Panel A, the coefficient on the fraction of land confiscated is consistently negative for 1950–55. In Table 5.5 Panel A, I regress productivity growth over 1955–60 on the land reform variable. The resulting coefficient is now insignificantly different from 0 (Regs. (1)–(2)).

Crucially again, however, the land reform program never spurs productivity growth. The claim that it does lies at the heart of the conventional wisdom: land reform raises the pace of economic growth. In fact, by several specifications, it lowers it over the first half of the 1950s. Although that drag disappears by the end of the decade, land reform never actually quickens the pace of the growth. It never boosts productivity. Instead, by the end of the 1950s, the areas most subject to the program merely recover from it – and cause productivity growth across the prefectures to converge.

5. Credit accessibility. – (a) Leases. At least in part, the land reform program appears to have retarded productivity growth by disrupting the credit market. Most obviously, it banned leases – and leases are a form of credit. Recall the terms of the program. It let no cultivator own more than 3 hectares of paddy land. It let absentee owners hold none at all. It let corporate owners hold none at all. It let no one lease out more than 1 hectare. And in a world where the market rental constituted half the yield, it capped the allowable rents at a quarter.

In pre-war Japan, village elites – successful farmers, sake brewers, and factory owners – extended credit to the agricultural sector by leasing land. Banks and local elites both provided credit, in other words, but took different approaches. Banks lent money, but local elites leased land (and occasionally added some loans besides). In effect, land reform stopped the elites from extending their credit as best they knew how.

(b) Loans. Given that leases and loans are substitutes, if farmers need funds but cannot lease, they will try to borrow what they need instead. For that money, in the post-reform years, they could turn to banks. In Regressions (4)–(8) of Table 5.4 Panel B, I regress productivity growth on the accessibility of a bank office (measured *before* the period). The coefficient on bank accessibility is consistently and significantly positive: the more bank branches per capita, the faster the rate of productivity growth. The effect is the same whether I regress productivity on all prefectures or only the 40 non-urban prefectures.

Bank accessibility offsets in part the harm that the land reform program caused. Although the program cut credit, in other words, an accessible bank branch could partially make good the damage. In Regs. (4)–(8), the

Table 5.5 *Land reform and productivity*

A. Determinants of Productivity

Dependent Variable	Prod'y gr 1955–60		Prod'y 1950		Prod'y 1955		Prod'y 1960	
	(1)	(2)	(3)	(4)	(5)	(6)	(7)	(8)
Frac paddies purch'd	.705	.236	23.230***	12.014	.777	10.810	22.860***	23.231**
	(1.00)	(0.26)	(3.23)	(1.48)	(0.09)	(1.07)	(2.83)	(2.40)
Prod growth, 35–40	.043	.077						
	(0.24)	(0.39)						
Productivity, 1940			.309**	.423***	.255	.190	.234	.319*
			(2.33)	(3.12)	(1.64)	(1.13)	(1.57)	(1.98)
Pop density		.113		2.105		-1.848		-.229
		(0.74)		(1.53)		(1.09)		(0.14)
Frac pop rural		.170		1.626		-.190		1.819
		(0.46)		(0.47)		(0.04)		(0.44)
Bank branch, PC		-1.452		-22.687**	11.181		-20.125	
		(1.41)		(2.18)	(0.87)		(1.63)	
Adj R2	-.02	-.002	.30	.39	.02	.03	.21	.22
N	46	46	46	46	46	46	46	46

B. Correlation Coefficients

	Prod'y 1950	Prod'y 1955	Prod'y 1960
Productivity 1950	1.0000		
Productivity 1955	0.1359	1.0000	
	0.3680		
Productivity 1960	0.6448	0.2398	1.0000
	0.0000	0.1085	

Notes: In Panel A, all regressions are OLS. The table gives the coefficient, followed by the absolute value of the t-statistic in parenthesis.***, **, *: statistically significant at the 1 percent, 5 percent, and 10 percent levels. n = 46.

In Panel B, the table gives the correlation coefficient, followed by the p-value on the line below.

Sources: See Table 5.4.

coefficient on the fraction of land confiscated remains negative, but is now smaller than in Panel A. In several specifications, it is statistically insignificant, but in Reg. (4) remains significantly negative.

(c) The problems. For several reasons, however, bank loans could not fully substitute for leases in the post-reform market for agricultural credit. Most obviously, local elites knew the community better than bank officers and could gauge more accurately the quality of local paddies and farmers. After all, they were local, and many farmed themselves. In the years before land reform, many farmers would have approached their landlord for money. Post-reform, they had few places to turn except the local bank.

Second, local elites and farmers lived and worked within the same dense network of social and economic ties. They both lived within a world of (generally) strong social capital. They both could invoke the force of informal sanctions against the other, should either breach community norms.

Third, land reform created a demand shock for which the banks would not have been prepared. To be sure, cultivators were richer post-reform, and would not have borrowed as much as before. They no longer paid rent. But they still would have needed funds for many improvements, and land reform had caused much of the village elite to drop out of the credit market. Having lost their land, they had less to lend, and were (one suspects) less eager to lend anything they still had. The resulting demand shock would have caught many banks off-guard. They would have lacked the staff they needed to handle the increased loan applications. And they would have lacked offsetting assets in their portfolios to diversify a massive increase in agricultural loans.

Fourth, banks could no longer protect themselves with a security interest in a farmer's field. Pre-reform, they could shield themselves against default by taking a security interest in a borrower's land. If the borrower defaulted, they could seize the land and sell it at auction. The process was simple: to an officer in the legal department of a bank in 1930, nothing about creating an enforceable security interest would have seemed hard.

Land reform eliminated a bank's ability to protect itself through a security interest. The law did not formally ban security interests. A bank could still take and record a security interest in land. But to stop tenants from selling their land back to their former landlords, the government had given local agricultural land committees a veto over all farmland transfers. Post-reform, a farmer could buy paddy land only if he applied to the committee and obtained its approval. He could buy land at bank auction only if he obtained committee approval in advance.

Necessarily, if a bank repossessed a paddy from a defaulting borrower, it could sell the farm at auction only to whatever group of farmers chose to obtain that preclearance. This is not a gamble banks have been willing to make. Reported one regional newspaper (Kan, 2011, 45 n.4):

> The reason that local banks have been reluctant to make agricultural loans lies in the law. Because the Agricultural Act [codifying the terms of the land reform program] restricts the transfer of farmland, that land provides little value as security.

A financial firm was more blunt:[21]

> Of all assets in which a lender can take a security interest, real estate is the one bank officers like best.... Among the different kinds of real estate, however, land that is hidden deep in the mountains, land that is part of an urban planning district, and land in agriculture have no value as a security. This is because – even if a bank were to take a security interest in such land – it cannot sell the land when the need arises."

Credit markets do eventually equilibrate, of course. In time (by 1955–60, according to Table 5.5, Pan. A, Regs. (1)–(2)), banks apparently adjusted to the new environment. Perhaps they added the staff they needed. Perhaps they rebalanced their asset portfolios. Crucially, however, the quantity of credit would have equilibrated at a lower level (i.e., lower than had there been no land reform) everywhere. After land reform, village elites no longer leased substantial land anywhere, and banks no longer lent on the basis of an agricultural mortgage anywhere.

6. Productivity levels. – In Regressions (3)–(8) of Table 5.5 Panel A, I use the Table 5.4 variables to predict productivity at a given time rather than productivity growth over a given period. The results confirm much of the analysis above: that land reform hit hardest some of the most productive areas, that those areas hit a steep decline, but that they recovered their relative status by the end of the decade. Regressions (3)–(4) illustrate their initial (1950) relative productivity: land reform redistributed the most land at the communities with the most productive farms. The positive coefficient on population density (almost significant at the 10 percent level) suggests that these communities lay just outside the cities along the coastal plains. Regressions (5)–(6) show the mid-decade decline: the areas hit hardest by the land reform program fell during the first half of the decade. Regressions (7)–(8) then demonstrate their eventual relative recovery: the areas hit hardest by the program recouped their earlier preeminence by 1960. The correlation coefficients in Panel B confirm similarly that the areas with the

---

[21] www.financial-i.co.jp/column/bank/20030410.html.

highest productivity at the time of the land reform (1950) recovered their relative standing by the end of the decade (1960).

C Did Land Reform Increase Paddy Construction?

Consider the possible effect of land reform on new paddy construction. If the conventional wisdom were true, one might expect the program not just to have induced farmers to raise the productivity on existing farms. One might expect it to have induced them to build new paddies as well.

Alternatively, if the land reform program interfered with the credit market (as the analysis above suggests), one might expect new paddy construction to have fallen in the communities hit hardest by land reform. After all, the land reform effectively banned leases. If investors could no longer lease any paddies they built, perhaps they built fewer paddies.

In Table 5.6 Panel A, I regress growth in paddies on the Table 5.4 Panel B variables. The coefficients on the fraction of paddies confiscated under land reform are uniformly insignificant: the land reform program neither increased nor decreased the rate at which people created new paddies.

In truth, by the 1950s Japanese investors were not creating new paddies anywhere. Instead, they were starting to take them out of production. Consider again Table 5.1. From 1887 to 1922, investors increased the amount of paddies by over 20 percent. Thereafter, paddy acreage stayed largely unchanged. According to Table 5.6 Panel B, during 1930–35, 1935–40, and 1950–55, at a majority of prefectures the amount of paddy land actually fell.

As the Japanese economy rebounded from World War II, Japanese pulled land and people out of agriculture. Through new plant varieties, fertilizers, and equipment, farmers steadily increased their yield. They produced more with fewer people and – often – with less land. The negative coefficient on bank accessibility in the Panel A regressions probably reflects the way local entrepreneurs used bank loans to shift resources out of agriculture and into industry.

D Where Did Tenancy Contracts Thrive?

1. Introduction – Most historians describe tenancy as a response to poverty: farmers cultivated leased land either because they lost the land they owned, or because they never owned any land in the first place. If true, the explanation implies that pre-war tenancy levels were the highest in the poorest communities.

Table 5.6 *Land reform and paddy construction*

A. Determinants of Paddy Area Growth

	Paddy Area Growth					
	1950–55	1950–55	1950–55	1955–60	1955–60	1955–60
Dependent variable	(1)	(2)	(3)	(4)	(5)	(6)
Frac paddies purch'd	.051	.108	.102	−.045	.050	.069
	(0.80)	(1.48)	(1.33)	(0.42)	(0.46)	(0.61)
Paddy area gr, 35–40	.211*	−.106	.031	.541**	−.140	.083
	(1.69)	(0.44)	(0.11)	(2.57)	(0.39)	(0.20)
Pop density		−.028	−.051		−.056**	−.120**
		(1.64)	(1.32)		(2.17)	(2.12)
Frac pop rural		−.012	−.020		−.008	.003
		(0.38)	(0.56)		(0.17)	(0.05)
Bank branch, PC		−.031	−.016		−.420***	−.494***
		(0.35)	(0.17)		(3.22)	(3.70)
Adj R2	.02	.02	−.05	.13	.32	.24
N	46	46	40	46	46	40
Prefectures	All	All	Non-Urban	All	All	Non-Urban

B. Paddy Area Growth – Summary Statistics

	Min	Mean	Median	Max
1920–25	−.894	.226	.006	9.824
1925–30	−.590	.171	.009	8.365
1930–35	−.061	.005	.001	.206
1935–40	−.165	−.005	−.001	.045
1950–55	−.065	−.003	−.006	.068
1955–60	−.071	.021	.018	.162

C. Paddy Area Growth – Correlation Coefficients

	1920–25	1925–30	1930–35	1935–40	1950–55	1955–60
1920–25	1.0000					
1925–30	−0.1153	1.0000				
	0.4455					
1930–35	0.0164	−0.0538	1.0000			
	0.9139	0.7195				
1935–40	0.0301	−0.0511	0.4013	1.0000		
	0.2835	0.7330	0.0052			
1950–55	−0.1615	−0.1764	0.1313	0.2210	1.0000	
	0.2835	0.2409	0.3846	0.1399		
1955–60	0.1069	0.1109	0.3690	0.4092	0.1966	1.0000
	0.4796	0.4630	0.0116	0.0047	0.1903	

Notes: In Panel A, all regressions are OLS. The table gives the coefficient, followed by the absolute value of the t-statistic in parenthesis.***,**,*: statistically significant at the 1 percent, 5 percent, and 10 percent levels. n = 46.
In Panel C, the table gives the correlation coefficient, followed by the p-value on the line below.
Sources: See Table 5.4.

If leases instead functioned as a credit extension, then different consequences would follow: lessors would have leased land most readily where
they could most confidently predict that their tenants would pay the
amounts due voluntarily – on time, in full. They would not have just relied
on the courts. After all, courts were slow, courts were expensive, and –
increasingly – courts (and mediation boards) did not necessarily let lessors evict non-paying tenants. When possible, lessors would have relied on
social norms and community ties.

If investors used leases to extend credit, in other words, we should
observe the highest tenancy levels not in the communities with the most
poverty, but in the communities with the highest levels of social capital.
Where social capital is high, people tend to fill the roles expected of them.
Bound by webs of friendship, kinship, trade, and religion, they more often
keep their promises. They do not just keep their promises because a court
would hold them liable if sued. They keep them out of deference to the
friends, families, and trading partners around them.

By contrast, where levels of social capital are low, people are less constrained by these social ties. Less tightly bound, they less strictly conform
to social norms of appropriate behavior. They divorce. They bear children
outside of marriage. They ignore expected roles, as do their children. And –
crucial to the study here – they less often pay their bills when due.

2. Data and variables – To explore suggestive evidence on this question
(the inquiry is necessarily more tentative than in Sections VI. A–C), I offer a
series of correlation coefficients. I first collect and create the following data
and variables. I include selected summary statistics in Table 5.2 Panel C.

(a) Tenant households. Fraction of farming households cultivating at
least some rented land, 1940. I take the data from Norin (1940; tokei hyo).

(b) Community income. Pre-war Japanese statistics do not give reliable measures of the now-standard indices of economic welfare. With
no income tax to collect, the government did not try to measure personal
income. Given the absence of reliable income statistics, I use several prox-
ies instead. First, I examine the heights of young children. The measure
reflects nutritional intake: whether families adequately fed their children.
The poorer a community, the shorter the children. Second, I ask whether
residents left Japan. The government did not reliably count the number of
residents who moved from village to city, but it did count those who left
the country. The poorer a community, the higher the fraction of residents
who left.

Girls height, age 7: Average height of 7-year-old girls, 1933. I take the
data from Monbu (1937).

Boys height, age 7: Average height of 7-year-old boys, from the same source.

Emigration rate: Total number of emigrants, 1899–1941, divided by the population in 1940. I take the data from Kokusai (1991) and Somu (2010).

(c) Social capital. Investors will more readily extend credit where social capital is high than where it is low – because where social capital is high, borrowers more reliably keep their promises. Where people live and work within webs of social obligations and expectations, they work harder to pay their debts. They pay them out of deference to their families, their friends, and their trading partners.

Typically, communities with strong networks of personal ties also enforce other norms. They urge their members to marry deliberately. They urge them to stay married. They urge them to bear their children within marriage. They urge them to send their children to school. Age at marriage, divorce rates, illegitimacy rates, and rates of school attendance thus tend to proxy for the level of social capital that binds a community together.

Divorce rate: Number of divorces in 1940, divided by the number of marriages. I take the data from Naikaku (1940).

Illegitimacy rate: Number of illegitimate births, divided by the total number of births, 1940. I take the data from Naikaku (1940).

Young wife rate: Number of brides under age 18, divided by the total number of brides, 1940. I take the data from Naikaku (1940).

Elementary school attendance: The percentage of children of elementary school age who are attending school, 1925. I take the data from Monbu (1925).

3. Incomes. – Turn first to the summary statistics of Table 5.3 Panel B. Consistently, they suggest that investors and farmers most often leased land in the wealthier farming communities. In 1940, 69 percent of the farming households in the median prefecture cultivated at least some rented land. At the half of the prefectures with more than the median fraction of tenant households, 7-year-old girls were 107.64 cm tall; at the half with less than the median fraction of tenant households, they were 107.10 cm. At the half with above-median tenancy, boys were 108.64 cm tall; at the half with below-median tenancy, they were 108.42 cm. From the half with above-median tenancy, 7.7 percent of the residents emigrated abroad between 1899 and 1940; from the half with below-median tenancy, 8.7 percent of the residents emigrated.

More generally, in Table 5.7 Panel A, I give the correlation coefficients between the fraction of tenant households and the three measures of economic welfare. Consistently, the coefficients are statistically significant at

Table 5.7 *The location of tenancy*

A. Incomes:

	Tenant Households	Girls Height	Boys Height	Emigration Rate
Tenant households	1.0000			
Girls height	0.5019	1.0000		
	0.0003			
Boys height	0.4621	0.6120	1.0000	
	0.0011	0.0000		
Emigration rate	−0.6529	−0.6187	−0.6079	1.0000
	0.0000	0.0000	0.0000	

B. Social Capital:

	Tenant households	Divorce rate	Illegit'y rate	Yg wife rate	Elementary sch attend
Tenant households	1.0000				
Divorce rate	−0.2518	1.0000			
	0.0878				
Illegitimacy rate	−0.5461	0.1474	1.0000		
	0.0001	0.3228			
Young wife rate	−0.2206	0.5921	−0.0234	1.0000	
	0.1363	0.0000	0.8760		
Elementary sch att	0.3058	0.0054	−0.1689	−0.1681	1.0000
	0.0366	0.9712	0.2563	0.2588	

Notes: The table gives the correlation coefficient, followed by the p-value on the line below.
Sources: Nochi kaikaku kiroku iinkai, ed., Nochi kaikaku tenmatsu gaiyo [Summary Account of Land Reform] (Tokyo: Nosei chosa kai, 1957); Norin sho ed., Norin sho tokei hyo [The Ministry of Agriculture & Forestry Statistics] (Tokyo: Norin sho, 1940); Naikaku tokei kyoku, ed., Jinko dotai tokei [Vital Statistics] (Tokyo: Naikaku tokei kyoku, 1940); Kokusai kyoryoku jigyodan,ed., Kaigai iju tokei [Foreign Emigration Statistics] (Tokyo: Kokusai kyoryoku jigyodan, 1991); Somu sho, Kokusei chosa hokoku [Population Survey] (Tokyo: Somu sho, 2010); Monbu sho, ed., Nihon teikoku monbusho nempo [The Japanese Imperial Ministry of Education Annual] (Tokyo: Monbu sho, 1925); Monbu sho, ed., Gakusei seito jido shincho taiju kyoi heikin ruinen hikaku, Meiji 33-Showa 9 nedo [Average Annual Heights, Weights, and Chest Circumference for Students and Children, 1900–1929] (Tokyo: Monbusho, 1937); Naikaku tokei kyoku, ed., Nippon teikoku tokei nenkan, v. 31 (Tokyo: Tokyo tokei kyokai, 1912).

better than the 1 percent level. Where tenancy rates are higher, young girls are taller, young boys are taller, and residents are less likely to move abroad.

4. Social capital – Investors and farmers were also most likely to lease land in communities with high levels of social capital. In those prefectures with above-median levels of tenant households, the divorce rate was 7.3

percent; in the below-median prefectures, it was 8.6 percent. In the prefectures with above-median levels of tenant households, the illegitimacy rate was 2.4 percent; in the below-median prefectures, it was 3.2 percent. In the prefectures with above-median levels of tenant households, 2.4 percent of the brides were below age 18; in the below-median prefectures, it was 2.8 percent. In the prefectures with above-median levels of tenant households, 96.51 percent of elementary-school age children attended school; in the below-median prefectures, 95.86 percent did.

In Table 5.7 Panel B, I report the correlation coefficient between the fraction of farm households renting at least some of their land and these several measures of social capital. The correlation between the tenancy rate and the divorce rate is negative and significant at the 10 percent level. The correlation between tenancy and the illegitimacy rate is negative and significant at the 1 percent level. The correlation between tenancy and the fraction of women marrying before age 18 is negative, but not statistically significant. And the correlation between the tenancy rate and elementary school attendance is positive and significant at the 5 percent level.

E Did Land Reform Promote Civic Engagement?

1. Introduction – Writers routinely claim that the Japanese land reform program promoted civic engagement. The newly independent farmers "prospered and became increasingly inclined to support the principles of democracy and capitalism," writes historian James McClain (2002, 548). In the "stable countryside," explains historian Marius Jansen (2000, 268), conservative politicians found "an almost invulnerable electoral base." Indeed, proclaims political scientist Kazuo Kawai (1960, 174):

When it is seen to what extent the desperation of the landless peasantry of so many Asian countries feed the fires of revolutionary unrest in those countries, the stability and social health which the successful land reform has given to rural Japan stand in significant contrast.

Did the land reform increase levels of political engagement?

2. Data and variables – I define the following additional variables, and include selected summary statistics on Table 5.2.

Voter turnout rate, 1947: The voter turnout rate in the 1947 election. The turnout rate is the number of votes cast, divided by the number of votes eligible to be cast. I calculate turnout rates from data given in Reed (2012).

Voter turnout rate, 1952: Calculated analogously.

Voter turnout rate, 1958: Calculated analogously.

Table 5.8 *Land reform and civic engagement*

Dependent Variable	Voter Turnout		Voter Turnout Change	
	1952	1958	1947–52	1947–58
Frac paddies purchased	−.269**	−.112	−.443**	−.191
	(2.27)	(1.10)	(2.47)	(1.23)
Voter turnout, 1947	.782***	.763***	−.502**	−.597***
	(5.26)	(5.92)	(2.23)	(3.06)
Adj R2:	.43	.45	.15	.15

Notes: The table gives the coefficient, followed by the absolute value of the t-statistic on the line below. All regressions are OLS. n =46.

Sources: Nochi kaikaku kiroku iinkai, ed., Nochi kaikaku tenmatsu gaiyo [Summary Account of Land Reform] (Tokyo: Nosei chosa kai, 1957); Steven R. Reed, Japan SMD Data Set, available at: www.fps.chuo-u.ac.jp/~sreed/DataPage.html.

Voter turnout change, 1947–52: The voter turnout rate in the 1952 election less the rate in the 1947 election, divided by the rate in the 1947 election.

Voter turnout change, 1947–58: Calculated analogously.

3. Discussion – If land reform promoted civic engagement, then voter turnout rates should have increased. More specifically, the difference between the rates before land reform (in 1947) and after (1952, 1958) should be largest where the program transferred the most land. Accordingly, in Table 5.8, I regress (i) the actual turnout rates and (ii) the change in turnout rates, on (iii) the fraction of paddies transferred and 1947 turnout rates.

The post-reform turnout rates do not depend on the fraction of land transferred. In general, turnout rates in 1947 predict turnout rates in the 1950s. The scope of the land reform does not. According to the first two regressions in Table 5.8, the fraction of land transferred is negatively associated with turnout rates in 1952 and 1958 (in one case significantly so). In the last two regressions, it is negatively associated with the change in turnout rates (in one case significantly so). More basically, the point of Table 5.8 is simply that land reform did not increase turnout.

The reason land reform should not have promoted civic engagement is simple: the program hit hardest those communities with the highest tenancy rates, but those communities were ones that already had high levels of social capital. Civic engagement correlates with other indices of social capital, but the land reform program redistributed land not at the communities with low social capital but at the communities with high. Given high levels of social capital at the outset, the program was not likely to increase civic engagement further.

VII Long-Term Changes

The land reform program caused damage that extended far beyond the numbers in these regressions. The regressions ask whether the program raised the growth rate at those prefectures where it redistributed the most land. They show that it did not. The prefectures where it redistributed the most land initially grew slowly, and the pace of growth only converged after several years.

The regressions do not ask what the land reform program did to growth rates more broadly. They capture the effect it had on *relative* growth rates, but not on growth across the country *as a whole*. As noted earlier (see Section III.B.2.), SCAP staff feared that the beneficiaries of its land reform program would unwind it. The staff could take from the owners and give to the cultivators, but worried that the cultivators would promptly sell the land back and pocket the cash. They seem not to have understood quite why investors and cultivators had negotiated the contracts that they had, but sensed that the underlying dynamics (whatever they might have been) could drive the parties to return to the earlier equilibrium.

To prevent the former landlords and former tenants from undoing the program, SCAP staff imposed a series of rules. Recall the terms of the rules, and consider their effect:

(i)   No one could own more than 3 hectares of paddy.[22] By 1950, farmers had not yet mastered the technologies that would let them extend economies of scale in rice production to larger fields, but they soon would. When they did, the 3-hectare rule would hold them to the older, less productive technology.

(ii) No one could lease out more than 1 hectare, and even on that hectare could charge only half the market price.[23] Again, the rule would soon prevent farmers from exploiting the new economies of scale.

(iii) No one could own paddy land unless he lived in the community, and no corporation could own a paddy.[24] The rule prevented farmers from reaping the benefits from a division of labor between investing and operating.

(iv) No one could transfer agricultural real estate without the permission of the local land committee.[25] The rule prevented farmers from using their land as security to borrow the funds they needed from a bank.

---

[22] Nochi ho [Agricultural Land Act], Law No. 229 of 1952, Sec. 3(b); see generally Tanabe (1974, 1036–61).

[23] Act, Sec. 24; see Tanabe (1974, 1050).

[24] Act, Sec. 6(a); see Tanabe (1974, 1042–43).

[25] Act, Sec. 3(a); see Tanabe (1974, 1039).

At the national level, the program almost certainly caused long-term damage. Most obviously, the 3-hectare ownership maximum (and 1-hectare leasing maximum) prevented farmers from exploiting the new economies of scale. Before 1940, few such economies were to be had. The new post-1950 technologies, however, introduced those economies en masse. The ban on absentee and corporate ownership prevented farmers from reaping the benefits from a division of labor between investing and operating.

And the law stopped both the first- and the second-best means of extending agricultural credit. The investors with the best local information had been local elites. By capping rentals at 25 percent of the yield, the law prevented them from using leases to extend credit. In most cases, the next-best alternatives were the banks. By banning land transfers without the permission of the local land committee, the law prevented farmers from using their land as security for bank loans.

Over the succeeding decades, the Japanese national legislature would loosen some of these rules. Ultimately, however, the restrictions that the SCAP staff had designed to prevent a return to pre-1940 tenure locked Japanese farmers into a miniscule scale whose inefficiency grew increasingly painful by the year. Over the course of the next decades, farmers would obtain access to technological improvements that required large outlays and large farms. There were improvements they could efficiently exploit only if they could leverage them over wide areas. Given the rules designed to lock-in the land reform program, there were improvements they could exploit only haphazardly at best.

VIII Conclusions

Land reform need not just reduce rural poverty, claim many development officials and scholars. It can raise productivity. It can promote civic engagement. Land reform will not always do this, they write, but it can – and in occupied Japan it did.

In fact, land reform in Japan did not raise productivity. Instead, it lowered the rate of productivity growth. The areas with the most land transferred under the program did not grow fastest during the succeeding years. Instead, they grew slowest.

Land reform slashed productivity growth by interfering with the allocation of credit. A lease is a capital market contract: both (a) a convenient way for local elites to invest in the agricultural sector and (b) a convenient way for local farmers to obtain the right to use additional farm land. During the pre-war period, wealthy villagers and ambitious farmers had economized on the cost of formal loans by using leasing contracts instead. Given the risk of default, wealthy villagers had been most likely to extend that credit in communities with relatively high levels of social capital.

By precluding the use of these leasing contracts, the land reform program increased the cost of capital to farmers, slashed the amount of credit, and reduced the accuracy with which investors could target the credit. To make matters worse, it simultaneously stopped banks from making good the credit shortfall created by what was effectively a leasing ban. Because SCAP staff feared that tenants might sell back their land to their former landlords, they banned paddy transfers except on the permission of a local agricultural land committee. Effectively, they stopped banks from auctioning foreclosed farmland and prevented farmers from offering their land as security for loans.

6

Contracting for Mercy in Buddhism

Hike anywhere in the Japanese mountains, and you will take narrow paths through dense forests. You will grab tree roots to pull yourself up mud-drenched furrows. You will scale the side of rocks.

No matter which mountain you climb, in shallow clearings by the side of your path you will occasionally find a small statuette. Eyes closed, the young child will have a peaceful expression. Usually, he (or she; the sex is often ambiguous) will wear a serene smile.

He is jizo (Kṣitigarbha, in Sanskrit), guardian of children and travelers. He is a bodhisattva – in Japanese Mahayana Buddhism, a being who has reached enlightenment but who, out of compassion for those still suffering, has declined to enter paradise. He remains instead in the mortal world to comfort and guide the rest of us.

A friend of mine recalled a hike he had taken some 15 years earlier. As his group passed a jizo, an older woman in the group had stopped, pressed her face into her hands, and started to sob. "Please forgive me," she seemed to mutter. After a pause, his group started to walk again. The woman wiped her tears, and privately explained to my friend that the Buddha had once sent her a baby but that the baby had never been born. Beyond that, my friend did not ask.

Chances are the jizo by the path will wear a red bib. An anonymous mother sewed it for him in penance. He will also sport a red cap, knitted by another mother in penance. He may even have offerings of a rice ball and a tangerine or two in front of him.

Pay attention when you return to Tokyo, and you will likely find the same young fellow near your home. He may stand at a small intersection. He may hide in a nook by the side of the road. He will be wearing a red bib and cap and, if lucky, have a rice ball and one or two tangerines.

Sometime during the first decades after World War II, jizo the guardian of children and travelers became the savior of miscarried and aborted souls. As the abortion rate skyrocketed with medical technology and postwar legalization, jizo became the savior of the boys and girls "who were not able to be born" – as temple pamphlets and websites so delicately put it.

Increasingly, temples began to offer memorial services for these children who "were not able to be born." They called the services "water-child memorials" (mizuko kuyo – with "water-child" being the fetus or unborn child) and charged a fee for the ritual. Many women ignored the temples: they had their abortions and moved on. Some, however, found the experience more troubling: they paid the fee for the ritual and turned to the temples for solace.

* * *

In Japan as elsewhere, religious institutions teach, maintain, and help enforce socially prescribed norms of moral behavior. They guide their parishioners through the most troubling times in the lives. They create and nourish the network of social and economic ties that bind a community together (and, importantly for this book, help enforce contracts among its members). Yet institutions are never free. They will themselves need to enter into the contracts that will let them raise the resources they need for their staff to do their work.

In contemporary Japan, Buddhist temples increasingly rely on fee-for-service finance. Increasingly, they raise the funds they need by selling rituals on the market. Of those rituals, the water-child memorials are merely the most notorious. The "eternal memorial" (the eitai kuyo) contracts are probably the more substantial. For centuries, families had interred the ashes of their ancestors in the local temple, and paid its priest regularly to perform memorials in their honor. In effect, some modern temples are trying to offer an "eternal" contract that substitutes a one-time up-front payment for the stream of future fees they otherwise might have collected.

This reliance on fee-for-service financing threatens to jeopardize the role that the temples have played on other dimensions – on the compassion and reassurance that they had provided the members of their community, on the moral norms that they had taught and encouraged among those members, on the network of community ties that they had so assiduously nourished. The problem stems from the fact that the temples sell their rituals in a competitive market. Bid down to marginal cost, they cannot use the fee revenue to cross-subsidize their other harder-to-price activities.

In this chapter, I study the contracting problem in the Japanese market for religious services. I first identify the problem (Section I). After reviewing the literature (Section II), I describe the shift to fee-for-service finance: the water-child memorial (Section III) and the eternal memorial (Section IV). I discuss the resulting contract problem (Section V) and describe attempts by committed priests to circumvent it (Section VI).

I The Contracting Problem

Within the pre-modern Japanese village, residents assigned their temple a central role. They held their family ceremonies and village festivals there. Through those ceremonies and festivals, they affirmed and reaffirmed their collective identity. They turned to the temple priests for moral guidance – and sometimes for more general advice and basic education. They looked to the priests for help as they passed through the existentially difficult times in their lives. And they relied on the priests to affirm collectively the norms and values that expected of each other.

Raised in the village, a good temple priest knew the residents. He knew their families. During Tokugawa Japan, some priests taught the village children basic literacy and numeracy. When villagers faced the profoundly liminal events like the death of a family member, a good priest knew how to counsel them through the crisis. A good priest knew how to teach and remind them of their basic ethical obligations.

Over the course of the last century and a half, Japanese have abandoned the villages in massive numbers. Yet temples are stationary institutions. They cannot readily move and reconstitute themselves. As a result, modern Japanese villages have far too many temples. The cities have far too few.

Village temples traditionally supported themselves through quasi-mandatory contributions from their local parishioner households (known as the danka). Given 150 years of migration, the village temples no longer have the danka households they need to support them. And so it is that enterprising priests have looked to new sources of revenue.

Temples traditionally provided three sets of complementary services, but they can readily price only one of these. First, temples offered support during the most difficult transitions in life: compassion, comfort, guidance, and mercy from (in the best of all worlds) a priest who has known a parishioner and his or her family for years. Second, they combined ethical instruction with the maintenance of networks of social capital through which they supported the moral norms so crucial to the community. Third, they offered the rituals by which community members could internalize that guidance and instruction.

The ritual temples could price and sell. The first two services are harder to price. Unfortunately for the temples, they now compete in a market for ritual against sellers who discount prices to marginal cost. If traditionally they used the ritual revenue to cross-subsidize the other services, they now find that much harder.

II Traditional Temple Finance

A The Village Temple

Throughout the Tokugawa period, most Japanese had lived within relatively stable villages. There, they lived within the dense networks of cross-cutting ties that together create social capital. Many migrated, to be sure. But most Japanese remained within communities with high levels of the repeated interactions through which they could obtain information about each other, and informally enforce on each other their collective sense of appropriate conduct.

The temple anchored the village. It was "woven into the fabric of everyday community life," wrote Steven Covell (2001, 49), and "local gatherings, community festivals, and the like all revolve[d] around the temple." With a bit more nostalgia, one commentator who was raised in a temple (Shimada 2018) explains:

Temples used to hold agricultural villages together.... When you were born, the priest gave you a name. You went to the temple school to learn ethics, and to learn to read and write. You played on the temple grounds. When you became an adult, if you were having trouble getting along with your parents, or if you were struggling because you were broke, you took your problems to the temple [priest].... As you grew old and realized you didn't have much time left, you told the priest what you wanted him to do at your funeral. You told him you were scared of dying, and he counseled you.

B The Registered Parishioners

To fund this central institution, community members collectively enforced on each other an obligation to support. Often, they paid the support by funding memorials, ceremonies, and festivals. Through their general obligation to support, however, the danka households ensured that the temple priest would be there to help them as needed. They needed him (usually him) for his emotional and social support, for his counsel. They needed him to remind them of the moral norms to which they would hold each other.

Collectively, the village needed the temple to coordinate the many cross-cutting ties and obligations among the members. As the locus of the networks of social and economic ties that supported the village social capital, the temple generated substantial positive externalities. By the very logic of collective action, community members would not be able to fund it adequately through voluntary contributions. Instead, they enforced on each other a commitment to contribute.[1]

C The Modern Migration

1. Nationally – Although rural villages a century ago did enforce the obligation to fund the local temple through their networks of social capital, very few Japanese live within those villages anymore. As a result, the village temples simply have too few people to support them (Covell 2005, 32; Nelson 2013, xv). By the closing decades of the nineteenth century, Japanese had begun to move in massive numbers from the towns and villages to urban centers. There, they found what were for them well-paying jobs in the new factories and commercial establishments. Through the early years of the twentieth century, they continued to migrate.

By contrast, the temples have not moved. The rural temples mostly have not yet closed, though many priests hold second jobs and some temples have no priests at all. Hypothetically, entrepreneurial (or missionary) priests might have moved to the cities to open new temples, but very few have. Consistent with this stasis, the number of temples has stayed remarkably constant. In 1880, there were 72,100 temples in Japan. In 1953, there were 74,300, and in 2013 77,300 (Bunka cho 2015, 12, 26).

As people moved, the temples lost their ability to fund their own activities. So long as people remained largely embedded within tightly structured villages, the temples had been able to use the social network to enforce the contributions they needed. As people began to move from the countryside to the city, the village temples retained their structure – but lost people. The cities gained the people – but without a tight social network through which to enforce temple contributions.

At root, Japanese temples face a crisis borne of geographical mismatch: the temples are no longer where the people are. Temples do not readily move.

---

[1] At the core of this support stood the danka – the families registered at the temple. The registration had begun as part of the Tokugawa government's anti-Christian policy. To identify those Christians, the government had ordered everyone to register at their local temple (Covell 2001, 2005; Rowe 2003, 94; 2005, 24; 2011, 22; Nelson 2013, xiv).

Table 6.1 *Population per temple, by municipality*

1.	Nishinomiya	6187.7
2.	Ashiya	5827.4
3.	Kawanishi	4469.2
4.	Itami	3700.5
5.	Akashi	3637.0
37.	Yabu	395.5
38.	Ichikawa	369.1
39.	Kamikawa	361.4
40.	Sasayama	335.4
41.	Asago	324.9

Sources: Total temples, from Hyogo no otera ichiran [List of Hyogo Temples], as of July 2020, from NokotsudoInfo, at www .nokotsudo.info/list/hyogo.html; population from Somu cho tokei kyoku, Kokusei chosa [Vital Statistics] (various years), available from www.e-stat.go.jp

People do. And since the late nineteenth century people have been moving in massive numbers. The villages that were so central to Tokugawa society have an excess of temples. The cities have a dearth.

2. Hyogo – Consider Hyogo prefecture. In 1920, only 28.8 percent of the residents of the prefectural capital of Kobe had been born in the city. Only 35.2 percent of the Himeji city residents had been born there, and only 35.4 percent of Amagasaki city residents. Over the next decade, the national population increased 15.2 percent to 64.5 million. The Hyogo prefectural population increased roughly in tandem: 15.0 percent to 2.6 million. The urban centers, however, grew much faster: Kobe grew 22.2 percent (to 787,616), Himeji grew 20.0 percent (to 62,171), and Amagasaki grew 30.2 percent (to 50,064). In that single decade, the new city of Nishinomiya grew an astonishing 38.5 percent (to 39,360).[2]

Table 6.1 illustrates this geographical mismatch. The table gives the five Hyogo municipalities with the greatest number of people per temple, and the five with the smallest. The five under-served areas are all part of the massive metropolitan area (home to the Nada breweries, Chapter 2) at the south of the prefecture along the Seto Inland Sea. Indeed, Nishinomiya, Kawanishi, and Itami are effectively suburbs to the giant city of Osaka to the east (population 19.2 million). On average, each temple in these areas

---

[2] Naikaku tokei (1920b pref. supp. v. 5); Naikaku (1930 supp.. 5).

serves at least 3,000 people (Kobe itself has a population per temple of 1503.6).

The five over-served areas are all in the mountainous area between the two coasts. People once lived there. A few still do. But far too few live there to maintain the temples that remain. Conventional wisdom has it that a temple needs 200–300 supporting households to survive (Covell 2001, ch. 2; 2005, 23). All five over-served areas have fewer than 400 people per temple. Even if everyone supported his or her local temple, there would be barely 100 households a piece.

D Land Reform

In the traditional village, the temple earned part of its income from its landholdings. Over the course of 1947–1948, the American-dominated military occupation (governing through the Japanese government) effectively expropriated a wide range of farm land and distributed it to the former renters (see Chapter 5).

Temples had leased out much of their farmland, of course. And what they leased, they mostly lost. Through this "land reform" program, the government confiscated 56,400 hectares of land from religious entities (Nakamura 2017, 123). For a typical "midsize temple," calculates Mark Rowe (2011, 27), the loss came to "approximately half of its yearly income." "In one swift move," writes Steven Covell (2005, 30), the government "eliminated a major source of income for temples, [and forced] an even greater reliance on income from ritual services or the development of other revenue streams."

III Modern Temple Finance

A The Voluntarist Non-Solution

Traditionally, Japanese Buddhist temples specialized in death (e.g., Rowe 2011). Death is the quintessential liminal event, of course. As sociologist Peter Berger (1967, 22) put it, it is the event in which "the fundamental order in terms of which the individual can 'make sense' of his life and recognize his own identity will be in process of disintegration."

To guide their community members through this liminal transition, Japanese temples classically provided two sets of complementary services. First, they supplied rituals: funerals and periodic commemorations of the dead. Second, they counseled, consoled, and encouraged those members through the stressful weeks and months. Crucially, the first set of services they could readily price; the second was much harder (Telser 1960, 1979). The second gave the first its religious significance; the first helped the parishioner internalize the second.

Japanese temples cannot rely on voluntary donations. First, unlike (for example) the most conservative Protestant and Jewish groups, Japanese temples are organizations that stand in low levels of tension with the secular world. They do not require their parishioners to reject the world. Instead, they accept the world as it is and help their parishioners live as a part of it. As Rodney Stark (Stark & Finke 2000; Stark & Bainbridge 1987) and Laurence Iannaccone (1992, 1994, 1998) show at length, groups that demand little from their adherents receive little.

The Stark–Iannaccone distinction has obvious financial consequences: A group that requires its members to shun a wide variety of common practices will attract and hold only those who place a value on group membership high enough to offset that cost. A group that requires none of that abstinence will include adherents who appreciate it much less. The group in high levels of tension can rely on its members for the necessary funding. The group in low levels of tension often cannot.

Second, Japanese Buddhism is not congregational. Parishioners do not attend weekly services, because Japanese temples do not offer them. Very few Japanese Buddhist temples conduct any weekly services at all. They hold events keyed instead to commemorative services for specific ancestors.

Japanese do visit their temples and shrines. Despite their putative secularization,[3] in 2009 (the last year the police released the number) 99.4 million people (out of a total population of 128 million) visited a shrine or temple between January 1 and 3 (2018 nen no, 2019). According to Alan S. Miller (1998, 363), a majority also claim to visit them "to offer prayers during difficult times."

But Japanese do not join with fellow parishioners for regular worship. As Iannaccone and Bose (2011, 326) explain, this non-congregational structure crucially shapes a temple's ability to raise funds. Congregational groups

---

[3] Ian Reader stresses that secularization and characterizes it as a post-war phenomenon. Reader (2011, 242) writes that "In 1970, there were 96,000 Buddhist temples in Japan," but only 75,866 by 2007. He further notes that by "2005 35.4% of Soto temples had no successor priest." Reader misreads his statistics. Take the total Buddhist temples operated by both incorporated and unincorporated religious entities. In 1970, there were 75,922 such temples; in 2007 there were 77,286 such temples (Bunka cho 2015, tab. 1-6). The priest shortage that Reader presents as post-war already plagued the temples before the war. In 1910, there were 71,770 temples in Japan (note how close this is to the figure at the end of the century). For these temples, there were 52,721 resident priests (Naikaku tokei 1920a, 435 tab. 406). There were 14,211 Soto temples, and they had 10,228 resident priests.

operate "like economic clubs." They stress "the collective … production of religious rewards," and rely on "mutual support." Non-congregational groups are "less capable of generating commitment" and fund themselves instead through fee-for-service transactions.

The result of this low-tension, non-congregational structure is straight-forward: Japanese do not give to their temples. In 2018, Americans (population 331 million) gave to their 380,000 churches $125 billion – $338 per capita.[4] In 2012, Japanese (population 126 million) gave to their 81,300 Shinto shrines and 77,400 Buddhist temples contributions (this includes the mandatory fees for funerals and memorial services) totaling 229 billion yen and membership fees of 54 billion (Bunka cho 2015, 12, 52–53). The amounts total 283 billion yen ($2.7 billion) – $22 per capita.

B The Complementary Service Problem in Japan

1. Introduction – Let me restate the problem: Japanese temples cannot readily fund the full range of their traditional functions through fee-for-service finance. They provide two broad sets of services: ritual on one hand, and counseling and teaching on the other. Although the first set they can readily price, the second they can price only haphazardly (see generally Telser 1960, 1979). The two function as complements and provide the highest value when supplied together. Yet because the temples cannot necessarily price the latter, they can provide their full range of services only if they receive generalized financial support or earn high enough prices on their priceable services to cross-subsidize the others.

The temples receive too little for the ritual to cross-subsidize comfortably. Although they can sell their ritual, they sell it within a highly competitive market. Some of their rivals are other temples. Other competitors are secular providers of funerary services. The latter do not maintain the fixed costs associated with a temple. Neither do they provide counselors willing to minister to troubled parishioners whenever necessary.

2. Competition in the market for ritual – (a) Funeral companies. Temples face their sharpest competition in death-related ritual from the specialty funeral companies. Until the 1970s, when someone died his or her family members called their local priest. The priest conducted the funeral service itself and coordinated the other suppliers involved in the requisite arrangements (Covell 2001, 236).

---

[4] Goshay (2020); Americans (2019).

No longer do families call the priest; instead, they call a professional funeral company, and that firm coordinates the event. As necessary, it hires priests on the spot market. The priests, in turn, offer these spot-market services during otherwise unoccupied times (Covell 2001, 236; Rowe 2000, 356–58). John Nelson (2017, 7) describes this market for priestly services as highly competitive, a "booming industry." The private funeral companies (Nelson 2017, 7), he writes, "offer cut-rate prices on Buddhist posthumous names (kaimyo), grave stones and sites, memorial services, interment options, and memorials for pets …."

(b) Dispatch services. The temples face high fixed costs: they maintain elaborate physical facilities and pay a priest even when he or she has nothing to do. The funeral homes do face some fixed costs: they maintain the buildings in which to hold the services.

Dispatch services dispense with all of this and focus relentlessly on price. Like the funeral homes, they hire priests by the hour – and avoid paying even opportunity costs by recruiting priests when they have nothing else to do. They rent funeral home space as needed – and try again to skirt opportunity costs by choosing those with idle capacity.

Take "Kakuyasu."[5] The term means something like "deep discount," and is the name of a website that dispatches priests. The site promises "EDLP" – Every-Day Low Prices. Consumers can buy the services of a priest to perform a funeral. They can ask for a "self-service funeral," a "next-day funeral," or a "water-child memorial." They can order commemoration rituals and can specify whether they want them done at a temple, at home, or at a grave site (separate prices for each). They can contract for a hearse to pick up a body. They can ask for a posthumous name for a deceased. And if they want the bones of the deceased interred in a distant temple, Kakuyasu will send them a mailing kit.

3. Selling the non-priced complements – Counseling is harder to price. Rituals are countable events, clear and sharply defined. Religious counseling is not necessarily so. Some Japanese priests do try to sell counseling by the hour. Some of them post a price on the web: typically 8,000 to 10,000 yen per hour. Others leave the amount of the fee to the person's discretion. One priest offers "color-light" therapy. Another website offers a corporate contract: the employer contracts with the website, and the website then gives its workers the right to talk to a priest on demand. Some priests offer home visits for a fee. Some handle the calls themselves.

---

[5] See website at https://kakuyasuso.jp/obosan/.

Others contract with an outplacement service – which often lets the caller specify the denomination. Home visits usually run about 35,000 yen.

Note that even secular counselors do not reach a very wide audience in Japan. In Japan, 14,000 psychiatrists practice medicine, and in the United States 30,000. In both countries psychiatrists seem to prescribe drugs more than they counsel. Clinical psychologists do offer counseling. In Japan, 35,000 clinical psychologists practice, and 106,000 licensed psychologists work in the United States.[6] As a result, Japan does indeed have the smaller market for clinical psychologists: 278 psychologists per 1 million in Japan; 320 in the United States More basically, however, even 320 psychological counselors per 1,000,000 citizens is a small number. In neither country do citizens support a large market for commercial counseling.

Urban Japanese know a by-the-hour priest will not counsel well anyway. The by-the-hour priest will not know the person who calls, and knowledge matters. The temple priest could lead his parishioners through a death in the family because he and the parishioners were both physically present – there, in the village. When a mother complained about a truant son, the priest could counsel both, and he could do so with the knowledge of their family background, because he was there – in the village. He and the parishioners had always been there. He had grown up in the village; he had succeeded to his father's post; he knew the parish. When a mother in the village died, the priest (usually) knew the (rough outlines of the) relationships that her children had had with her and with each other.

Traditionally, in other words, the temple priest was there when the villagers needed him. He could counsel. He could teach. And he could provide the rituals that would help them negotiate their way through the transitions. Knowledgeable counseling takes place within a social context. The traditional mainstream religions integrated their members into a cosmic order – but a distinctly human cosmic order involving a community of specific people. Not for nothing did Durkheim define religion as the collective worship of the community itself. When clerics in the mainstream religious traditions counseled and taught their parishioners, they counseled them in ways that integrated them into the collective human community about them. There is a reason people instinctively bristle at the notion of internet-based religious advice. Abstracting a cleric's counseling from a

---

[6] Psychiatrists in Japan: website of Japanese Society of Psychiatry and Neurology, available at: www.jspn.or.jp/modules/residents/index.php?content_id=2. Psychiatrists in the U.S.: Harrar (2020). Psychologists in Japan: Website of the Japanese Society of Certified Clinical Psychologists, available at: www.jsccp.jp/person/about.php. Psychologists in the United States.: Datapoint (2016).

specific human community misses the fundamentally social dimension to religion itself.

IV Fee-for-Service Finance – The Water-Child Memorials

A Introduction

To generate the support it can no longer receive from its parish community (its danka), Japanese temples have moved their fee-for-service finance increasingly front and center. More specifically, they have begun aggressively to market several rituals. The most notorious are the memorial services for aborted children (this Section IV). More financially disruptive are the advance payment contracts for all future death-related memorials (Section V).

B Abortion in 2022

Through an initial statute in 1948 and its amendment in 1952, the Japanese government legalized abortion so long as the "health of the mother" were at stake. The potential health threats included "economic" threats. Effectively, the government had made abortion available upon demand.[7]

Almost invariably, commentators have described the resulting abortion rate in Japan as high. It was: at its peak in 1957, the ratio of abortions to live births reached 71.6 percent (Table 6.2). Yet from that high, the rate has steadily declined. By 1975, it had fallen to 35.3 percent, by 1995 to 28.9 percent, and by 2017 to 17.4 percent. Prior to the 1973 Roe v. Wade decision, abortion legality in the United States had varied by state. During the years after Roe, however, the ratio of abortions to live births in Japan and in the United States have tracked each other almost perfectly. In 1980, the ratio stood at 37.9 in Japan and 35.9 in the United States By 2015, it had fallen to 17.5 in Japan and 18.8 in the United States.

C The Memorials

1. The phenomenon – Within the field of Japanese religious studies, the water-child memorial service has generated an unusually sharp exchange.[8]

---

[7] Yusei hogo ho [Eugenics Protection Act], Law No. 156 of 1948, Sec. 14(a)(iv)(abortion allowed when mother's life in danger); Law No. 141 of 1952 (abortion allowed for "health of the mother" for "physical or economic reasons").

[8] Harrison (1999, 770) writes that the services "generally consist of several basic elements: an invocation, a verbal listing of the dead or of those commissioning the service, chanting

Table 6.2 *Abortion trends over time*

	Abortions (Japan)	Abortions/Live Births (%) (Japan)	Abortions/ /LB (%) (U.S.)
1950	320,150	13.7	
1955	1,170,143	67.6	
1957*	1,122,316	71.6	
1960	1,063,256	66.2	
1965	843,248	46.2	
1970	732,033	37.8	
1975	671,597	35.3	
1980	598,084	37.9	35.9
1985	550,127	38.4	35.4
1990	456,797	37.4	34.5
1995	343,024	28.9	31.1
2000	341,146	28.7	24.6
2005	289,127	27.2	23.3
2010	212,694	19.9	22.8
2015	176,388	17.5	18.8
2017	164,621	17.4	

Notes: * Peak post-war abortion rate
Sources: Kokuritsu Shakai hosho jinko mondai kenkyujo, Jinko tokei shiryo shu [Materials on Population Statistics] (2019), as available at www.ipss.go.jp/syoushika/ tohkei/Popular/P_Detail2018.asp, based on data from Ministry of Health & Labor; Center for Disease Control, Division of Reproductive Health, Abortion Surveillance System (various years)

Bardwell Smith (1988) was one of the first scholars to discuss the phenomenon in the English-language literature. Smith described it sympathetically, and as a largely therapeutic response to a woman's close encounter with death. The ritual reflected the "emotional problems encountered by large numbers of Japanese women following an abortion experience," said he (1988, 3, 9), and allowed them "to acknowledge death, even a death that one has willed." Not "all women," and perhaps not even "most women" – but a "large number of women" found the experience troubling, and many of them turned to the water-child memorial.

> of texts as offerings to accrue some kind of merit for the dead, prayers to appropriate deities to watch over the dead, an invitation to participants to come forward to make an offering. The giving of a name ... and the creation of a place ... to mark the continued presence of the dead are also common elements in the practice of *mizuko kuyo* ...."

William LaFleur (1990, 1992, 1995, 1999) continued Smith's largely sympathetic approach. LaFleur noted the way that Japanese Buddhist cosmology did not draw the line between human and non-human life as sharply as did the Christian tradition. From the moment of conception, the fetus or child (the temples and parishioners always call it a child or baby, never a fetus) clearly had human life.

Within this world, LaFleur detailed the tension that Japanese men and women (but especially women) feel as they contemplate a pregnancy they had not wanted. The tension is between (i) respect for the life of the child to be and (ii) hopes for the quality of the life for that new child and the other members of the family. Although Buddhists condemned the taking of the new life, he explained, they also respected this tension. Usually, he (1990, 532) wrote, they "took the position that abortion was what we call a 'necessary evil' – although their term was a 'necessary sorrow.'"

Toward this approach, Helen Hardacre (1997) responded harshly in the extreme. Styling her project self-consciously "feminist," Hardacre (1997, e.g., 92, 251, xxi) repeatedly described the ritual as both "fetocentric" and "misogynistic." The temples had generated the demand for their ritual through "an intense media advertising campaign" that stressed the harm that vengeful spirits of the aborted fetuses could wreak. Mizuko kuyo "was advanced as the 'answer' to a 'problem,'" she (1997, 251) writes, "created mostly by those purveying the rites in question." It was and is, she continued, invented and promoted by "entrepreneurial religionists" (a phrase she considered derogatory). It is a "fad," fanned by a "media blitz," but one which by 1997 was already "dying out."

Scholars questioned the causal connection between Hardacre's "media blitz" and the water-child ritual. The "blitz" about vengeful fetal spirits did not begin until the 1970s, but by Hardacre's (1997, 94 tab. 5) own evidence the temples were already offering the ritual before 1965. George Tanabe (1998, 378) thought the tie between water-child memorial and vengeful ghosts "unclear (or clearly tenuous)." Ian Reader (1998, 154) declared that Hardacre supported her causal claim "with surprisingly little evidence." Elizabeth Harrison (1995, 74, 76) thought Hardacre gave Japanese women far too little credit. "[M]any of them," she continued, "are actively choosing for themselves to do mizuko kuyo, because it helps them make sense of and deal with disturbing and unresolved issues in their lives."[9]

---

[9] See also Meredith Underwood (1999, 751): Hardacre had lost sight of, she wrote, "not women but women's agency."

2. By denomination – Journalists and scholars in the 1990s focused on several temples dedicated specifically to the water-child memorial service. Yet for ordinary Japanese women troubled by their abortion, those prominent institutions matter less than the neighborhood temple. Writing in 1997, Hardacre (92) estimated that "mizuko kuyo is practiced at roughly 40–45 percent of the religious institutions." Plausibly, observers suggest that even temples that do not advertise the ritual may sometimes perform it upon request.

To canvass the market, I take the temples in Hyogo prefecture. Located next to metropolitan Osaka, Hyogo stretches from the Kobe metropolis (population 1.5 million) on the Seto Inland Sea, to prime rice (and sake rice, Chapter 2) paddy fields inland, to the isolated villages and hot springs resorts along the coast of the Sea of Japan (see Chapter 4).

In the first column on Table 6.3, I give the number of Hyogo temples by denomination. Among the 3,743 total, Jodo shin temples are the most numerous by far (1148), followed by Shingon (798). Jodo, Soto, and Rinzai each have 300+ temples, and Tendai and Nichiren have the fewest.

Note that the Tendai and Shingon denominations developed out of the Buddhism that arrived from China in the eighth and ninth centuries. The Jodo and Jodo shin denominations date from the twelfth and thirteenth centuries and focus on a faith in the mercy of the Amida Buddha in leading a believer to the "Pure Land." Zen (Soto and Rinzai are both Zen denominations) arrived in Japan in the thirteenth century. The Nichiren faith

Table 6.3 *Hyogo temples, total and Mizuko, by denomination*

	Total Temples %		Mizuko Temples	Mizuko/Total
Tendai	166	(4.4)	7	.0422
Shingon	798	(21.3)	27	.0338
Jodo	369	(9.9)	5	.0136
Jodo shin	1148	(30.7)	0	0
Nichiren	166	(4.4)	10	.0645
Soto Zen	392	(10.5)	8	.0204
Rinzai Zen	356	(9.5)	6	.0169
Other	348	(9.3)	7	.0201
Total	3743	70	.0187	
	If exclude Jodo shin:		.0270	

Sources: Total temples, from Hyogo no otera ichiran [List of Hyogo Temples], as of July 2020, from NokotsudoInfo, at www.nokotsudo.info/list/hyogo.html; mizuko temples, by internet search, July 2020

developed as an indigenous Japanese denomination (also during the thirteenth century) and focuses on the Lotus sutra.

The denominational distribution in Hyogo roughly tracks national patterns. Oda (2003, 41) details the national distribution as of 1959. He identifies 41.8 percent of the temples in Japan as Jodo or Jodo shin, 29.0 percent as Soto or Rinzai, 21.2 percent as Tendai or Shingon, and 8.0 percent Nichiren. The comparable figures for Hyogo from Table 6.2 are 40.6 percent, 20.0 percent, 25.7 percent, and 4.4 percent.

In the second column of Table 6.3, I give the number of Hyogo temples identified on the Internet as offering water-child memorial services. Most of these temples advertise the ritual on their own website; a few are identified through other sources like websites for women's services. The Hyogo temples identifiable on the Internet as offering water-child memorial come to 70 temples (1.9 percent).

Obviously, Table 6.3 does not mean that only 2 percent of Hyogo temples offer the water-child memorials; it means that only 2 percent of Hyogo temples can be identified on the Internet as temples that offer the service. The vast majority of temples are small, chronically underfunded operations with no presence on the Internet at all. Of the 3,743 Kobe temples, only 151 have a website.

Note that the Jodo shin denomination has taken a public stand against water-child memorial services. As one temple (Joshoji, in Kobe) explains it:[10]

In the Jodo shin denomination, there is no special ceremony for commemorating a water-child. According to Buddhist teachings, a "life" is born the moment the soul enters the mother's womb. Although we call it a "water-child," in terms of reverence for life, its birth is no different from the birth of any other form of life. It is a soul that did not enter our world, but one which we must recognize as a fine human being….

There may have been a variety of causes and reasons for what happened, but it is a fact that a precious life was lost. It is crucial that we recognize this fact directly.

3. By municipality – Table 6.4 explores which cities have temples that publicly offer water-child memorial ceremonies. Of the 41 municipalities in Hyogo, 30 have at least one temple whose provision of the water-child memorial can be confirmed on the Internet. The metropolitan centers of Kobe, Himeji, and Amagasaki all have multiple such temples. Of the remaining municipalities, six have at least two such temples, eighteen have at least 1, and eleven have none. Of the municipalities with no such temple, the largest is Takasago. Note, however, that twenty eight of the fifty-six temples in

---

[10] See temple website at www.jyoshoji.com/buddhist/.

Table 6.4 *Water-child memorial temples, by municipality*

	Population Temples	Mizuko Temples	All Temples
Kobe	1,544,000	14	1027
Himeji	536,000	10	378
Amagasaki	453,000	6	128
Tanpa	68,000	5	168
Kakogawa	267,000	3	98
Kasai	48,000	3	77

Notes: Water-child memorial temples are those temples whose provision of water-child memorial can be confirmed publicly on the Internet.

Sources: Mizuko temples: internet search as of July 2020; total temples, from Hyogo no otera ichiran [List of Hyogo Temples], as of July 2020, from NokotsudoInfo, at www.nokotsudo.info/list/hyogo.html; population from Somu cho tokei kyoku, Kokusei chosa [Vital Statistics] (various years), available from www.e-stat.go.jp

Takasago are Jodo shin temples. The other 10 municipalities without such a temple are all municipalities with less than 41,000 population.

4. As the priests involved describe it – Some temples perform water-child memorial services regularly, and others perform it when requested – but perform it they do. The 1970s "media blitz" over the ritual has completely disappeared. The tales of the vengeful ghosts of the aborted children have almost disappeared. What remains is a simple story of death, suffering, and sorrow. It is a story of the remorseful women and the priests who counsel them, largely as Smith and LaFleur told it nearly thirty years ago.

The Enmanji is a suburban Osaka (Shingon) temple dating to the eighth century. On its website, its priests answer some of the questions that they receive.[11] "Will my water-child haunt?" asked one parent (probably a mother). "A water-child does not haunt," answered the priest:

We still get questions like this at the Joko Enmanji. But no matter where you look in the Buddhist sutras, you will find nothing about this. What is more, a water-child's heart is clear and pure. With his limitlessly beautiful heart, how could a water child ever feel jealous or hold a grudge?

One mother asks, "can someone like me – the worst kind of human – even be forgiven?" The priest replies that many mothers lament, "I did the worst thing." "I have no right to be happy," they tell him. But the priest

---

[11] Tengoku no akachan Q & A [Baby in Heaven, Q & A]. Available at www.enmanji.com/mizukoga2.htm.

simply reassures: "Just as you wish for the happiness of your parents, your child is wishing for your happiness from the bottom of his heart." "How then should I pray to our baby in paradise?" asks a mother. "Just pray your honest feelings," answers the priest:

Maybe all you can do at first is to cry. Maybe you can't communicate how you feel. Maybe all you can say is "I'm sorry." ... But at Enmanji, we don't encourage you to pray "I'm sorry" forever. Once your heart has begun to clear, try to communicate your love and thankfulness.

Writing on "The Lotus Leaf" Buddhist counseling website, another priest talked of the requests he receives for the water-child memorial:[12]

Once in a while, someone comes to my temple and asks, "would you do a water-child memorial?" Sometimes the man comes along, but usually the woman comes by herself.... The man ought to be there too, and when he's not it makes me angry.
    I read the sutras [and hold the water-child memorial ceremony,] but here's what I tell the woman. "Let's pledge to the Buddha and to your baby that you'll never do this again." "Get married, and with a good partner proudly give birth. Raise those babies to be fine children. That's the penance you need to perform. That's your act of remembrance."

V Fee-for-Service Finance – The Eternal Memorials

A Introduction

Like churches and synagogues in the West, indeed like most mainstream religious faiths everywhere, Japanese temples guide their community members through the deaths of their family members and friends. In part, they did this by providing memorial services on a regular basis. As they did, the family members reciprocated by donating (though the fee was usually at least informally required) funds to the temple.

Increasingly, temples are offering to perform the memorials forever. An "eternal memorial" (the "eitai kuyo"), they call it. For people who sign up and pay for the service during their lifetime, they promise an unending stream of memorials. Rather than trust a person's heirs to pay for memorial services on a regular basis, in other words, they are asking the person while still alive to pay the present value of those future payments up-front.

---

[12] Mizuko kuyo ni tsuite [Regarding Water-child memorial], Hasunoha. Available at https://hasunoha.jp/questions/32426.

B The Eternal Memorial

1. The service. – Traditionally, the village temple ran the funerals for its registered parishioner households. Often, it provided them with a grave yard as well. Crucially, the registered parishioners did not just hold the funerals at the local temple. They held an on-going stream of memorial services.

For each service, parishioners gave the priest a contribution. There was seldom anything voluntary about the amount, of course. Parishioners held the services for each of the deceased at carefully delineated intervals, for amounts set by the priest, and at their registered temple. At root, neither the temple nor the parishioners transacted on a competitive market. At root, it was not a fee for a service at all. It was payment on an obligation to support the temple in its continuing ministry to the community.

Through the new "eternal memorial" contract, enterprising temples now offer a perpetual stream of future memorial services for a single lump-sum advance payment. They offer the arrangement to anyone, registered parishioner or no. They began selling the contracts in the 1980s and 1990s (Rowe 2011, 4–5). Typically, they called a contracting person a "member" (kaiin) of the temple (or an affiliated society) rather than part of any traditional registered parishioner arrangement (danka).

Ostensibly, the temples created the contract for people without children. Unable to assure a temple of future payments, childless men and women had sometimes found it hard to arrange a funeral with a temple that relied on a standard registered parishioner arrangement. Even people with children, however, soon began buying eternal memorial contracts.

In essence, the contract enabled the temples not just to borrow against future services, but to precommit to a price. Under the traditional system, parishioners who held a funeral for a parent at the family temple obligated themselves to an endless stream of future memorial-for-cash transactions. The temple, however, priced the transactions as time went by. In effect, the registered parishioners left themselves captive to the temple's good well: they paid whatever price the temple might demand, or they reneged on their obligations to their ancestors. The eternal memorial contract eliminated the problem of ex post temple opportunism.

2. The premium arrangement. – The Myokoji offered a premium eternal memorial contract.[13] A Nichiren temple nestled in the Niigata mountains, Myokoji claims to date from the fourteenth century. After abolishing its registered parishioner structure, it turned to a membership organization

---

[13] See temple website at https://myoukouji.or.jp/annon/.

it calls the Annonbyo. To inter and commemorate its members' bones, it has added to its 16,000 square meter temple complex an exquisite park. It charges a membership fee of 850,000 yen, and for that price agrees to pray for its members in perpetuity.

3. The cut-rate alternative. – The antithesis to the Myokoji's eternal memorial program may be that of the Saitama Soto Zen temple named the Kenshoin.[14] Eiju Hashimoto serves as its head abbot and claims to want to transform it from a temple with a funerary focus to an institution that addresses all aspects of life. He wants to make it a community, he explains, a place for people not just to study meditation and calligraphy, but to obtain help with things like health care and insurance too. Where temples like the Myokoji display exquisitely designed websites with professionally produced photographs, the Kenshoin website looks more like a newspaper want ad section from several decades back. It posts advertisements to a variety of graveyards, priest-dispatch services, water-child memorial services, and even to memorial services for pets.

It is hard to quarrel with creating community, but Hashimoto's website primarily shows a devotion to price-cutting. He runs a Zen temple, yet the one thing missing is any sense of religious faith. People worry about health care and insurance to be sure, but sometimes they endure agonizing nights after a death in the family. Hashimoto mostly just sells rituals that are cheap. The eternal memorial service that the Myokoji sold for 850,000 yen, the Kenshoin sells for 30,000. Should someone want to inter a parent's bones without bothering to visit the temple, the Kenshoin will send him a cardboard box. Deposit 35,000 yen in the Kenshoin bank account, put the bones in the box, and mail it in. Hashimoto promises to take care of the rest – forever.

VI Ministering in the Face of the Contracting Problem

A Counseling

None of this is new to the community of Japanese priests. They realize how hard it is to fund the counseling, guidance, and teaching that priests had traditionally provided. They realize (even if they may not articulate it quite this way) that altruism seldom generates a stable economic equilibrium. But the most committed among them have worked hard to provide those services anyway.

---

[14] See Danka seido (2017); Asayama 2018, and the temple website at www.kenshouin.com.

Japanese priests realize that many Japanese see temples as funerary machines. They realize that many Japanese see them as crassly mercenary. "Can I visit a priest at a temple where I'm not a registered parishioner, and ask for counseling," asks one person on a Yahoo website.[15] "Sure, I think so," answers another. "But I look at the priest at the temple where I'm a registered parishioner…. With lots of these priests, it's just not worth asking questions about life. Unless a priest's got a really good reputation, it's a waste of time. Most of them are just in it for 'the money.'" Well, answers another reader, "the point of the temple is to help resolve problems, so sure, they'll let you talk to them. But it's not like they're counselors or medical specialists. Don't count on getting an answer that satisfies you. You may want consolation, but find yourself scolded instead. If you're prepared for that, go ahead."

For all the priests who effectively (not formally) inherit a temple from their father and exploit it for the revenue and tax advantages, some of the others take their ministry seriously. Some priests offer counseling without even trying to make it pay. They straightforwardly invite people (registered parishioners or no) to come for counseling on the web, by telephone, or in person. They assure them that they do not charge for the service.[16]

Some of the priests quit good positions in the private sector to take these jobs. Men and women with established careers do not drop their profession to work as a priest for the money. If a temple generated a substantial revenue stream, the priest would have conveyed it to one of his children. The only temples available to priests who come to the ministry from the outside are the temples that no priest's child wanted.

And yet some men and women join the ministry anyway. Ryumyo Hato serves as priest at the Joren'in, a Shingon temple in Tokyo.[17] Hato worked nine years as an engineer before becoming a priest. "There are lots of people who are suffering," he writes, "but don't know where to turn. It used to be that a person like that would go to the temple priest. But people are reluctant to do that these days. I thought maybe they would find it more comfortable to come to [a secular] counseling room. So I became a psychological counselor as well, and spend time outside of the temple too." Hato works as a counselor in an office during the week, and in the temple on the weekends.

[15] https://detail.chiebukuro.yahoo.co.jp/qa/question_detail/q1297105602.
[16] Renshoji (http://renshouji.jp/consul/); Shosanji (https://www.shosanji.jp).
[17] See: https://kakedera.com/staff.html.

Several of these more concerned priests tend the Bonze Bar in the Yotsuya district of Tokyo. They do this to talk to the people who come by. Hato volunteers there too. "I actually can't drink much," he explains, "so I had to start as a real novice and learn the names of drinks…. I talk about Buddhism. I talk about psychology. Sometimes we tell jokes…. The Bonze Bar is a space for healing for men and women who work in the office and carry burdens that no one knows about."[18] Some 12 to 13 priests take turns at the bar. "It's the place to go alone," writes one woman (Takahashi 2015). "Problems that you can't tell your friends or your lover, problems that you can't share with your colleagues at work – a priest will generously listen."

Some temples operate cafes. They specify times when a priest will be there to chat. Some specify times when a female priest will be there.[19]

Some priests operate counseling websites. The most popular may be the "Lotus Leaf."[20] Operating since 2012, nearly 300 priests answer inquiries as needed on line. Over 50 of them have volunteered to counsel people individually. For this, again, they charge nothing.

B Fostering Social Capital

Some temple priests self-consciously try to build social capital in their local neighborhoods. They do not build that capital in order to facilitate contract enforcement. They do not care about contracting problems at all. Yet for all the reasons discussed by Putnam, Coleman, and so many other scholars, social capital does build and strengthen an environment that lets its members more cost-effectively contract. Some temple priests self-consciously work to build that capital. Within the urban or suburban settings in which they find themselves, the priests work to build the dense networks of social connections that people once had in the villages. They work to build, in short, a community.

Take those Hyogo temples with websites. Many of them offer a wide range of services that have nothing to do with Buddhism, but everything to do with social capital. Several of them offer yoga lessons (e.g., Ujiyamadera, in Kobe). Others provide courses in flower arranging (Shorinji in Tanpa), gourmet cooking classes (Kogenji, in Tanpa), or (think Robert Putnam

---

[18] See: https://kakedera.com/staff.html.
[19] See, for example, websites at: https://kuma-zenstyle.jp/1089; https://hitoyoshifusui.com/archives/1171; https://rocketnews24.com/2019/05/22/1210556/.
[20] https://hasunoha.jp; see Soryo (2016).

in Italy) choral societies (Zenkyoji, in Nishinomiya). The Saishoji in Amagasaki runs a discussion group on social issues (e.g., LGB relations) and specifically promises not to mention Buddhism. Some temples run nursery schools (Zenkyoji, in Nishinomiya), while others offer summer camps (Honganji branch, in Kobe), run weekend programs for children (Honganji branch, again), sponsor baseball teams (Myofukuji, in Sasayama), operate children's activity centers (Kohonji, in Kawanishi), or organize boy scout troops (Jofukuji in Kawanishi). At least one held a social for singles (Shokoji, in Kobe), and another – literally – held bingo games (Rengeji, in Toyooka).

C Making Ends Meet

Takashi Uriu (2015) worked as a systems engineer before becoming a priest. In a recent essay, he describes his life at a small temple. A few priests are rich, he writes, but they are rare. Most priests cannot feed their families on their temple income. To pay their bills, they look for a second job.

> I serve in the Jodo shin denomination …. Our founder Shinran came down from the mountain and walked among the people. Many resident priests think it important to do the same. They make ends meet as a laborer, and walk the way of the nembutsu [calling on Amidha Buddha for mercy] with their parishioners."

Of course, some of the towns where the temples find it hard to stay solvent are also the towns where a priest will find it hard to locate a second job. If he does, his employer may not sympathize with the demands of the priesthood.

> Because of this, I registered with a priest-dispatching service. I immediately started getting many requests, and was going east and west every day.

He was surprised, says Uriu:

> I had thought that the people who would use these services were people who didn't want to spend time with a priest. I thought they used the service simply because they had to – they needed to hold a funeral….
>
> I was wrong. At the wake and the funeral, we carry on ordinary conversations. Everyone is really interested [in the Buddhist message], and asks all sorts of questions. Some of them later asked for Buddhist services. Some of them wrote me letters, or said that they wanted to hear more….
>
> Maybe some people think, "it's not that Buddhism is important. [The people at the wake] are just thinking about the person they've lost." But these days lots of people do a funeral and memorial without a priest. The fact that they'd go on the Internet and ask for a priest means, I think, that they care about Buddhism.

As Victor Turner put it many years ago, the funeral is a liminal event. Uriu continued:

These are occasions so full of sadness that the family members cannot even put it into words. When we come to such places, we realize the limits to "companionship" among human beings. And each time we realize those limits, I want to convey the true compassion, the compassion of the Buddha.

His fellow priests do not necessarily sympathize:

Once at a study group, a resident priest from a big temple said, "I don't want to run around to funeral homes with my head bowed, trying to increase the number of parishioners. That's unseemly." But unseemly as it is, we do it because there's something more important here. Priests who get lots of funeral requests and have hired cars pick them up at the temple will never understand this....

Uriu may as well have quoted Graham Greene's "whiskey priest" in The Power and the Glory:

We're priests, but we ... drink. We marry. We worry about our own lives, and we send our children to schools.... In ordinary life, there's virtually no difference between someone who's a priest, and someone who's not.

So why are people paying several 10,000's of yen to have people like us come and hold a commemoration? It must be because they appreciate a deeper Buddhist truth here.

Personally, I don't care if people think it's a commercial product. Sure, there're big problems with the priest-dispatch services ... on Amazon.com. I know that. "But if I'm called, I'll go. I'll do my best to speak to the grief. And in the midst of that grief, I'll do my best to convey [the truth at the heart of] Buddhism."

VII Conclusions

As the Japanese government liberalized access to abortions after the war, women began aborting their children (they never call them fetuses) in large numbers. Soon, many women began asking temples to perform commemorative ceremonies for these children. Women still do. Temples respond by advertising their commemorative ritual and posting the fees which they charge for the service.

Traditionally, priests stood ready to offer counseling and ritual as needed during the existentially troubling passages in life. They maintained the temple as the central institution in the village, and the focus around which residents maintained their webs of economic, social, and personal ties. In exchange for all this, local communities effectively kept the temples on retainer. Yet as non-congregational religious groups in low levels of tension with the surrounding society (as Iannaccone and Stark put it), Japanese temples could never rely on their parishioners to give voluntarily; such groups never can. Instead, they counted on the tightly intertwined social network within the local community to enforce the obligation to give.

Like firms in most of the traditional religions, Japanese temples offer complementary services. They offer the counseling by which their parishioners can make sense of the existential crises they face. They teach and remind them of the moral code by which the community members expect each other to live. And they offer the rituals through which to internalize those explanations and reminders. The counseling and teaching on one hand, and the ritual on the other, acquire their plausibility only in tandem – yet temples find that counseling and teaching hard to price, while they sell their ritual in a competitive market.

Over the course of the twentieth century, Japanese migrated out of these richly structured villages to the more anomic cities. Without a coercive village structure, the non-congregational low-tension temples could no longer rely on (what was in effect) a retainer-fee. With that first-best contract unavailable, temples saw no option but to compete aggressively in a fee-for-service market. Of the available contracts, the most notorious remains the commemorative ritual for aborted children.

7

Conclusions

The eighteenth- and nineteenth-century Omi merchants in Japan relied heavily on social ties to augment their access to information and increase their transactional reliability. They relied as heavily as their peers in the classic Landa-Bernstein-Greif accounts. The Tokugawa economy was growing. Producers were starting to specialize by region. If only they could sell their goods more widely, they could capture scale economies and capitalize on their comparative advantage. To meet their demand for large-scale interregional trade, the Omi merchants began to establish branches around the country. They travelled widely, buying from each community and selling as they went. Regional producers needed the markets in order to innovate. By creating more broadly national markets, the Omi merchants gave them exactly that opportunity.

To maintain honesty within their networks of agents and branch offices, the Omi merchants (Chapter 1) created their own "ethnic" ties. They hired people from a common geographical area. They intermarried. They shared a common religious tradition. They sent a young man to a branch office only after they had trained and observed him in the home office for multiple years. To maintain his loyalty, they required him to return to the home office every few years. In effect, they cultivated around their office the dense network of social ties that collectively constitute social capital.

Regional brewers (Chapter 2) determined to create premium terroir sake faced an extraordinarily complex contracting problem. They needed to convince farmers to grow unusual varieties of delicate and temperamental sake-optimized rice. They needed to convince the farmers to lavish the rice with high levels of care. Yet they did not address the complex contracting problem with complex agreements. Instead, they negotiated extraordinarily simple contracts: terminable at the end of the year, paying extremely high prices, and embedded – once again – within a dense network of deliberately created social capital.

Given the returns to modern equipment, many fishermen (Chapter 3) face economies of scale they cannot afford. To survive, some entrepreneurial fishermen are moving deliberately upscale. Rather than sell on the mass market, they create and service a niche market for premium, high-quality fish. To compete in this market, the entrepreneurial fishermen purposely raise the stakes: On the internet sales sites, they post their broader reputations as a bond. In doing so, they increase their vulnerability to a dissatisfied customer. In effect, the fisherman creates among his customers the network of overlapping ties that together constitute closed social capital. In the process, he builds a network that lets him more credibly promise high quality – precisely because his buyers can contact each other, learn how he has behaved in the past, and punish him if he reneges.

Japan contains one of the largest deposits of geothermal energy in the world, yet has an extraordinarily small number of electrical plants to exploit it (Chapter 4). It has few plants because their wells would threaten the hot springs resort industry. Electrical utilities would like to commit to compensating the hot springs hotels for any damages they might cause – but given the difficulty of showing causation in court, cannot do so credibly. The hot springs hotels would like to negotiate in good faith – but given that each hotel potentially has a right to hold up the entire plant, cannot credibly promise that all subsequent hotels will negotiate in good faith. The developers who have succeeded in this industry over the last two decades are disproportionately those with roots in the community itself.

Young would-be farmers (Chapter 5) in pre-war Japan needed land to till. They could borrow the money to buy it from banks, but the out-of-town staff at the banks lacked much information about who would make the best farmers. Alternatively, they could borrow from wealthy local families. These local elites knew the area and the people. Embedded in the network of community social ties, they knew which farmers were most conscientious and which lands were most productive. Should a farmer consider reneging on a contract, they had access to the networks that would collectively impose the sanctions necessary to encourage compliance. Although these local elites lacked the university education necessary to document court-enforceable security interests, leases let them advance the funds without the elaborate documentation. Rather than lend the farmer the money and have him buy the land, they bought the land (if they did not already own it) and leased it to the farmer. If the farmer failed to pay, the investor evicted him from the land and moved on.

Japanese Buddhist temples (Chapter 6) had traditionally relied on the high levels of social capital within the local village to enforce the giving they needed to stay solvent. When men and women began to leave the villages for the anomic cities, the temples found themselves without the necessary funds. In response, they turned from what had been an effective village retainer contract to an individual fee-for-service model of finance. Unfortunately for the temples, they market their priceable services (primarily ceremonies connected to deaths) within competitive markets. Unable to sell above marginal cost, they have been unable to cross-subsidize their other – less priceable – services.

* * *

Together, these examples illustrate several of the most basic problems and opportunities in contract structure. The transacting parties in these examples faced informational constraints. The brewery did not know the level of care a farmer would take in growing the rice. The restaurant did not know whether the distant fisherman would provide the quality of fish it needed for its evening offerings. In fact, it did not know whether the fisherman would send anything at all. The out-of-town bankers in the mountain village did not know the farming abilities of the local young men. They did not know character. The hotels did not know the extent to which a geothermal plant would lower the output of their own hot springs.

Most of the examples also illustrate ways that contracting parties try to avoid the cost of litigation. By keeping their contracts to one-year arrangements, the brewers limited the scale of damages they would incur if the transaction collapsed. By structuring a credit extension as a lease rather than a loan, local elites could retrieve their investment in agriculture simply by evicting the farmer.

Many of the examples involve parties working to make their assurances credible. Toward that end, they relied heavily on dense networks of social connections. To make credible their promise to be fair, brewers gathered their supplying farmers into a close network in which the farmers could readily learn of any misconduct in which the brewer might engage. Premium fisherman drew their customers into a network of other customers. Those geothermal developers who succeed in building a new plant were disproportionately developers with extensive connections within the local community.

The contracting parties, in other words, deliberately create and cultivate social capital. In wealthy modern democracies, they simultaneously manipulate formal legal institutions. But they do not ignore the social structures within which they live. Instead, they recognize and leverage the benefits that those structures provide. They use the structures to obtain information – about their agents, about their counter-parties, about their markets, and about their competitors. They use the structures to maintain the threat of social sanctions. Given the role that the network of social ties can play, they deliberately create and cultivate those ties and embed their agreements within it.

Bibliography

2018 nen no hatsumode ninzu rankingu [Ranking of New Year's Visits in 2018], Manegy, Dec. 41, 2018, available at: www.manegy.com/news/detail/793.

Abe, Hiromitsu. 2012. "Chiiki to shizen enerugii" kyozon ni mukete [Toward the Coexistence of "The Locality and Natural Energy."] *Beppu daigaku kokusai keiei gakkaiu shi Global Management*, 2: 72–82.

Abe, Takaki. 2009. Nihon ni okeru engan gyogyo no kyodotai kanri [The Monitoring of Collective Bodies in the Japanese Coastal Fishing Industry]. *Fukushima daigaku chiiki sozo*, 20: 6285.

Ackerberg, D. A. & M. Botticini. 2002. Endogenous Matching and the Empirical Determinants of Contract Form. J. Pol. *Econ.*, 110: 564–91.

Ackerberg, Daniel A. & Maristella Botticini. 2000. The Choice of Agrarian Contracts in Early Renaissance Tuscany: Risk Sharing, Moral Hazard, or Capital Market Imperfections. Explorations *Econ. Hist.*, 37: 241–57.

Adachi, Mikio. 1959. Kosaku chotei ho [Tenancy Mediation Act]. In Nobushige Ukai, et al., eds., *Nihon kindai ho hattatsu shi [The History of the Development of Modern Japanese Law]*, vol. 7. Tokyo: Keiso shobo, pp. 37–86.

Akerlof, George A. 1970. The Market for "Lemons": Quality Uncertainty and the Market Mechanism. *Quarterly Journal of Economics*, 84: 488–500.

Akita keizai. 2019. Kappatsuka suru honken no jinetsu hatsuden kaihatsu [Geothermal Electrical Generating Gains Momentum in Our Prefecture]. Akita keizai, 2019.

Akita no shinsei shuzo [Akita's New Sake Production], Nihon keizai shimbun, Nov. 28, 2019.

Allen, D. W. & D. Lueck. 2002. *The Nature of the Farm: Contracts, Risk, and Organization in Agriculture.* Cambridge: MIT Press.

Ambros, Barbara R. 2012. *Bones of Contention: Animals and Religion in Contemporary Japan.* Honolulu: University of Hawai'i Press.

Americans Donated $125 Billion to Religion in 2018. ECFA. [2019]. Available at: www.ecfa.org/Content/Americans-Donated-125-Billion-to-Religion-in-2018-29-of-All-Charitable-Giving

Ando, Yoshio, ed. 1979. *Kindai Nihon keizai shi yoran [Overview of Early Modern Japanese Economic History]*, 2d ed. Tokyo: University of Tokyo Pres.

Anon. 2016. Umaku ikanai chiho wo mokaraseru "chiho kochi" [The "Local Coach" Who Helps Struggling Areas Make Money]. Gacchiri Mandee, Apr. 18, 2016. Available at: https://lovely-lovely.net/busienss/handaichiba-2.

Aquaculture North America. 2019. First Tuna Hatchery Established in North America, Aquaculture North America, April 1, 2019.

Arimoto, Yutaka, Tetsuji Okazaki & Masaki Nakabayashi. 2010. Agrarian Tenancy in Prewar Japan: Contract Choice and Implications on Productivity. *Developing Economies*, 48, 293–318.

Asahi shimbun moto kisha [Former Reporter for Asahi Shimbun], Zakzak, Aug. 5, 2014.

Asayama, Minoru. 2018. Danka haishi to "Nagaya jiin" ["Nagaya Temples," and the Abolition of Danka]. Notes, June 21, 2018. https://note.com/monomono117/.

Ashenfelter, Orley & Karl Storchmann. 2016. The Economics of Wine, Weather, and Climate Change. *Rev. Environmental Econ. & Pol.*, 10: 25–46.

Ashenfelter, Orley. 2007 Peredicting the Quality and Prices of Bordeaux Wines. Am. Assn. of Wine Economists Working Paper, Apr. 2007.

Atuna: Know Your Business. Available at: https://atuna.com/pages/tuna-fishing-statistics。

Baba, Kenji, et al. 2015. Jenetsu shigen wo meguru hatsuden … [Electrical Generation Based on Geothermal Resources …]. *Kankyo kagaku kaishi*, 28: 316–29.

Babb, James. 2005. Making Farmers Conservative: Japanese Farmers, Land Reform and Socialism. *Social Science Japan Journal*, 8, 175–95.

Baird, Douglas G. 2003. In Coase's Footsteps. U. Chi. L. Rev.

Banerjee, A. V. 1999. Prospects and Strategies for Land Reform. Proceedings Ann. World Bank Conf. Development Econ., 253–84.

Basu, Kaushik. 1984. *The Less Developed Economy: A Critique of Contemporary Theory*. Oxford: Basil Blackwell.

Beardsley, Richard K., John W. Hall & Robert E. Ward. 1959. *Village Japan*. Chicago: University of Chicago Press.

Benetti, Daniel D., Gavin J. Partridge & John Stieglitz. 2016. Overview on Status and Technological Advances in Tuna Aquaculture Around the World. In Daniel D. Benetti, Gavin J. Partridge & Alejandro Buentello, eds. 2016. *Advances in Tuna Aquaculture*. Amsterdam: Elsevier, pp. 1–20.

Benkeimaru ni tsuite [About the Boat, Benkei-maru], Available at: https://benkeimaru .com/about

Berger, Peter L. 1967. *The Sacred Canopy: Elements of a Sociological Theory of Religion*. New York: Doubleday.

Berman, Sheri. 1997. Civil Society and the Collapse of the Weimar Republic. *World Pol.*, 49: 401–29.

Bernstein, Lisa. 1992. Opting Out of the Legal System: Extralegal Contractual Relations in the Diamond Industry. *J. Legal Stud.*, 21: 115–58.

Bernstein, Lisa. 1996. Merchant Law in a Merchant Court: Rethinking the Code's Search for Immanent Business Norms. *U. Penn. L. Rev.*, 144: 1765–1821.

Bernstein, Lisa. 1999. The Questionable Empirical Basis of Article 2's Incorporation Strategy: A Preliminary Study. *U. Chi. L. Rev.*, 66: 710–80.

Bernstein, Lisa. 2015. Beyond Relational Contracts: Social Capital and Network Governance in Procurement Contracts. *J. Legal Anal.*, 7: 561–621.

Bernstein, Lisa. 2019. Contract Governance in Small-World Networks: The Case of the Maghribi Traders. *Northwestern Univ. L. Rev.*, 113: 1009.

Berry, R. Albert, & William R. Cline. 1979. *Agrarian Structure and Productivity in Developing Countries*. Baltimore: Johns Hopkins University Press.

Besley, T. & M. Ghatak. 2010. Property Rights and Economic Development. In D. Rodrik & M. Rosenzweig, eds., *Handbook of Development Economics*, v. 5. Netherlands: North Holland, pp. 4525–95.

Bestor, Theodore C. 2004. *Tsukiji: The Fish Market at the Center of the World*. Berkeley: University of California Press.

Binswanger, Hans P., Klaus Deininger & Gershon Feder. 1995. "Power, Distortions, Revolt and Reform in Agricultural Land Relations." In Jere Behrman & T. N. Srinivasan, eds., *Handbook of Development Economics*. Amsterdam: Elsevier, pp. 2659–772.

Bisson, T. A. 1941. *Shadow Over Asia: The Rise of Militant Japan*. New York: Foreign Policy Association.

Bisson, T. A. 1944. *America's Far Eastern Policy*. New York: Institute of Pacific Relations.

Bisson, T. A. 1945. *Japan's War Economy*. New York: Institute of Pacific Relations.

Blake, Cary. 2013. 8 Keys to a Better Wine Grape Grower Contract, May 22, 2013, available at www.farmprogress.com

Bluefin Tuna Farming Business, Struggles of Commercial Enterprises. 2021. Fish Information & Services, Jan. 5, 2021.

Bourdieu, Pierre. 1985. The Forms of Capital. In J.G. Richardson, ed., *Handbook of Theory and Research for the Sociology of Education*. New York: Greenwood, 241–58.

Bowen, Roger. 1988. "Japanese Peasants: Moral? Rational? Revolutionary? Duped?" *J. Asian Stud.*, 47, 821–32.

Brooks, Anne Page. 1981. Mizuko Kuyo and Japanese Buddhism. *Japanese J. Religious Stud.*, 8: 119–47.

Buentello, Alejandro, Manabu Seoka, Keitaro Kato & Gavin J. Partridge. 2016. Tuna Farming in Japan and Mexico, Advances in Tuna Aquaculture, supra, pp. 189–216.

Bumu no saki ni arumono … [Beyond the Boom …], Sake bunka kenkyujo News Letter, Nov. 25, 2015.

Bunka cho. 2015. Shukyo kanren tokei ni kansuru shiryoshu [Materials Relating to Religious Statistics]. Tokyo: Bunka cho.

Burt, Ronald S. 1997. The Contingent Value of Social Capital. *Adm. Sci. Q.*, 42: 339–65.

Burt, Ronald S. 2000. The Network Structure of Social Capital. *Res. Org'l Behav.*, 22: 345–423.

Casadesus-Masanell, Ramon & Daniel F. Spulber. 2000. The Fable of Fisher Body. *J.L. & Econ.*, 43: 67.

Center for Disease Control, Division of Reproductive Health. Various years. Abortion Surveillance System.

Chambers, Simone & Jeffrey Kopstein. 2001. Bad Civil Society. *Pol. Theory*, 29: 837–65.

Cheung, Steven N. S. 1969. *The Theory of Share Tenancy*. Chicago: University of Chicago Press.

Cheung, Steven N. S. 1969. Transaction Costs, Risk Aversion, and the Choice of Contractual Arrangements. *J.L. & Econ.*, 12: 23–42.

Chiorazzi, Michael. 1985. Tax Reform during President Reagan's First Four Years: A Selective Bibliography. *L. & Contemporary Prob.*, 48: 301–09.

Coase, R. H. 1937. The Nature of the Firm. *Economica*, 4: 386.

Coase, R. H. 1960. The Problem of Social Cost. *J.L. & Econ.*, 3: 1–44.

Coase, R. H. 2000. The Acquisition of Fisher Body by General Motors. *J.L. & Econ.*, 43: 15.

Coleman, James S. 1988. Social Capital in the Creation of Human Capital. *Am. J. Soc.* 94: S95–S120.

Coleman, James S. 1990. *Foundations of Social Theory.* Cambridge: Harvard University Press.

Cooter, Robert & Janet T. Landa. 1984. Personal versus Impersonal Trade: The Size of Trading Groups and Contract Law. *Int'l Rev. L. & Econ.* 4: 15–22.

Costello, John. 1988. *Mask of Treachery.* London: Collins.

Covell, Stephen G. 2001. Living Temple Buddhism in Contemporary Japan: The Tendai Sect Today. Princeton Ph.D. dissertation.

Covell, Stephen G. 2005. *Japanese Temple Buddhism.* Honolulu: University of Hawai'i Press.

Daiginjo jidai no ishizue [The Foundations of the Daiginjo Age], Sake bunka kenkyujo News Letter, Jan. 25, 2014.

Danka no inai "Minna no otera Kenshuin" ["Everyone's Temple, Kenshuin", No Danka], as of July 2020. Available at https://dailoguetemple.com.

Danka seido haishi de shunyu 4 bai [Revenue Quadruples with Abandonment of Danka System]. 2017. Aera, Aug. 3, 2017.

Dassai" de Nihonshu no katsuro wo hiraita "Yamaguchi no chiisana shuzo" [The Small Yamagata Brewery that Opened a Path for Sake with Dassai], Nippon.com, Dec. 16, 2013. Available at: www.nippon.com/ja/features/c00618/

Datapoint: Where Are the Highest Concentrations of Licensed Psychologists? American Psychological Association, March 2016. Available at: www.apa.org/monitor/2016/03/datapoint.

Deininger, Klaus & Rogier van den Brink. 2000. How Land Reform Can Contribute to Economic Growth and Poverty Reduction. Available at: http://siteresources .worldbank.org/INTARD/825826-1111148606850/20431879/Zimbabwe.pdf

Deininger, Klaus. 2012. Land Policy Reforms, pp. 213–259. Available at: http://web .worldbank.org/WBSITE/EXTERNAL/TOPICS/EXTPSIA/0,contentMDK:2050335 3~pagePK:148956~piPK:216618~theSitePK:490130,00.html.

Deloitte Thomas Consulting. 2016. *Heisei 27 nendo shin enerugii to donyu sokushin kiso chosa [Basic Survey for the Promotion of the Introduction of New Energies, Etc., 2015].*

Demsetz, Harold. 1967. Towards a Theory of Property Rights, *Am. Econ. Rev.*, 57: 347–59.

Denno, Hiroko. 2018. Nechi tani no terowaaru wo katareru sake [The Sake that Speaks of the Nechi Valley Terroir]. Feb. 27, 2018, Sirabee.

Dietz, Thomas. 2012. Contract Law, Relational Contracts, and Reputational Networks in International Trade: An Empirical Investigation into Cross-Border Contracts in the Software Industry. *L. & Soc. Inquiry*, 37: 25–57.

Dore, Ronald P. 1959. *Land Reform in Japan.* London: Oxford University Press.

Dore, Ronald P. 1978. *Shinohata.* New York: Pantheon.

Dorner, Peter. 1972. *Land Reform and Economic Development.* Middlesex: Penguin Books.

Dower, John W. 1993. *Japan in War & Peace: Selected Essays.* New York: New Press.

Dower, John W. 1999. *Embracing Defeat.* New York: W.W. Norton.

Dower, John W. 2000. The Historian in His Times: E.H. Norman and Japan, in E. Herbert Norman, Japan's Emergence as a Modern State: Political and Economic Problems of the Meiji Period (60th Anniversary Edition) (Vancouver: UBC Press, 2000), page 252.

Dower, John W. 2003a. Occupations and Empires: Why Iraq Is Not Japan. San Jose Mercury News. May 9, 2003.

Dower, John W. 2003c. A Warning from History: Don't Expect Democracy in Iraq. Boston Rev., Feb./Mar. 2003.

Drixler, Fabian. 2008. *Infanticide and Fertility in Eastern Japan: Discourse and Demography, 1660–880*. Cambridge: Harvard University Press.

Economist. 2002. Zimbabwe: From Breadbasket to Basket Case. Economist, June 27, 2002.

Effect of Terminating Ethnic Subsidies. J. Empirical Legal Stud., 15: 192.

Ehara, Sachio & Tetsuro Noda. 2014. Jinetsu hatsuden to onsen riyo no kyosei ni kanren suru giron [Issues Relating to the Coexistence of Geothermal Electrical Generation and Hot Springs Useage]. *Onsen kagaku*, 64: 310–24.

Ellickson, Robert C. 1986. Of Coase and Cattle: Dispute Resolution among Neighbors in Shasta county. *Stan. L. Rev.*, 38: 623.

Ellickson, Robert C. 1991. *Order without Law: How Neighbors Settle Disputes*. Cambridge: Harvard University Press.

Endo, Jun'ichi. 2016. Yutaka na shizen wo tsugi no sedai he [Pass the Plentiful Nature to the Next Generation]. Kanko keizai shinbun, Aug. 6, 2016.

Epstein, Richard A. 2008. Is Group Selection Necessary? An Alternative Interpretatin of Homogeneous Middleman Groups: Comments on Janet Landa's Paper, *J. Bioecon.* 10: 279–85.

Eswaran, Mukesh & Ashok Kotwal. 1985. A Theory of Contractual Structure in Agriculture. *Am. Econ. Rev.*, 75: 352–67.

Facts and Details. 2012. Bluefin Tuna Fish Farming. Available at: https://factsanddetails .com/world/cat53/sub340/item2188.html

FAO (Food and Agriculture Organization of the United Nations). 2020. *The State of World Fisheries and Aquaculture*. Rome.

Feldman, Eric. 2006. The Tuna Court: Law & Norms in the World's Premier Fish Market. *California Law Review*, 94: 313.

Firstenfeld, Jane. Buy, Lease or Contract? Wines & Vines, June 2008.

Flath, David. 2000. *The Japanese Economy*. Oxford: Oxford University Press.

Ford, Stephen A. & Wesley N. Musser. 1994. The Lease-Purchase Decision for Agricultural Assets. *Am. J. Agricultural Econ.*, 76: 277–85.

Fujii, Akihiko. 2015. Nagasaki ken ni okeru kuromaguro yoshoku gyo no genjo to kadai [Circumstances and Issues in the Nagasaki Bluefin Tuna Farming Industry]. Shima, Mar. 2015, at 42.

Fukui, Shin'ichi. 2011. *Sengo shi wo yominaosu [Re-reading Post-war History]*. Tokyo: Kodansha.

Fukumi, Takao. 1928. *Teito ni okeru baiin no kenkyu [Study of Prostitution in the Capital]*. Tokyo: Hakubun kan.

Furuichi, Akitoshi. 1996. Sakamai to shin shokuryo ho [Sake Rice and the New Foodstuffs Act], *Jokyo*, 91: 178.

Gardner, Richard A. 1998. Matters of Life and Death: The Middling Way as a New Buddhist Humanism. *Eastern Buddhist*, 31 (N.S.): 109–24.

Gekkeikan K. K., ed. 1987. *Gekkeikan: 350 nen no ayumi [Gekkeikan: A 350 Year Journey]*. Kyoto: Gekkeikan, K. K.

Geothermal Power: Japan Has World's Third Largest Geothermal Reserves, 60 percent of Which Can Be Developed, Japan for Sustainability, Sept. 11, 2014, available at: www.japanfs.org/en/news/archives/news_id035043.html.

Ghai, Dharam, Azizur Rahman Khan, Eddy Lee & Samir Radwin. 1979. *Agrarian Systems and Rural Development*. London: Macmillan.

Ghatak, M. & S. Roy. 2007. Land Reform and Agricultural Productivity in India: A Review of the Evidence. *Oxford Rev. Econ. Pol.*, 23: 251–69.

Glacier Partners. 2009. Geothermal Economics 101: Economics of a 35 MW Binary Cycle Geothermal Plant. Available at: https://web.archive.org/web/20130521174852/http://www.georestore.com/cms_files/Geothermal%20Economics%20101%20-%20Glacier%20Partners.pdf.

Goodhue, Rachel E., Dale M. Heien, Hyunok Lee & Daniel A. Sumner. 2002. Contract Use Widespread in the Grape Industry, California Agriculture, May-June 2002, at 97–102.

Gordon, Andrew. 2003. *A Modern History of Japan*. New York: Oxford University Press.

Goshay, Charita. 2020. 'Difficult Days Are Ahead for America's Churches, Faith Institutions, "Akron Beacon Journal, Aug. 22, 2020. Available at: www.beaconjournal.com/story/news/local/2020/08/22/lsquodifficult-days-are-aheadrsquo-for-americarsquos-churches-faith-institutions/42282593/

Goto umare goto sodachi … [Born and Raised on Goto …], Sept. 2015. *Koho Goto*, 134: 4–5.

Goto, Aya, et al. 1999. Oral Contraceptives and Women's Health in Japan. *JAMA*, 282: 2173.

Grape Purchase Agreement – sample posted on web by Napa Valley Grapegrowers.

Greif, Avner. 1993. Contract Enforceability and Economic Institutions in Early Trade: The Maghribi Traders' Coalition. *Am. Econ. Rev.*, 83: 525–48.

Greif, Avner. 2012. The Maghribi Traders: A Reappraisal? *Econ. Hist. Rev.*, 65: 445–69.

Grossman, Sanford J. and Oliver D. Hart. 1986. The Costs and Benefits of Ownership: A Theory of Vertical and Lateral Integration. *Journal of Political Economy*. 94: 691–719.

Guinnane, Timothy W., & Ronald I. Miller. 1997. The Limits to Land Reform: The Land Acts in Ireland, 1870–1909. *Econ. Dev. Cult. Change*, 45, 591–612.

Gunnlaugsson, Einar, Halldor Armannsson, Sverrir Thorhallsson & Benedikt Steingrimsson. 2014. Problems in Geothermal Operation – Scaling and Corrosion. Presented at Short Course VI on Utilization of Low- and Medium-Enthalpy Geothermal Resources …", El Savador, Mar. 23–29, 2014.

Gyogyo shugyo doko chosa. 2017. Heisei 29nen gyogyo shugyo doko chosa hokokusho [Survey Report on the Direction in Employment in Fishing].

Gyokyo kyokatsu jiken … [Fishing Union Blackmail Case …], Ise shimbun, Dec. 17, 2020.

Gyokyo to jiba marikon … [Fishing Union and Local Marine Construction …], NetIVNews, Jan. 19, 2010.

Gyoshi san chokuso ichiba [Direct Delivery Market from Fishermen]. N.D. Available at: https://umai.fish/product-date

Gyoson kasseika no arikata kentokai. 2015. Gyoson no genjo [The Current State of Fishing Villages].

Hadfield, Gillian K. & Iva Bozovic. 2016. Scaffolding: Using Formal Contracts to Support Informal Relations in Support of Innovation, 2016 *Wisc. L. Rev.* 981-1032.

Halonen-Akatwijuka, Maija. 2019. Oliver Hart: Incomplete Contracts and the Theory of the Firm. Lindau Nobel Laureate Meetings, Nov. 29, 2016. Available at: www.lindau-nobel.org/oliver-hart-incomplete-contracts-and-the-theory-of-the-firm/

Hane, Mikiso. 1982. *Peasants, Rebels, & Outcastes: The Underside of Modern Japan*. New York: Pantheon.

Hara, Akira. 2007. "Hi senryo ka no sengo henkaku [Post-war changes under Occupation]. In Ishii, Kanji, Akira Hara & Haruhito Takeda, eds., *Nihon keizai shi 4 [Japanese Economic History 4]*. Tokyo: Tokyo daigaku shuppankai, pp. 261–310.

Hardacre, Helen. 1997. *Marketing the Menacing Fetus in Japan*. Berkeley: University of California Press.

Harrar, Sari. 2020. Inside America's Psychiatrist Shortage, Psycom, Sept. 8, 2020. Available at: www.psycom.net/inside-americas-psychiatrist-shortage

Harrison, Elizabeth G. 1995. Women's Responses to Child Loss in Japan: The Case of *Mizuko kuyo. J. Feminist Stud. Religion*, 11: 67–100.

Harrison, Elizabeth G. 1999. Strands of Complexity: The Emergence of Mizuko Kuyo in Postwar Japan. *J. Am. Acad. Religion*, 67: 769–96,

Hart, Oliver & John Moore. 1990. Property Rights and the Nature of the Firm. *J. Pol. Econ.*, 98: 1119–58.

Hatarakeru onna no hitoha hitori nokorazu hatarako [Women Able to work Should All Work],

Hatsuki, Hironori. 2015. Waga kuni no suiden nogyo wo meguru shomondai (I) [Problems Involving Our Country's Rice Paddies (I)]. *Nogyo kenkyu*, 28: 103–33.

Hatsumode sanpai shasu rankingu [Ranking of New Year's Visitors], Memorva, Jan. 14, 2009, available at: https://memorva.jp/ranking/japan/hatsumoude_2009.php.

Hayami, Yujiro, & Saburo Yamada. 1991. *The Agricultural Development of Japan: A Century's Perspective*. Tokyo: University of Tokyo Press.

Hayami, Yujiro. 1988. *Japanese Agriculture under Siege: The Political Economy of Agricultural Policies*. Houndmills: Macmillan.

Hayashi, Futoshi. 2017. Shuzo kotekimai ryutsu ni okeru chokusetsu torihiki no zoka yoin [Reasons for the Increase in Direct Transactions in the Distribution of Sake Rice], *Nogyo shijo kenkyu*, 26: 54–65.

Hayashi, Yuka. 2014. Tasting Bluefin Tuna Raised in University Lab, Wall St. J., Nov. 15, 2014.

Hewes, Laurence I., Jr. 1950. *Japanese Land Reform Program, Report Number 127, Mar. 15, 1950*. Washington, DC: SCAP Natural Resources Section.

Higuchi, Yuichi. 2005. Soryokusen taisei to shokuminchi [The Total War System and the Colonies], in Norio Hayakawa, ed., *Shokuminchi to senso sekinin [The Colonies and War Responsibility]* (Tokyo: Yoshikawa kobun kan), at 53.

Hillmann, Henning & Brandy L. Aven. 2011. Fragmented Networks and Entrepreneurship in Late Imperial Russia. *Am. J. Soc.*, 117: 484–538.

Himi shi. 2019. Suisan tokei [Fishing Statistics]. Available at: www.city.himi.toyama.jp/material/files/group/9/suisantoukei2019.pdf.

Himi shi. 2021. "Himi kan buri" gyokaku joho [The Catch Volume of "Himi Winter Yellowtail"], Feb. 8, 2021. Available at: www.city.himi.toyama.jp/gyosei/soshiki/suisan/1/1823.html

Hirogaru sakamai seisan (ka) [Growing Sake Rice Production (II)], Nihon keizai shimbun, Jan. 20, 2018.

Hogo ken sakamai shinko kai. 1961. Hyogo no sakamai [The Sake-Optimized Rice of Hyogo]. [Kobe]: Hyogo ken sakamai shinko kai.

Hokuriku nosei kyoku. Ippan kigyo no nogyo sannyu ga dekiruyo ni narimashita [General Firms may Now Enter the Agricultural Sector]. Jan. 2008.

Holmstrom, Bengt & Paul Milgrom. 1991. Multitask Principal-Agent Analyses: Incentive Contracts, Asset Ownership, and Job Design. *J.L. Econ. & Org.*, 7: 24–52.

Hoshino, Eiki & Dosho Takeda. 1987. Indebtedness and Comfort: The Undercurrents of Water-child memorial in Contemporary Japan. *Japanese J. Religious Stud.*, 14: 305–20.

Hosoi, Jun, et al. 2018. Shuzo kotekimai shin hinshu "Sankei nishiki" no ikusei [The Development of Seikei nishiki, a New Variety of Sake Rice]. *Hokuriku sakumotsu gakkai ho*, 53: 9–11.

Hoston, Germaine A. 1986. *Marxism and the Crisis of Development in Prewar Japan.* Princeton: Princeton University Press.

Hymans, Jacques E. C. 2020. Losing Steam: Why Does Japan Produce So Little Geothermal Power. *Soc. Sci. Jpn. J.*, 24: 45–65.

Hymans, Jacques E. C. & Fumiya Uchikoshi. 2022. To Drill or Not to Drill: Determinants of Geothermal Energy Project Siting in Japan. *Environmental Pol.*, 31: 407–28.

Hyogo no otera ichiran [List of Hyogo Temples], as of July 2020, from NokotsudoInfo, at www.nokotsudo.info/list/hyogo.html.

Iannaccone, Laurence R. & Feler Bose. 2011. Funding the Faiths: Toward a Theory of Religious Finance. In Rachel M. McCleary, *The Oxford Handbook of the Economics of Religion*. Oxford University Presspp. 323–340.

Iannaccone, Laurence R. 1992. Sacrifice and Stigma: Reducing Free-riding in Cults, Communes, and Other Collectives. *J. Pol. Eco.*, 100: 271–92.

Iannacone, Laurence R. 1994. Why Strict Churches Are Strong. *Am. J. Soc.*, 99: 1180–1211.

Iannacone, Laurence R. 1998. Introduction to the Economics of Religion. *J. Econ. Lit.*, 36: 1465–95.

Ibusuki shi "Chi no megumi" wo katsuyo he [Ibusuki City to Turn to Use of the "Blessings of the Earth" …], Kankyo bijinesu onrain, Dec. 20, 2019.

Ichinokura. N.D. Ichinokura [Ichinokura]. Available at: https://ichinokura.co.jp.

Iga, Masaya. 2008. Seishu kyokyu taikei ni okeru shuzogyosha to sakamai seisansha no teikei kankei [The Relationship Between the Sake Breyers and the Sake-Optimized Rice Producers under the Sake Supply Structure], *Chiri gaku hyoron*, 81: 150–78.

Ikeda, Hiroki. 2008. *Kinsei Nihon no daijinushi keisei kenkyu [Research into the Structure of Large Landowners in Early Modern Japan]*. Tokyo: Kokusho kanko kai.

International Scientific Committee for Tuna and Tuna-Like Species in the North Pacific Ocean. 2016. 2016 Pacific Bluefin Tuna Stock Assessment, July 2016. Available at: http://isc.fra.go.jp/pdf/ISC16/ISC16_Annex_09_2016_Pacific_Bluefin_Tuna_Stock_Assessment.pdf.

IRENA. 2017. Geothermal Power: Technology Brief. Available at: www.irena.org/-/media/Files/IRENA/Agency/Publication/2017/Aug/IRENA_Geothermal_Power_2017.pdf.

ISEP, Shizen enerugii hakusho 2017 [Natural Energy White Paper]. Available at: www.isep.or.jp/jsr/2017report

Ishida, Masaya. 2012. Miriyo no onsensui de hatsuden [Electrical Generation with Unused Hot Springs Water], Smart Japan, Oct. 15, 2012.

Ishida, Masaya. 2013. Kokutei koen no naka de jinetsu hatsuden … [Geothermal Electricity Generation within Quasi-National Parks …]. Smart Japan, July 29, 2013.

Ishida, Masaya. 2015a. Fukushima ken no onsen de jinetsu hatsuden wo kaishi [Fukushima Prefecture Hot Springs Begin Geothermal Electrical Generation]. Smart Japan, Nov. 25, 2015.

Ishida, Masaya. 2015b. Jumin 26 nin ga tachiageta jinetsu hatsudensho [The Geothermal Electrical Generating Plant Built by 26 Citizens]. Smart Japan, June 26, 2015.

Ishida, Masaya. 2015c. 42 MW no jinetsu hatsudensho ga shigatsu in kensetsu kaishi… [Construction on the 42 MW Geothermal Plant Begins in April], Sumaato Japan, Feb. 3, 2015. Available at: www.itmedia.co.jp/smartjapan/articles/1502/03/news021.html.

Ishiguro, Kenta. 2015a. "Gosei shu to sanzoshu no tojo" … [The Appearance of Synthetic Sake and Treble Sake" …], Sake Times, Apr. 8, 2015.

Ishiguro, Kenta. 2015b. Showa 30 nendai kohan kara Showa 40nendai kohan … [From the late Showa 30s to the Late Showa 40s …], Sake Times, June 2, 2015.

Ishiguro, Kenta. 2015c. Sanzoshu … [Treble sake …], Sake Times, June 2, 2015.

Isobe, Toshihiko. 1979. Agrarian Reform in Asia: The Japanese Experience. In Seminar Report [Agricultural Development Council], 19 (Apr), p. 4.

Ito, Hisao. N.D. Nihon ni okeru jinetsu hatsuden to kadai [Issues Regarding Geothermal Electrical Generation in Japan].

Ito, Sogoro. 1981. Sakamai to jishu ryutsu mai seido ni tsuite [Sake Rice and the Directly Traded Rice System], *Jokyo*, 76: 640–43.

Jackson, Matthew O., Tomas Rodriguez-Barraquer & Xu Tan. 2012. Social Capital and Social Quilts: Network Patterns of Favor Exchange. *Am. Econ. Rev.*, 102: 1857–1897.

Jansen, Marius B. 2000. *The Making of Modern Japan*. Cambridge: Harvard University Press.

Jatlaoui, Tara C., et al. 2019. Abortion Surveillance – United States, 2019. *Surveillance Summaries*, 68(11): 1–41.

Jidai no henka ni taio … [Responding to Changes in the Times …], pdf, hanbaijigyou-34. Available at: jfa.maff.go.jp

Jimoto wo daihyo suru Nihon shu wo [A Sake to Represent the Local Community], Sake Times, July 18, 2018.

Jinetsu hatsuden ga hantai sareru riyu [The Reasons for the Opposition to Geothermal Electrical Generation]. N.D. Available at: https://hidemaro25.exblog.jp/19500208/.

Jinetsu hatsuden ni kansuru shomondai no seiri [Resolution of Problems Relating to Geothermal Electrical Generation]. 2012. Available at: www.pref.fukushima.lg.jp/download/1/geo_121012_3.pdf

Jinetsu hatsuden to onsen no kyozon [The Coexistence of Geothermal Electrical Generation and Hot Springs]. Hanajijii no burogu, Nov. 14, 2011. Available at: http://hanaming.cocolog-nifty.com/blog/2011/11/67-bf61.html.

Jiyu na seisan shoki tsukamu [Free Production, Grab Commercial Opportunity], Nihon keizai shimbun, Jan. 19, 2018.

Josephson, Jason Ananda. 2012. *The Invention of Religion in Japan*. Chicago: University of Chicago Press.

Kadono, Atsunobu, et al. 2011. Hyogo ken Kita Harima chiiki ni okeru "Yamada nishiki" no scisan kankyo kaiseki [Analysis of Production Environment for Yamada Nishiki Sake Rice in the Kita-Harima Area of Hyogo]. Kanko kagaku kenkyu, 4: 9–14.

Kagoshima Prefectural Visitors Bureau. N.D. Buri [Yellowtail.]. Available at: www.kagoshima-kankou.com/s/gourmet/fish/buri/

Kagoshimaken. 2019. Heisei 30 nendo jinetsu shigen wo ikashita machizukuri jigyo [Town Development Through Geothermal Resources, 2018].

Kaicho, kowan koji … [Chairman, Harbor Construction …], Asahi shimbun, June 30, 2020.

Kaishain kara gyoshi ni tenshoku! [Company Man Becomes Fisherman!], Apr. 2020. Inaka kurashi no hon, available at: https://inaka.tkj.jp/archives/4209/

Kaiyo seibutsu shigen bumon. 2008. Maiwashi wa naze takai? [Why Are Sardines Expensive]. Univ. Tokyo Atmosphere & Ocean Research Inst., Mar. 2008. Available at: www.aori.u-tokyo.ac.jp/research/topics/2008/2008_ORI04.html.

Kamitaki, Naoshi. 2017. Nihon ni okeru jinetsu hatsuden no genjo [The Currnt Situation of Geothermal Electrical Generation in Japan], Dec. 19, 2017 (Saisei kano enerugii keizaigaku koza [Renewable Energy Economics Lecture]). Available at: www.econ .kyoto-u.ac.jp/renewable_energy/wp-content/uploads/2018/04/20171219-gai.pdf.

Kan, Shokin. 2011. Kagoshima ken no shin'yo kinko, shin'yo kumiai ni okeru chiiki kaseika ni tuite (3) [Regarding the Regional Activation of the Credit Institutions and Credit Cooperatives in Kagoshima Prefecture]. *Chiiki sogo kenkyu*, 38, 43–56.

Kaneda, Hiromitsu. 1980. Transcript of presentation. In Lawrence H. Redford, ed., *The Occupation of Japan: Economic Policy and Reform*. Norfolk: The MacArthur Memorial, pp. 133–146.

Kangoshi shisho … [Nurse Stabbed …], Asahi shimbun, June 29, 2020.

Kankyo enerugii seisaku kenkyu jo. 2017. Shizen enerugii hakusho [Natural Energy White Paper]. Available at www.isep.or.jp/jsr/2017report.

Kankyo enerugii seisaku kenkyu jo. 2020. Nihon no shizen enerugii no genjo [The Current State of Natural Energy in Japan]. Available at: www.isep.or.jp/

Kankyo sho. 2012. Onsen shigen no hogo ni kansuru gaido rain (jinetsu hatsuden kankei) [Guidelines Regarding the Protection of Hot Springs Resources (Regarding Geothermal Electrical Generation)]. Available at www.env.go.jp/nature/onsen/docs/ chinetu_guideline.pdf.

Kanzen yoshoku maguro no shukka kaishi … [Delivery of Closed-cycle Farmed Tuna Begins …], Nikkei, Mar. 7, 2018.

Karakulak, F., Saadet, Bayram Oeztuerk & Taner Yildiz. 2016. From Ocean to Farm: Capture-Based Aquaculture of Bluefin Tuna in the Eastern Mediterranean Sea, in Advances in Tuna Aquaculture, supra, pp. 59–76.

Katayama, Osamu. 2016. Gyogyo no fukkatsu ni kakeru … [Gambling on a Renaissance in Fishing]. Keizai jaanarisuto Katayama Osamu, Nov. 2, 2016. Available at: http:// katayama-osamu.com/wordpress/2016/11/35930/.

Katz, Avery. 1996. Taking Private Ordering Seriously. *U. Pa. L. Rev.*, 144: 1745.

Kawagoe, Toshihiko. 1993. Land Reform in Postwar Japan. In Juro Teranishi & Yutaka Kosai, eds., *The Japanese Experience of Economic Reforms*. Houndmills: Macmillan Press, pp. 178–204.

Kawagoe, Toshihiko. 1995. Sengo Nihon no nochi kaikaku [Land Reform in Postwar Japan], *Keizai kenkyu*, 46, 249–259.

Kawaguchi, Mitsuo & Masayo Fujimoto. Gekkeikan kabushiki gaisha [Gekkeikan, K.K.]. Doshisha Business Case, March 2007.

Kawai, Kazuo. 1960. *Japan's American Interlude*. Chicago: University of Chicago Press.

Kawanami, Yoshiko. Jinetsu hatsuden to onsen [Geothermal Electrical Generation and Hot Springs], Kankyo kanri, Nov. 2013, at 49.

Kawano, Shigeto. 1969. Effects of Land Reform on Consumption and Investment of Farmers. In Kazushi Ohkawa, Bruce F. Johnston & Hiromitsu Kaneda, eds., *Agriculture and Economic Growth: Japan's Experience*. Princeton & Tokyo: Princeton University Press & University of Tokyo Press, pp. 374–397.

Kawashima, Takeyoshi, Toshitaka Shiomi & Yozo Watanabe, eds. 1964. *Onsenken no kenkyu [A Study of Hot Springs Rights]*. Tokyo: Keiso shobo.

Keijo [Seoul] nippo, June 12, 1918 (evening ed.), quoted in Takeshi Fujinaga, Shokuminchi Chosen ni okeru kosho seido no kakuritsu katei [The Establishment Process for the Licensed Prostitution System in Colonial Korea], Nijusseiki kenkyu, Dec. 2004.

Keiyaku saibai de hinshitsu kojo [Raising Quality by Contract Cultivation], Nihon keizai shimbun, Jan. 20, 2018.

Keizai sangyo sho. 2020. Jinetsu hatsu den no donyu kakudai ni muketa keizai sangyo sho no torikumi [Work of METI Towardd the Expanded Introduction of Geothermal Electrical Generating].

Kensatsu, kowan riken nerai wo kyocho …[Prosecution Stresses Aim for Bay-Related Subsidies], Nishi Nihon shimbun, Jan. 10, 2021.

Kensatsu, kowan riken nerai wo kyocho …[Prosecution Stresses Aim for Bay-Related Subsidies], Nishi Nihon shimbun, Dec. 26, 2019.

Kirishima onsen wo mamoru kai. 2015. Hatchobara jinetsu hatsuden … [Hatchobara Geothermal Electrical Generation …], Jan. 21, 2015. Available at: www.kirisima.org/.

Kitano, Shin'ichi & Naotoshi Yamamoto. 2013. Kokunai maguro yoshoku gyo no kakudai to ote shihon no sannyu jittai [The Expansion of the Domestic Tuna Farming Industry and the Entrance of Large Capital]. *Norin gyo mondai kenkyu*, 49: 329–335.

K.K. Kaneko shoten. 2016. "Okome hinshu" sakutsuke wariai Heisei 28 nendo sokuho [Fraction of Production by Rice Variety], Okome no chishiki [Knowledge about Rice], Aug. 9, 2016, available at: https://kome.kaneko-shouten.co.jp/knowledge/name/.

Klein, Benjamin & Keith Leffler (1981). The Role of Market Forces in Assuring Contractual Performance. *J. Pol. Eco.* 89:615–41.

Klein, Benjamin, Robert G. Crawford & Armen A. Alchian. 1978. Vertical Integration, Appropriable Rents, and the Competitive Contracting Process. *J.L. & Econ.*, 21: 297–326.

Kobayashi, Kazunori. 2004. Brewing Japanese Sake from Nature's Gifts, Japan for Sustainability Newsletter, July 31, 2004.

Koike, Harutomo. 1995. Shuzo kotekimai no seisan, ryutsu no genjo to kadai [The Circumstances and Issues in the Production and Distribution of Sake-Optimized Rice]. *Nokei ronso*, 51: 161–70.

Kokonoe machi jinetsu shigen no hogo oyobi katsuyo ni kansuru jorei [Rules Regarding the Protection and Use of Geothermal Resources in Kokonoe Village]. Kokonoe machi jorei No. 33, Dec. 18 of 2015.

Kokuritsu Shakai hosho jinko mondai kenkyujo. 2019. Jinko tokei shiryo shu [Materials on Population Statistics], as available at www.ipss.go.jp/syoushika/tohkei/Popular/P_Detail2018.asp.

Kokusai kyoryoku jigyodan, ed. 1991. Kaigai iju tokei [Foreign Emigration Statistics]. Tokyo: Kokusai kyoryoku jigyodan.

Kokuzei cho. N.D. "Seishu no seiho hinshitsu hyoji kijun" no gaiyo [Summary of "Standards for the Display of Productive Process and Product Quality of Sake"]. Available at: www.nta.go.jp/taxes/sake/hyoji/seishu/gaiyo/02.htm

Kokuzei cho. 2018a. Sake repoto [Sake Report], March 2018, available at: www.nta.go .jp/taxes/sake/shiori-gaikyo/shiori/2018/pdf/000.pdf

Kokuzei cho. 2018b. Seishu seizogyo no gaikyo [Summary of the Sake Manufacturing Industry]. Available at: www.nta.go.jp/taxes/sake/shiori-gaikyo/seishu/2018/pdf/all.pdf.

Kokuzei cho. 2018c. Seishu seizo gyo sha no yushutsu gaikyo [Summary of Exports by Sake Manufacturers].

Kokuzei cho. 2020. Osake no chiri teki hyoji (GI) wo shitte imasuka [Do you Know of the Geographical Indication for Sake?], 2020. Available at: www.nta.go.jp/publication/pamph/sake/03.pdf

Kokuzei cho. 2020. Saikin 5 nenkan no ikken atari no jigyo shotoku ... [Business Income per Case in Last 5 Years ...], as of July 2020, available at: www.nta.go.jp/publication/statistics/kokuzeicho/minkan/top.htm.

Kokuzei cho. 2020. *Seishu seizogyo no gaikyo [A Summary of Rice Production]*, National Tax Agency: Feb. 2020.

Kokuzei cho. 2020a. Minkan kyuyo jittai tokei chosa kekka [Survey Results for Private Sector Pay]. Available at: www.nta.go.jp/publication/statistics/kokuzeicho/jikeiretsu/01_02.htm#page-top

Kondo, Kaori. 2015. Jinetsu hatsuden no genjo to kadai [The Current State of and Issues Relating to Geothermal Electrical Generation], [National Diet Library] *Issue Brief*, 837: 1.

Korede toppu made ikeru ... ["Now We Can Reach to the Top" ...], Nishi Nihon shimbun, Aug. 26, 2021.

Kosai, Yutaka. 1986. *The Era of High-Speed Growth: Notes on the Postwar Japanese Economy*. Tokyo: University of Tokyo Press. Transl: Jacqueline Kaminski.

Kouri bukka tokei chosa ni yoru kakaku suii. 2021. Buri 200g kakaku suii, kako 80ka getsu [Yellowtail 100g, Price trends, Past 80 months]. Available at: https://jpmarket-conditions.com/1111/.

Kudokai toppu saiban ... [Trial of the Kudokai Leadership ...], Bijinesu jaaneru, Mar. 19, 2021.

Kumamoto, Kazunori. 1990. Iriai gyogyo no kenri shutai [The Subject of Rights in Common in Fisheries]. *Meiji gakuin ronso*, 5: 33-45.

Kunifuda, Hiroyuki. N.D. Shudo [The Way of Sake], available at www.kikusui-sake.com/home/jp/fun/shudo/

Kuromaguro no kanzen yoshoku [Full Lifecycle Farming of Blue-fin Tuna], Kinki daigaku suisan kenkyujo, N.D., Available at: www.flku.jp/aquaculture/tuna/.

Kuromaguro no yoshoku bijinesu ... [The Farming Business of Bluefin Tuna], Newswitch, Jan. 2, 2021. Available at: https://newswitch.jp/p/25308.

Kusama, Yasoo. 1930. Jokyu to baishofu [Waitresses and Prostitutes] (Hanjin sha).

Kyokatsu higisha no taiho [Arrest of Blackmail Suspect], Mie Prefectural Police Headquarters, July 14, 2020, available at: www.police.pref.mie.jp/sp/accident/detail.php?no=20200714175612

LaFleur, William R. 1990. Contestation and Consensus: The Morality of Abortion in Japan. *Philosophy East & West.*, 40: 529–42.

LaFleur, William R. 1992. *Liquid Life: Abortion and Buddhism in Japan*. Princeton: Princeton University Press.

LaFleur, William R. 1995. Silences and Censures: Abortion, History, and Buddhism in Japan: A Rejoinder to George Tanabe. *Japanese J. Religious Stud.* 22: 185–96.

LaFleur, William R. 1999. Abortion, Ambiguity, and Exorcism. *J. Am. Acad. Religion*, 67: 797–808.

Landa, Janet T. 1981. A Theory of the Ethnically Homogeneous Middleman Group: An Institutional Alternative to Congract Law. *J. Legal Stud.*, 10 349–362.

Lyon, Peyton V. 1991. The Loyalties of E. Herbert Norman. *Labour/LeTravail*, 28, 219–59.

Macaulay, Stewart. 1963. Non-Contractual Relations in Business: A Preliminary Study. *Am. Soc. Rev.*, 28: 55–67.

Macaulay, Stewart. 1985. An Empirical View of Contract. *Wisc. L. Rev.* 465–82.

Magaloni, Beatriz, Barry R. Weingast & Alberto Diaz-Cayeros. 2008. Why Developing Countries Sabotage Economic Growth: Land Reform in Mexico. Unpublished, available at: irps.ucsd.edu/assets/001/502977.pdf.

Maguro kansen yoshoku no genjo wo shiru [Learn the Current status of Closed-Cycle Tuna Farming]. Nikkei4946.com, Jan. 19, 2015.

Maguro yoshoku.net, available at: www.yousyokugyojyou.net/index10_6.htm

Maikoku kiko. 2014. Seishu no doko [Trends in Sake], Kome ni kansuru chosa repoto H26-5. Available at: www.komenet.jp/pdf/chousa-rep_H26-5.pdf

Maruha Nichiro no kanzen yoshoku … [Maruha Nichiro's Closed-Cycle Farming …], Maruha Nichiro, Oct. 21, 2019. Available at: www.maruha-nichiro.co.jp/corporate/news_center/channel/kuromaguro.html.

Marumoto shuzo. N.D. Utsukushii sakezukuri wa komezukuri kara [Beautiful Sake Brewing Begins with Beautiful Rice Farming]. Available at: http://kamomidori.co.jp.

Masten, Scott E. 1984. The Organization of Production: Evidence from the Aerospace Industry. *J.L. & Econ.*, 27: 403–417.

Masten, Scott E., James W. Meehan, Jr., Edward A. Snyder. 1991. The Costs of Organization. *J.L. Econ. & Org.*, 7: 1–25.

Matsuo, Hajime. 2017. Sakamai wo meguru tohoku no josei [Circumstances in Tohoku about Sake Rice]. *Fudo shisutemu kenkyu*, 24: 42–45.

Matsuzaki, Yukio. 2016. Onsenchi wo saisei funo ni suru jinetsu kaihatsu [The Geothermal Development that Makes Recovery Impossible for Hot Springs]. Kanko keizai shimbun, Oct. 8, 2016.

McClain, James L. 2002. *Japan: A Modern History*. New York: W.W. Norton & Co.

McCloskey, Donald N. 1991. The Prudent Peasant: New Findings on Open Fields. *J. Econ. Hist.*, 51, 343–355.

METI. 2018. Shigen enerugii kankei yosan no gaiyo [Summary of Budget Relating to Rources and Energy].

METI. 2019. Enerugii hakusho [Energy White Paper]. 2019. Available at: www.enecho.meti.go.jp/about/whitepaper/2019html/2-1-4.html

METI. 2020. Jinetsu hatsuden no donyu kakudai ni muketa keizai sangyo sho no tori-kumi [METI Moves toward Expanding Use of Geothermal Electrical Generation], Jan. 20120. Available at: www.enaa.or.jp/?fname=gec_2019_5_1.pdf.

Miller, Alan S. 1998. Why Japanese Religions Look Different: The Social Role of Religious Organizations in Japan. *Rev. Religious Res.* 39: 360–70.

Minami, Ryoshin. 1986. *The Economic Development of Japan: A Quantitative Study*. Houndmills: Macmillan.

Ministry of Environment. 2010. Onsen riyo jokyo [Hot Springs Usage]. Available at: www.env.go.jp/nature/onsen/data/index.html

Ministry of Environment. 2014. Onsen ho dai 3 jo ni motozuku kussaku no ruikeika ni tsuite [Toward a Typology of Cases not Requiring a Drilling Permit Under Section 3 of the Hot Springs Act], 2014, p. 65. Available at: www.env.go.jp/nature/onsen/council/chinetsukaisei/chinetsukaisei3/siryo1-2.pdf

Ministry of Environment. 2015. Shingikai: Onsen no hogo to riyo, dai 5 kai [Study Session: The Protection and Useage of Hot Springs, Session 5], Feb. 9, 2015, supp. mat. 2: Goi keisei ni itatta jirei [Examples that Resulted in Agreement]. Available at: www.env.go.jp/nature/onsen/council/kadai/05kadai/siryo2.pdf.

Ministry of Environment. N.D. Akitaken Yuzawashi jinetsu kaihatsu adobaizaa Iwata shi he no hiaringu kekka no gaiyo [Summary of Hearings with Mr. Iwata, Akita prefecture Yuzawa City Geothermal Development Advisor. www.env.go.jp/nature/ onsen/council/kadai/05kadai/sanko4.pdf

Missick, Christopher Matthew. 2015. Three Basic Models for Grape Purchase Contracts. Feb. 25, 2015, available at: www.avvo.com.

Mitchell, C. Clyde. 1949. Land Reform in South Korea. *Pacific Affairs*, 22, 144–154.

Miwa, Ryoichi. 2012. *Gaisetsu Nihon keizaishi [Summary of Japanese Economic History]*. Tokyo: Tokyo daigaku shuppan kai.

Miwa, Yoshiro & J. Mark Ramseyer. 2000. Rethinking Relationship-Specific Investments: Subcontracting in the Japanese Automobile Industry, *Mich. L. Rev.* 98: 2636.

Miwa, Yoshiro & J. Mark Ramseyer. 2005. The Good Occupation. Available at http:// papers.ssrn.com/sol3/papers.cfm?abstract_id=729463.

Miwa, Yoshiro & J. Mark Ramseyer. 2006. Japanese Industrial Finance at the Close of the nineteenth Century: Trade Credit and Financial Intermediation. *Explorations Econ. Hist.* 43, 94.

Miwa, Yoshiro. 2014. Japan's Economic Planning and Mobilization in Wartime, 1930s-1940s (Cambridge University Press).

Miyajima, Satoshi. N.D. Dochaku no kura, "Shinano nishiki" [The Brewery of the Earth: Shinano nishiki]. Available at: www.miyajima.net/?hajimeni.

Miyazaki ken. 2020. Honken no suisangyo, gyoson no genjo [The State of the Fishing Industry and the Fishing Villages in Our Prefecture]. Available at: www.pref.miyazaki .lg.jp/suisanseisaku/shigoto/suisangyo/documents/55187_20201012091614-1.pdf

Mnookin, Robert H. & Lewis Kornhauser, Bargaining the Shadow of the Law: The Case of Divorce. *Yale L.J.* 88: 950 (1979).

Moehwald, Ulrich. 2004. Rural Society. In Josef Kreiner, Ulrich Moehwald & Hans Dieter Oelschleger, eds., *Modern Japanese Society*. Leiden: Brill, pp. 257–276.

Monbu sho, ed. 1925. *Nihon teikoku monbu sho nempo [The Japanese Imperial Ministry of Education Annual]*. Tokyo: Monbu sho.

Monbu sho, ed. 1937. *Gakusei seito jido shincho taiju kyoi heikin ruinen hikaku, Meiji 33-Showa 9 nendo [Average Annual Heights, Weights, and Chest Circumference for Students and Children, 1900–1929]*. Tokyo: Monbu sho.

Monbu sho, ed. 1939. *Dai-Nippon teikoku bonfu sho, dai 66 nempo [66th Annual Report of the Ministry of Education of the Great Japanese Empire]*. Tokyo: Monbu sho (reprinted 1979).

Mori, Taro. 1983. Muramai ni tsuite [Regarding Muramai]. Jokyo, 78: 124.

Morikuni, Osamu. 2017. Maguro kanzen yoshoku … [Full Lifecycle Farming of Tuna …], Nihon keizai shimbun, Dec. 3, 2017.

Moriya, Yuki. 2016. Hatsuden jigyo wo fukko to machi zukuri no ashigake ni [Electrical Generation as a Step Toward Recovery and the Building of Community]. Available at: www.tsukubabank.co.jp/corporate/info/monthlyreport/pdf/2016/08/201608_ 10.pdf.

Moriyama, Kenta. 2017. Mura hachibu ni natta gyoshi san ni … [To the Fisherman Who was Ostracized …], Nippon taberu Times, April 20, 2017. Available at: https://taberutimes.com/posts/25237.

Murray, Charles. 2012. *Coming Apart: The State of White America, 1960–2010*. New York: Crown Forum.

Nagashima, Hiromi. 2018. 23 nen buri! [After 23 Years!]. EMIRA, May 21, 2018. Available at: https://emira-t.jp/special/6070/.

Naikaku tokei kyoku, ed. 1912. *Nippon teikoku tokei nenkan*, v. 31. Tokyo: Tokyo tokei kyokai.

Naikaku tokei kyoku, ed. 1940. *Jinko dotai tokei [Vital Statistics]*. Tokyo: Naikaku tokei kyoku.

Naikaku tokeikyoku, cd. 1920a. *Nihon teikoku tokei nenkan*. Tokyo: Tokyo tokci kyokai.

Naikaku tokkei kyoku. 1920b. *Kokusei chosa hokoku [Report on Vital Statistics]*. Tokyo: Tokyo tokei kyokai (Prefectural supplement v. 5).

Naikaku tokkei kyoku. 1930. *Kokusei chosa hokoku [Report on Vital Statistics]*. Tokyo: Tokyo tokei kyokai (Supplement v. 5).

Nakamura, Hisato. 2017. Nihon no jiin to keieigaku [Japanese Temples and Management Science]. *Gendai shakai kenkyu*, 15: 121–31.

Nakamura, Takafusa. 1983. *Economic Growth in Prewar Japan*. New Haven: Yale University Press. Transl. Robert A. Feldman.

Nakamura, Takafusa. 1995. *The Postwar Japanese Economy: Its Development and Structure, 1937–1994*. Tokyo: University of Tokyo Press, 2d ed.

National Geographic. 2020. Geothermal Energy. Available at: www.nationalgeographic.org/encyclopedia/geothermal-energy/.

NEDO. 2014. Saisei kano enerugii gijutsu hakusho [Renewable Energy Technology White Paper] 2d ed.

Nelson, John K. 2012. Japanese Secularities and the Decline of Temple Buddhism. *J. Religion in Japan*, 1: 37–60.

Nelson, John K. 2013. *Experimental Buddhism: Innovation and Activism in Contemporary Japan*. Honolulu: University of Hawai'i Press.

Nelson, John. 2017. An Experimental Approach to Buddhism and Religion. *Int'l J. Dharma Stud.*, 5:16.

New Energy Foundation. 2020. Website of New Energy Foundation, www.nef.or.jp/award/kako/h29/p01.html.

Nihon jinetsu gakkai. 2010. Jinetsu hatsuden to onsen riyo to no kyosei wo mezashite [Toward the Coexistence of Geothermal Electrical Generation and Hot Springs Useage]. Available at: https://grsj.gr.jp/wp-content/uploads/Onsen_kyosei_report_200215.pdf.

Nihon no nochi seido to nochi seisaku [Japanese Agricultural Land System and Policy], Norin kinyu, July 2007, 346–356.

Nihon nogyo isan. 2021. Himi no jizoku kano na teichi ami gyogyo [Himi's Sustainable Fixed Net Fishing Industry]. Available at: www.maff.go.jp/j/nousin/kantai/attach/pdf/giahs_3_himi-9.pdf

Nihon okome kyokai. 2018. Kodawari no sake zukuri ha okeme zukuri kara [Making the Best Sake Starts with Making the Rice], Nihon okome kyokai. Available at: https://rice-assoc.jp/eat-gohan/120-2018-08-08-14-07-22.html.

Nihon onsen sogo kenkyujo. N.D. Nihon no onsen deeta [Data about Japanese Hot Springs]. Available at: www.onsen-r.co.jp/data/.

Nihon saidai kyu no jinetsu hatsudensho ... [Largest Class of Geothermal Electrical Generating Plant in Japan ...]. Sankei nyusu, Aug. 26, 2019. Available at:. www .sankei.com/economy/news/190826/pr1908260011-n1.html.

Nihon seisaku toshi ginko. 2013. Hanshinkan ni okeru shuzo me-ka- no kofukakachika senryaku [The High Value-Added Strategy of the Sake Brewers Between Osaka and Kobe], Report, April 2013. Available at: www.dbj.jp/pdf/investigate/area/kansai/pdf_ all/kansai1304_01.pdf.

Nihonshu no korekara [The Future of Sake], Hobo Nikkan Itoi shimbun. 2017. Available at www.1101.com/juku/hiroba/3rd/free-317/06.html.

Nihonshu no yushutsu, kako saiko no 222 oku yen ni [Exports of Japanese Sake Reach Record 22.2 Billion yen], Nippon.com, Feb. 15, 2019a.

Nihonshu renesansu [Sake Renaisance]. Asahi shimbun, Dec. 30, 2019.

Niigata no Sake: 3 [The Sake of Niigata: 3], Asahi shimbun, Oct. 10, 2019.

Ninomiya, Mari. 2012. Edoki kara Showa shoki (1657nen – 1931 nen) no Nada shuzoka to Tokyo sake tonya tono torihiki kankei no henka [Changes in the Trade Relations between the Nada Brewers and the Tokyo Sake Brokers from the Edo Period to Early Showa [1657–1931], *Fukuoka daigaku shogaku ronso*, 57: 51–80.

Ninomiya, Mari. 2013. Meijiki kara Taishoki ni okeru Nada shuzo gyo [The Nada Brewing Industry from the Meiji Period to the Taisho Period]. *Fukuoka daigaku shogaku ronso*, 57: 307–40.

Ninomiya, Mari. 2014. Shurui sangyo ni okeru seisan ryutsu kisei [Production and Distribution Regulation in the Alcoholic Beverage Industry]. *Fukuoka daigaku shogau ronso*, 58: 469–495.

Ninomiya, Mari. 2015. Seishugyo ni okeru kindai gijutsu no donyu to seishu no doshit-suka [The Introduction of Modern Techniques in Sake Production and the Increasing Similarity of Sake]. *Fukuoka daigaku shogaku ronso*, 59: 471–501.

Nishinomiya shuzo, K.K., ed. 1989. *Nihon sakari: Nishinomiya shuzo 100 nen shi [Nihon Sakari: A 100 Year History of the Nishinomiya Brewery]*. Nishinomiya: Nishinomiya shuzo, K.K.

No to ieru shuzo no kai [The Association of Brewers Who Can Say Farm]. N.D. Available at: https://agri-sake.com

Nochi kaikaku kiroku iinkai, ed. 1957. Nochi kaikaku tenmatsu gaiyo [Summary Account of Land Reform]. Tokyo: Nosei chosa kai.

Nochi kaikaku shiryo hensan iinkai, ed. 1980. Nochi kaikaku shiryo shusei [Collected Materials on Land Reform], vol. 11. Tokyo: Nosei chosa kai.

Nochi kaikaku shiryo hensan iinkai, ed. 1981. Nochi kaikaku shiryo shusei [Compilation of Material on Agricultural Land Reform], vol. 13. Tokyo: Nosei chosa kai.

Nomoto, Ryohei. 2015. Haneda kuko hatsu, shinbutsuryu shisutemu ... [From Haneda Airport, The New Distribution System ...], Another Life, Oct. 5, 2015. Available at: https://an-life.jp/article/669/?para=5.

Nomoto, Ryohei. 2017. Haneda ichiba – chosoku yuso ... [The Haneda Market – Ultra-high-speed Delivery ...]. Kokusai bunka kenshu, Summer 2017.

Norin chukin sogo kenkyujo. 2019. Gyokyo ni okeru baishu hanbai ni kansuru jittai chosa [Empirical Survey on Transations by Fishing Unions], Nokin, Mar. 18, 2019.

Norin sho, ed. 1928. *Kosaku jijo chosa [Survey of Tenancy Circumstances]*. Tokyo: Norin sho.

Norin sho, ed. 1956. *Nochito kaiho jisseki chosa [Survey of Performance of Agricultural Land Liberation]*. Tokyo: Norin sho.

Norin sho, ed. 2012. *Norin suisan tokei [Agriculture, Forestry and Fishery Statistics].* Tokyo: Norin sho.

Norin sho, ed. *Various years. Norin sho tokei hyo [Ministry of Agriculture Statistical Tables].* Tokyo: Norin sho.

Norin suisan sho, ed. 2003. *Nogyo sensasu ruinen tokeisho [Agricultural Census: yearly Statistics].* Tokyo: Norin suisan sho.

Norin suisan sho. 2018a. Shuzo koteki mai no nosanbutsu kensa kekka ... [Examination Results of Sake-specific Rice ...], 2018. Available at: www.maff.go.jp/j/seisaku_tokatu/kikaku/sake_02seisan.html.

Norin suisan sho. 2018b. Gyokakuryo ga gensho shite iru riyu wo oshiete kudasai [Please Give Me the Reason for the Plummeting Catch]. www.maff.go.jp/j/heya/kodomo_sodan/0007/04.html.

Norin suisan sho. N.D. Kaigan jigyo [Seashore Works]. Available at: www.maff.go.jp/j/nousin/bousai/bousai_saigai/b_kaigan/.

Norin suisan sho. N.D. a Kome seisanryo joi ni tsuite [On the Major Producers of Rice]. Available at: www.maff.go.jp/j/kids/crops/rice/farm.html.

Oana, Fujio. 1970. Shuzogyo no suii [Trends in the Brewing Industry], *Jokyo,* 65: 307–311.

Oda, Masayasu. 2003. Nihon ni okeru Bukkyo shoshuha no bunpu [The Distribution of Buddhist Denominations in Japan]. *Komazawa chiri,* 39: 37–58.

Odaka, Konosuke. 1975. Nihon tochika ni okeru Chosen no rodo keizai [Korean Labor Economy Under Japanese Control], *Keizai kenkyu,* 26: 145.

OECD. 2009. Evaluation of Agricultural Policy Reforms in Japan. Available at: www.oecd.org/agriculture/agriculturalpoliciesandsupport/42791674.pdf.

Ohsato, Katsuma, ed. 1966. Meiji iko honpo shuyo keizai tokei [Principal Economic Statistics for Our Nation Since the Meiji Period] (Bank of Japan).

Okamura, Tadahiko. 2017 Zenkoku no nessui katsuyo oyobi bainarii hatsuden no jirei [The Hot Water and Binary Generators in the Country]. Sept. 27, 2017.

Okawa, Taketsugu. 1979. *Sengo Nihon shihon shugi to nogyo [Post-war Capitalism and Agriculture].* Tokyo: Ochanomizu shobo.

Okome no chishiki [Information about Rice], Aug. 9, 2016, available at: https://kome.kaneko-shouten.co.jp/knowledge/name/.html

Okuda, Shin'ichi. 2013. Jisaki gyogyoken no hoteki seishitsu to kyukan no kaihai [The Legal Character of Coastal Fishing and the Reorganization of Customs]. *Nihon fudo-san gakkai shi,* 27–3: 82–89.

Okura sho, ed. 1926. Ginko soran [Banking Almanac], vol. 32. Tokyo: Okura sho.

Ono, Seiichiro. 2014. 2010 nendai shoto ni okeru Nihon no maguro yoshoku gyo [Tuna Farming in Japan in the early 2010s]. *Bull. Fisheries Lab. Kinki Univ.,* 14: 1–24.

Ono, Yoshio. 2019. Shuzogyo keieisha no henkaku kodo [Transformation of Brewery Managers], *Shiga daigaku keizaigakubu kenkyu nenpo,* 26: 13–38.

Onsen de hatsuden!? Jinetsu enerugii de Fukushima wo Kosei saseru ["Generate Electricity from Hot Springs!? Using Geothermal Energy to Revive Fukushima], June 11, 2018. Kokocara. Available at: https://kokocara.pal-system.co.jp/2018/06/11/power-generation-in-tsuchiyu-hot-spring.

Osake sutatisutikkusu [Sake Statistics]. N.D. Available at: www.kitasangyo.com/pdf/e-academy/osake-statistics/osake_statistics_1805.pdf

Otera de "shakai mondai' kangaerutte!? [Think About "Social Problems" at the Temple!?]. 2016. Sankei west, Dec. 9, 2016.

Oyama, Masao. 2014. Jinetsu hatsuden to onsen no kyozon no mondai [Problems in the Coexistence of Geothermal Electrical Generation and Hot Springs]. *Onsen kagaku.* 63: 341–52.

Ozeki, K.K., ed. 1996. *Ozeki: 280 nen shi [Ozeki: A 280 Year History].* Nishinomiya: Ozeki, K.K.

Perrin, Richard. 1992. *Japanese Studies from Pre-History to 1990: A Bibliographical Guide.* Manchester: Manchester University Press.

Popkin, Samuel L. 1979. *The Rational Peasant.* Berkeley: The University of California Press.

Portes, Alejandro. 1998. Social Capital: Its Origins and Applications in Modern Sociology. *Ann. Rev. Sociol.,* 24: 1–24.

Posner, Eric A. 1998. Symbols, Signals, and Social Norms in Politics and Law. *J. Legal Stud.,* 27: 765–97.

Posner, Eric A. 2002. *Law and Social Norms.* Cambridge: Harvard University Press.

Posner, Richard A. 1997. Social Norms and the Law: An Economic Approach. *Am. Econ. Rev.,* 87: 365–69 (P&P).

Posner, Richard A. 1998. Social Norms, Social Meaning, and Economic Analysis of Law: A Comment. *J. Legal Stud.,* 27: 553–65.

Posner, Richard A. & Eric B. Rasmusen. 1991. Creating and Enforcing Norms, with Special Reference to Sanctions. *Int'l Rev. L. & Econ.,* 19: 369–82.

Putnam, Robert D. 1995. Bowling Alone: America's Declining Social Capital. *J. Democracy,* 6: 65–78.

Putnam, Robert D. 2000. *Bowling Alone: The Collapse and Revival of American Community.* New York: Simon & Schuster.

Raff, Daniel M. G. & Lawrence H. Summers. 1987. Did Henry Ford Pay Efficiency Wages? *J. Labor Econ.,* 5: S57–S86.

Rajvanshi, Ullas. 2018. Effect of Mineral Scaling on Geothermal Wells. TUDelft.

Ramseyer, J. Mark, & Eric B. Rasmusen. 2018. Outcaste Politics and Organized Crime in Japan: The

Ramseyer, J. Mark & Eric B. Rasmusen. 2020. Ostracism in Japan. SSRN No. 3706315, Oct. 6, 2020.

Ramseyer, J. Mark, & Minoru Nakazato. 1998. *Japanese Law: An Economic Approach.* Chicago: University of Chicago Press.

Ramseyer, J. Mark. 1989. Water Law in Imperial Japan: Public Goods, Private Claims, and Legal Convergence. *J. Legal Stud.,* 18, 51.

Ramseyer, J. Mark. 2012. Why Power Companies Build Nuclear Reactors on Fault Lines: The Case of Japan, *Theoretical Inquiries in Law,* 13: 457.

Ramseyer, J. Mark. 2015. The Fable of Land Reform: Leases and Credit Markets in Occupied Japan. *J. Econ. & Mgmt Strategy* 24: 934.

Ramseyer, J. Mark. 2015. Social Capital and the Formal Legal System: Evidence from Prefecture-Level Data in Japan. *J. Legal Anal., JLA,* 7: 421.

Ramseyer, J. Mark. 2019. On the Invention of Identity Politics: The Buraku Outcastes in Japan. *Rev. L. & Econ.* 16: 95, et seq.

Ramseyer, J. Mark. 2020. The Story of Japan's Ohmi Merchants, by Kunitoshi Suenaga, Japan Forward, Nov. 12, 2020.

Reader, Ian. 1998. Review. *Asian Folklore Stud.* 57: 152–55.

Reader, Ian. 2011. Buddhism in Crisis? Institutional Decline in Modern Japan. *Buddhist Stud. Rev.* 28: 233.

Reed, Steven R. 2012. Japan SMD Data Set. Available at: www.fps.chuo-u.ac.jp/~sreed/DataPage.html.

Reiheld, Alison. 2015. "The Event That Was Nothing": *Miscarriage as a Liminal Event.* *J. Soc. Phil.* 46: 9–26.

Reiwa gannen ni okeru kokunai no kuromaguro yoshoku jisseki ni tsuite [Regarding the Domestic Bluefin Tuna Farming in 2019]. Suisan sho, Mar. 31, 2020. Available at: www.maff.go.jp/j/press/saibai/s00331.html.

Renewable Energy. 2017. Shizen enerugii katsuyo repoto [Natural Energy Useage Report], July 25, 2017. Available at: www.renewable-ei.org/column_r/REappliation_20170725.php.

Richman, Barak D. An Autopsy of Cooperation: Diamond Dealers and the Limits of Trusdt-Based Exchange. *J. Legal Anal.*, 9: 247 (2017).

Riley, Dylan. 2005. Civic Associations and Authoritarian Regimes in Interwar Europe: Italy and Spain in Comparative Perspective. *Am. Soc. Rev.*, 70: 288–310.

Risoteki na onsen hatsuden [The Ideal Hot Springs Electrical Generator], Nov. 6, 2018, Kirishima onsen wo mamoru kai. Available at www.kirisima.org/.

Rowe, Mark Michael. 2011. *Bonds of the Dead: Temples, Burial, and the Transformation of Contemporary Japanese Buddhism.* Chicago: University of Chicago Press.

Rowe, Mark. 2000. Stickers for Nails: The Ongoing Transformation of Roles, Rites, and Symbols in Japanese Funerals. *Japanese J. Religious Stud.*, 27: 353–78.

Rowe, Mark. 2003. Grave Changes: Scattering Ashes in Contemporary Japan. *Japanese J. Religious Stud.*, 30: 85–118.

Rowe, Mark. 2004. Where the Action Is: Sites of Contemporary Soto Buddhism. *Japanese J. Religious Stud.*, 31: 357–88.

Ryoko shimbun. 2015. Jinetsu kaihatsu kanwa ni hantai [Against Liberalization of Geothermal Development]. June 5, 2015. Ryoko shimbun. Available at: www.ryoko-net.co.jp/?p=12357.

Sackton, Frank. 1980. Transcript of presentation. In Lawrence H. Redford, ed., *The Occupation of Japan: Economic Policy and Reform.* Norfolk: The MacArthur Memorial, pp. 123–33.

Saegert, Susan & Gary Winkel. 2004. Crime, Social Capital, and Community Participation. *Am. J. Community Psychol.* 34: 219–233.

Saikaku, Ihara. 1963. The Life of an Amorous Woman. New York: New Dimensions, Ivan Morris, transl. (N.B.: Ihara is the family name, but the author is known as Saikaku).

Saitama jishu ni kodawaru Ishii shuzo [Ishida Brewery, Caring about Saitama Local Sake], Sake Times, Dec. 1, 2017.

Saito, Maiko. 2015. Sakamai no scisan wo meguru jokyo [Circumstances Surrounding the Productin of Sake Rice]. Kokuritsu kokkai toshokan, Issue Brief, 880, Nov. 10, 2015.

Saito, Osamu & Toshiaki Yamada. 2017. Seishu wo meguru Inobeeshon to baryu cheen [Innovation and Value Chain Surrounding Sake-Optimized Rice]. Fudo shisutemu kenkyu, 24: 18.

Sakamai no saiko mine [The Peak of Sake Rice], available at www.kikumasamune.co.jp.

Sando, Atsuko. 2018. Shinka tsuzukeru Nihon shu (19) [Japanese Sake Continues to Progress (19)], Guide to Japan, Nov. 28, 2018.

Sando, Atsuko. 2019. "Nihonshu" Now: Sustainable Grower Brewer Izumibashi Shuzo, Guide to Japan, Jan. 11, 2019.

Sasaki, Megumi. 2019. Jinetsu hatsudensho no yojo netsu katsuyo wo kento … [Studying the use of Excess Heat at Geothermal Electrical Generating Plant …], Nikkei Business, Dec. 18, 2019.

Sasaki, Takeshi, et al., eds. 2005. *Sengo shi dai jiten zoho shinpan [Encyclopedia of Post-war History: Expanded Edition]*. Tokyo: Sanseido.

Sato, Akio. 2002. *Seikatsu shukan byo wo yobosuru shoku seikatsu [Eating Habits that Prevent Diseases Caused by Living Habits]*. www.eps1.comlink.ne.jp/~mayus/index .html

Satyanath, Shanker, Nico Voiglaender & Hans-Joachim Voth. 2017. Bowling for Fascism: Social Capital and the Rise of the Nazi Party. *J. Pol. Eco.*, 125: 478.

SCAP. 1945. "Memorandum for Imperial Japanese Government," AG 602.6 (9 Dec. 45) CIE. Available in Nochi (1957, 111) and Hewes (1950, 96).

Schonberger, Howard B. 1989. Aftermath of War: Americans and the Remaking of Japan, 1945–1952.

Science Journal. 2012. Kaigai de chaku chaku to susumu "jinetsu hatsuden" ["Geothermal Generating" Proceeds Steadily Abroad]. Saiensu jaaneru. Aug. 16, 2012. Available at: http://sciencejournal.livedoor.biz/archives/4141911.html.

Scott, James C. 1976. *The Moral Economy of the Peasant*. New Haven: Yale University Press.

Seesaa Blog. Chotto zeitaku na okuri mono [Gifts that Are a Bit of a Luxury]. Available at: http://petitluxurylife.seesaa.net/article/477455104.html.

Sekai he habatakutame ni "Terowaaru" kara Nihon shu wo kataru [To Travel to the World, Tell of Sake Through "Terroir"]. Sake Times, Sept. 3, 2019.

Shakai jigyo kenkyu jo. 1936. Shuro shone shojo rodo jijo chosa [Survey of Working Conditions of Working Boys and Girls] (Chuo shakai jigyo kyokai).

Shapiro, Carl & Stiglitz, Joseph E. 1984. Equilibrium Unemployment as a Worker Discipline Device. *American Economic Review*, 74: 433–444

Shibuya, Yukio. 2016. Seishu seizogyo no nogyo sannyu ni kansuru ichi kosatsu [Studies in the Reasons for Entry by Sake Brewers into Farming], *Nogyo keiei kenkyu*, 54: 73–78.

Shibuya, Yukio. 2020. Seishu seizogyo ni yoru nogyo sannyu no jittai bunseki [An Empirical Analysis of the Entry in Agriculture by the Sake Brewing Industry], in Yukio Shibuya, ed., Naze kigyo ha nogyou ni sannyu suru no ka [Why do Firms Enter Agriculture]. Norin tokei shuppan, 2020, at 83.

Shimada, Hisanori. 2018. Otera 3.0: Otera wo appudeeto shiyo [Temple 3.0: Let's Update the Temple]. Shimasan no otera, Dec. 10, 2018. Available at: https://shima-sun.com/ temple-be-updating/お寺をアップデート.

Shimazono, Susumu. 1998. The Commercialization of the Sacred: The Structural Evoluton of Religious Communities in Japan. Soc. Sci. Japan J., 1: 181–98.

Shimizu, Yozo. 2007. Sengo kiko to keizai fukko 1 [The Post-war Crisis and Economic Recovery 1]. In Hara, et al, pp. 311–56.

Shin enerugii sangyo sogo kaihatsu kiko. 2016. TSC Foresight (12), June 2016.

Shin enerugii zaidan. 2018. Shin ene daisho [New Energy Award]. Available at: www .nef.or.jp/award/kako/h30/b_02.html.

Shinano machi sei yoran shiryo hen [Vital Statistics for Shinano machi: Materials]. 2019. Available at: www.town.shinano.lg.jp/docs/228.html.

Shishido, Zen'ichi. 2019. Japanese Contracting Practices: Realities and Changes.

Shoji, Shunsaku. 1999. *Nihon nochi kaikaku shi kenkyu [Studies in the History of Japanese Land Reform]*. Tokyo: Ochanomizu shobo.

Smethurst, Richard J. 1986. *Agricultural Development and Tenancy Disputes in Japan, 1870–1940*. Princeton: Princeton University Press.

Smethurst, Richard J. 1989. A Challenge to Orthodoxy and Its Orthodox Critics, *J. Japanese Stud.*, 15, 417–437.

Smith, Adam. 1992 (1776). *The Wealth of Nations*. Oxford: Oxford University Press.

Smith, Bardwell. 1988. Buddhism and Abortion in Contemporary Japan: Water-child memorial and the Confrontation with Death. *Japanese J. Religious Stud.*, 15: 3–24.

Smith, Henry E. 2008. Governing Water: The Semicommons of Fluid Property Rights. *Ariz. L. Rev.*, 50: 445.

Smith, Robert J. 1978. *Kurusu: The Price of Progress in a Japanese Village*. Stanford: Stanford University Press.

Soin gyokyo kumiaicho no kyokatsu jiken [The Extortion Case involving the Head of the Soin River Fishing Union], Ise shimbun, Aug. 31, 2020.

Sojitsu ga torikumu honmaguro yoshoku jigyo ni tsuite [Regarding the Bluefin Tuna Farming Business in Which Sojitsu will Engage], Nihon boeki kai geppo, July-Aug. 2013, at 24–25.

Somu cho tokei kyoku. Various years. Kokusei chosa [Vital Statistics], available from www.e-stat.go.jp.

Somu sho, ed. 2010. Kokusei chosa hokoku [Population Survey]. Tokyo: Somu sho.

Sorifu, ed. 1952. Nihon tokei nenkan, Showa 26 nenban [Japan Statistical Annual, 1951]. Tokyo: Nihon tokei kyokai.

Soryo sodan saito [Priest Consultation Site], Nihon keizai shimbun, Oct. 15, 2016. Available at:. www.nikkei.com/article/DGXLASDG01H0Z_V11C16A0CR0000

Stark, Rodney & Roger Finke. 2000. *Acts of Faith: Explaining the Human Side of Religion*. Berkeley: University of California Press.

Stark, Rodney & William Sims Bainbridge. 1987. *A Theory of Religion*. New Brunswick: Rutgers University Press. 1987 (1996 reprint).

Steiman, Harvey. 2014. Terroir? What Exactly Do You Mean? Wine Spectator, Apr. 8, 2014.

Stiglitz, Joseph E. 1974. Incentives and Risk Sharing in Sharecropping. *Rev. Econ. Stud.*, 41, 219–255.

Stolle, Dietlind & Thomas R. Rochon. 1998. Are All Associations Alike: Member Diversity, Associational Type, and the Creation of Social Capital. *Am. Behavioral Scientist*, 42: 47–65.

Storr, Virgil Henry & Ginny Seung Choi. 2019. *Do Markets Corrupt Our Morals? Cham*, Switzerland: Palgrave Macmillan.

Storr, Virgil Henry. 2009. Why the Market? Markets as Social and Moral Spaces. *J. Markets & Morality*, 12: 277–96.

Suenaga, Kunitoshi. 2019. The Story of Japan's Ohmi Merchants: The Precept of Sanpo-yoshi. JPIC. (tr. Larry Greenberg).

Suenaga, Kunitoshi. 2019. The Story of Japan's Ohmi Merchants: The Precept of Sanpo-yoshi. Translated by Larry Greenberg. Tokyo: Japan Publishing Industry Foundation for Culture, 2019, pp. 170 + index.

Sugihara, So, et al. 2012. Sakamai to saibai dojo no kagaku teki seishitsu ha kankei suruka [Does Soil Chemical Characteristics Affect the Brewer's Sake Rice Quality]. Nihon dojo hiryo gakkai.

Suisancho. 2018. Suisan hakusho [Fisheries White Paper]. Available at: www.jfa.maff
    .go.jp/j/kikaku/wpaper/h30_h/trend/1/sankou_4_4.html

Suisancho. N.D. Gyogyo seisan no jokyo no henka [The Change in the Circumstances
    of Fisheries Production]. Available at www.jfa.maff.go.jp/j/kikaku/wpaper/ro1_h/
    trend/1/t1_f1_html.

Sunaga, Taiichiro. Chiho no "asa dore" sengyo … [The "Caught This Morning" Local
    Fishing …]. Nikkei bijinesu, Sept. 26, 2016.

Suzuki, Atsushi & Osamu Takada. 2017. Senshin shuzo kotekimai sanchi no iji hatten
    yoin to kadai [Factors and Problems in the Maintenance and Development of Good
    Locations for Growing Sake-Optimized Rice]. *J. Rural Problems*, 53: 139–47.

Suzuki, Yoshiyuki. 2015. *Nihon shu no kingendai shi [Modern and Early Modern History
    of Sake]*. Tokyo: Yoshikawa kobunkan.

Swift, Philip. 2013. Review. *Japan Rev.*, 25: 188–90.

Tachiba wo riyo … [Use of Position …]. Yahoo! nyuusu, Dec. 25, 2020, Ise shimbun,
    Dec. 25, 2020.

Takada, Ikki. 2020. Shinkoku more kingaku [Unreported Amounts], Gentosha Gold
    Online, Apr. 18, 2020.

Takagi, Masaru. 2008. *Nochi seido: nani ga mondai nanoka [The Agricultural Land
    System: Where's the Problem]*. Tokyo: K.K. Taisei shuppansha.

Takahashi, Yukari. 2015. Obosan tachiga jinsei sodan [Priests Offer Consultation about
    Life], July 2015. Available at: www.enjoytokyo.jp/solo/detail/263/?__ngt__=TT11587
    e20c002ac1e4ae01c-c3sU1UnSXs0FTufa1m4Xx.

Takayama, Kazuyoshi. 2017. Zetsumetsu wa kore de nakunaru? [Will This End
    Extinction?]. Nikkei, June 20, 2017. Available at: https://project.nikkeibp.co.jp/
    mirakoto/atcl/food/h_vol13/.

Takayama, Taisuke & Tomoaki Nakatani. 2017. Nochi riisu tokku donyu ni yoru
    kigyo to no nogyo sannyu no inpakuto hyoka [The Impact of the Entry of Firms
    into Agriculture through the Introduction of the Special Farmland Leases]. *Noson
    keikaku gakkai shi*, 36: 77.

Takemae, Eiji. 2002. *The Allied Occupation of Japan*. New York: Continuum.

Takeyasu, Hideko, et al. 2018. Hyogo yamada nishiki seisansha no genjo to kadai [The
    Circumstances and Issues Relating to the Hyogo Producers of Yamada Nishiki].
    Gendai shakai kenkyu ronshu, 12: 65–91.

Tamanohikari Sake Brewing Co. N.D. Kome, mizu, koji, kokoro iki [Rice, Water, Yeast,
    Spirit]. Available at: www.tamanohikari.co.jp/identity/.

Tanabe, George J., Jr. 1998. Review. *Japanese J. Religious Stud.*, 25: 377–80.

Tanabe, Katsumasa. 1974. *Nihon tochi seido shi [History of Japanese Land System]*.
    Tokyo: Nihon tochi seido shi kanko kai.

Teitaikyo ni "mono goi, aka" bogen … Saibansho ga Ji Man-won shi ni yuzai hanketsu
    [Slandering the CDH as "beggars, reds," Court Convicts Ji Man-won, Hankyoren,
    Nov. 10, 2018, available at: http://japan.hani.co.kr/arti/politics/32072.html.

Tell NOAA Note to Reverse Conservation Measures for Atlantic Bluefin, International
    Game Fish Association, Available at: https://igfa.org/2019/09/09/tell-noaa-not-to-
    reverse-conservation-measures-for-atlantic-bluefin/?gclid=EAIaIQobChMI-Nfo-
    9C78gIVBOXjBx3WGAyYEAAYASAAEgIjifD_BwE

Telser, Lester G. 1960. Why Should Manufacturers Want Fair Trade? *J.L. & Econ.*, 3:
    86–105.

Telser, Lester G. 1979. A Theory of Monopoly of Complementary Goods. *J. Bus.*, 52: 211–30.

Tennen maguro to yoshoku maguro no chigaitte nani? [What's the Difference Between Wild and Farmed Tuna?], Gurume-tei, July 6, 2020. Available at: https://gurume-tei .com/blog/maguro-aquacultureornature.html.

Teruoka, Shozo. 2003. *Nihon no nogyo 150 nen [150 Years of Japanese Agriculture].* Tokyo: Yuhikaku.

Tohoku Nihon shu terowaaru purojekuto kento kai. 2015. Tohoku Nihon shu terowaaru purojekuto. August, 2015.

Tohoku nosei kyoku. N.D. Tohoku, Nihonshu terowaaru purojekuto [Northeastern Sake Terroir Project]. Available at www.maff.go.jp/tohoku/

Toku A chiiki shitei no yurai [The Origins of the Special A Area Designation], available at www.kikuhime.co.jp

Torii, Kyoshi. 2005. *Gyogyousha ni yoru kuromaguro yoshoku keieitai no bunseki [An Analysis of the Managerial Entities by Those in the Fishing Industry for Bluefin Tuna Farming].* Kinki University Fisheries Research Center. 21st Century COE 2003–04 Interim Program Report, pp. 221–26.

Torii, Kyoshi. N.D. Shokibo keieitai ni yoru maguro yoshokugyo no keiei tenkai to kadai [The Developments and Issues the Management of the Tuna Farming Industry by Small-Scale Managerial Entities]. Available at: www.gyokei.sakura.ne.jp/dp/Vol1/ No2.pdf.

Toro no hana seisansha kyogyo tai.N.D. Nihon ichi no kuromaguro yoshoku wo meza-shite [Toward the Best Farmed Bluefin Tuna in Japan]. Available at: zengyoren.or.jp

Toyota tsusho, K. K. 2020. Toyota tsusho, jizoku kanona … [Toyota Trading: Replicable …], Nihon boeki kai geppo, Mar. 2020, at 8.

Tsukue wo tatakuhodo agaru gyogyo hosho [Fishing Compensation – It Rises with the Number of Times You Pound the Table]. Wedge Report, March issue, Feb. 21, 2012.

Tsuna doriimu Goto … [Tuna Dream Goto …], Toyota tsusho, K.K., July 23, 2015.

Turner, Victor. 1967. Betwixt and Between The Liminal Period in Rites of Passage. 1967. Reproduced in Betwixt & Between: Patterns of Masculine and Feminine Initiation. ed. Louise Carus Mahdi, Steven Foster, and Meredith Little. La Salle, IL: Open Court.

U.S. Department of Energy. 2008. Hydrothermal Power Systems. Available at: https:// web.archive.org/web/20081013155410/http://www1.eere.energy.gov/geothermal/ powerplants.html#drysteam.

Uechi, Joju, et al. 2016. Jinetsu hatsuden kaihatsu wo meguru funso no yoin bunseki [Factor Analysis of Disputes Relating to Geothermal Electrical Generation]. Keikaku gyosei, 39: 44.

Umemura, Mataji, et al. 1966. Noringyo [Agiculture and Forestries]. Tokyo: Toyo keizai shimpo sha. (Hitotsubashi Long-term Economic Statistics series, vol. 9).

Underwood, Meredith. 1999. Strategies of Survival: Women, Abortin, and Popular Religion in Contemporary Religion. *J. Am. Acad. Religion*, 67: 739–68.

United Nations. 1976. *Progress in Land Reform, Sixth Report.* New York: United Nations.

Uriu, Takashi. 2015. Watashi wa Amazon de" Chumon" sareru soryo [I Am a Priest One Can "Order" Through Amazon]. Riree koramu, Dec. 20, 205. Available at: http:// shinshuhouwa.info/column/archives/1134.

Ushiomi, Toshitaka. 1954. *Gyoson no kozo [The Structure of Fishing Villages].* Tokyo: Tokyo daigaku shakai kagaku kenkyujo.

Wagatsuma, Sakae. 1944. Minpo taii [Overview of Civil Code], vol. 1. Tokyo: Iwanami shoten.

Waita kai. N.D. Waita kai ni tsuite [Regarding the Waita kai], website of Waita kai. https://waita-kai.com/about-waitakai/

Wanner, Christoph, Florian Eichinger, Thomas Jahrfeld & Larryn W. Diamond. 2017. Causes of Abundant Calcite Scaling in Geothermal Wells in the Bavarian Molasse Basin, Southern Germany. *Geothermics*, 70: 324–38.

Washington Wine Industry Foundation. 2015. Getting Paid: Tools for Washington Grape Growers. Available at: [Reproducing advice from NJ's Outer Caostal Plain Vineyard Association.]

Watanabe shuzoten. N.D. Nechi otokoyama [Nechi Otokoyama]. Available at: https://nechiotokoyama.jp.

Watanabe, Manabu. 2014. Dare ga heishi ni nattano ka (1) [Who Became a Soldier (1)]. Shakai gakubu kiyo, 119: 1.

Werblowsky, R. J. Zwi. 1991. Water-child memorial: Notulae on the Most Important New Religion of Japan. *Japanese J. Religious Stud.* 18: 295–354.

West, Nigel. 1982. *The Circus: M15 Operations, 1945–1972*. New York: Stein & Day.

Williamson, Oliver E. 1975. *Markets and Hierarchies*, New York: Free Press.

Williamson, Oliver E. 1985. *The Economic Institutions of Capitalism*, New York: Free Press.

World Bank. 1993. *The East Asian Miracle: Economic Growth and Public Policy*. Oxford: Oxford University Press.

Yamada nishiki hassho no sato [The Place where Yamada Nishiki Began], available at www.kikuhime.co.jp.

Yamada, Hiromichi & Sahashi Hirama. 1923. Tokei yori mitaru karyubyo [Venereal Diseases Seen Through Statistics] (Nanzan do).

Yamagata ken kogyo gijutsu sentaa. 2015. Tohoku chiiki ni okeru Nihon shu terowaaru no kanosei ni tsuite [Regarding the Potential for Sake Terroir in the Tohoku Area]. Available at: www.maff.go.jp/tohoku/seisan/sake/terroir/attach/pdf/index-2.pdf.

Yamaguchi san no Nihonshu … [Yamaguchi Sake], Nihon keizai shimbun, Aug. 29, 2018.

Yamaguchi, Adam, & Zach Slobig. 2011. Can Bluefin Tuna Farms Work? Los Angeles Times, July 21, 2011.

Yamakata, Hirayuemon, ed. 1977. Hakutsuru 230nen no ayumi [Hakutsuru: A 230 Year Journey]. Kobe: Hakutsuru shuzo K.K.

Yamamoto, Shun'ichi. 1983. Nihon kosho shi [A History of Licensed Prostitution in Japan] (Chuo hoki shuppan).

Yamane, Koyuki. 2018. Beppushi ga onsen hatsuden ni "matta" [Beppu Shouts "Stop" to Geothermal Electrical Generation], Nikkei xTech, May 31, 2018. Available at: https://xtech.nikkei.com/dm/atci/feature/15/031400070/053100059/.

Yamauchi, Shigeki & Akira Nagano. 2014. Engan gyogyo chiki ni okeru gyogyo seisan-sei … [The Productivity of Coastal Fishing …]. Japan Section of the Regional Science Association International, annual meeting, Oct. 3–5, 2014. Available at: www.jsrsai .jp/Annual_Meeting/PROG_51/ResumeC/rC08-3.pdf.

Yamazaki, Motomu. 2019. Kappatsuka suru honken no jinetsu hatsuden kaihatsu [Booming Geothermal Electrical Generating in Our Prefecture]. Akita keizai, Aug. 2019.

Yoshida, Honami, et al. 2016. Contraception in Japan: Current Trends. *Contraception*, 93: 475–477.

Yoshoku maguro ha naze umai [Why Is Farmed Tuna Delicious?], Gyoppy.yahoo.co.jp, May 8, 2020.

Zen saibankan keireki soran henshu iinkai, ed. 2010. Zen saibankan keireki soran [Overview of Careers of All Judges]. Tokyo: Konin sha.

Zenkoku gyogyo shugyosha kakuho ikusei sentaa. N.D. Okiai, enyo gyogyo ni tsuite [Regarding the Offshore and Deep-sea Fishing Industry]. Available at: https://ryoushi.jp/gyogyou/okai-enyou/.

Zenkoku kinsho mezasu [Aiming for a National Gold Prize], Nihon nogyo shimbun, Oct. 8, 2019.

Zenkoku no Nihon shu rankingu 2020 [National Sake Rankings, 2020]. Sake Time, April 11, 2020a.

Zenkoku ryokan hoteru seikatsu eisei dogyo kumiai rengo kai. 2013. Jinetsu hatsuden no genjo to kosatsu [Thoughts and the Current Circumstances of Geothermal Electrical Generation].

Index